Effective COM

Effective COM

*50 Ways to Improve Your COM and
MTS-based Applications*

Don Box
Keith Brown
Tim Ewald
Chris Sells

ADDISON-WESLEY

An imprint of Addison Wesley Longman, Inc.
Reading, Massachusetts • Harlow, England • Menlo Park, California
Berkeley, California • Don Mills, Ontario • Sydney
Bonn • Amsterdam • Tokyo • Mexico City

Many of the designations used by manufacturers and sellers to distinguish their products are claimed as trademarks. Where those designations appear in this book and Addison-Wesley was aware of a trademark claim, the designations have been printed in initial caps or all caps.

The authors and publisher have taken care in the preparation of this book, but make no expressed or implied warranty of any kind and assume no responsibility for errors or omissions. No liability is assumed for incidental or consequential damages in connection with or arising out of the use of the information or programs contained herein.

The publisher offers discounts on this book when ordered in quantity for special sales. For more information, please contact:

Corporate, Government and Special Sales Group
Addison Wesley Longman, Inc.
One Jacob Way
Reading, Massachusetts 01867
(781) 944-3700

Library of Congress Calatoging-in-Publication Data

Effective COM: 50 ways to improve your COM and MTS-based
    applications / Don Box . . . [et al.].
        p.   cm.
    Includes index.
    ISBN 0-201-37968-6
    1. Application software—Development. 2. Object-oriented
programming (Computer science) 3. COM (Computer architecture)
4. Microsoft Transaction server. I. Box, Don, 1962-
QA76.76.D47E34   1999
005.2'76—dc21   98-46027
                                                                            CIP

Executive Editor: J. Carter Shanklin
Project Editor: Krysia Bebick
Production Coordinator: Jacquelyn Young
Copyeditor: Cindy Kogut
Composition: Barbara Northcott
Cover Design: Simone Payment

ISBN 0-201-37968-6
Text printed on recycled and acid-free paper.
1 2 3 4 5 6 7 8 9 10–VB–0201009998
First printing, December 1998

Contents

Preface

The evolution of the Component Object Model (COM) has in many ways paralleled the evolution of C++. Both movements shared a common goal of achieving better reuse and modularity through refinements to an existing programming model. In the case of C++, the preceding model was procedural programming in C, and C++'s added value was its support for class-based object-oriented programming. In the case of COM, the preceding model was class-based programming in C++, and COM's added value is its support for interface-based object-oriented programming.

As C++ evolved, its canon evolved as well. One notable work in this canon was Scott Meyers' *Effective C++*. This text was perhaps the first text that did not try to teach the reader the basic mechanics and syntax of C++. Rather, *Effective C++* was targeted at the working C++ practitioner and offered 50 concrete rules that all C++ developers should follow to craft reasonable C++-based systems. The success of *Effective C++* required a critical mass of practitioners in the field working with the technology. Additionally, *Effective C++* relied on a critical mass of supporting texts in the canon. At the time of its initial publication, the supporting texts were primarily *The C++ Programming Language* by Stroustrup and *The C++ Primer* by Lippman, although a variety of other introductory texts were also available.

The COM programming movement has reached a similar state of critical mass. Given the mass adoption of COM by Microsoft as well as many other development organizations, the number of COM developers is slowly but surely approaching the number of Windows developers. Also, five years after its first public release, there is finally a sufficiently large canon to lay the tutorial groundwork for a more advanced text. To this end, *Effective COM* represents a homage to Scott Meyers' seminal work and attempts to provide a book that is sufficiently approachable that most working developers can easily find solutions to common design and coding problems.

Virtually all existing COM texts assume that the reader has no COM knowledge and focus most of their attention on teaching the basics. *Effective COM* attempts to fill a hole in the current COM canon by providing guidelines that transcend basic tutorial explanations of the mechanics or theory of COM. These concrete guidelines are based on the authors' experiences working with and training literally thousands of COM developers over the last four years as well as on the communal body of knowledge that has emerged from various Internet-based forums, the most important of which is the DCOM mailing list hosted at `DCOM-request@discuss.microsoft.com`.

This book owes a lot to the various reviewers who offered feedback during the book's development. These reviewers included Saji Abraham, David Chappell, Steve DeLassus, Richard Grimes, Martin Gudgin, Ted Neff, Mike Nelson, Peter Partch, Wilf Russell, Ranjiv Sharma, George Shepherd, and James Sievert. Special thanks go to George Reilly, whose extensive copyediting showed the authors just how horrible their grammar really is. Any errors that remain are the responsibility of the authors. You can let us know about these errors by sending mail to `effectiveerrata@develop.com`. Any errata or updates to the book will be posted to the book's Web page, `http://www.develop.com/effectivecom`.

The fact that some of the guidelines presented in this book fly in the face of popular opinion and/or "official" documentation from Microsoft may at first be confusing to the reader. We encourage you to test our assertions against your current beliefs and let us know what you find. The four authors can be reached *en masse* by sending electronic mail to `effectivecom@develop.com`.

Intended Audience

This book is targeted at developers currently using the Component Object Model and Microsoft Transaction Server (MTS) to develop software. *Effective COM* is not a tutorial or primer; rather, it assumes that the reader has already tackled at least one pilot project in COM and has been humbled by the complexity and breadth of distributed object computing. This book also assumes that the reader is at least somewhat familiar with the working vocabulary of COM as it is described in *Essential COM*. The book is targeted primarily at developers who work in C++; however, many of the topics (e.g., interface design, security, transactions) are approachable by developers who work in Visual Basic, Java, or Object Pascal.

What to Expect

The book is arranged in six chapters. Except for the first chapter, which addresses the cultural differences between "100% pure" C++ and COM, each chapter addresses one of the core atoms of COM.

Shifting from C++ to COM

Developers who work in C++ have the most flexibility when working in COM. However, it is these developers who must make the most adjustments to accommodate COM-based development. This chapter offers five concrete guidelines that make the transition from pure C++ to COM-based development possible. Aspects of COM/C++ discussed include exception handling, singletons, and interface-based programming.

Interfaces

The most fundamental atom of COM development is the interface. A well-designed interface will help increase system efficiency and usability. A poorly designed interface will make a system brittle and difficult to use. This chapter offers 12 concrete guidelines that help COM developers design interfaces that are efficient, correct, and approachable. Aspects of interface design discussed include round-trip optimization, semantic correctness, and common design flaws.

Implementations

Writing COM code in C++ requires a raised awareness of details, irrespective of the framework or class library used to develop COM components. This chapter offers 11 concrete guidelines that help developers write code that is efficient, correct, and maintainable. Aspects of COM implementation discussed include reference counting, memory optimization, and type-system errors.

Apartments

Perhaps one of the most perplexing aspects of COM is its concept of an apartment. Apartments are used to model concurrency in COM and do not have analogues in most operating systems or languages. This chapter offers nine concrete guidelines that help developers ensure that their objects operate properly in a multithreaded environment. Aspects of apartments discussed include real-world lock management, common marshaling errors, and life-cycle management.

Security

One of the few areas of COM that is more daunting than apartments is security. Part of this is due to the aversion to security that is inherent in most developers, and part is due to the fairly arcane and incomplete documentation that has plagued the security interfaces of COM. This chapter offers five concrete guidelines that distill the security solution space of COM. Aspects of security discussed include access control, authentication, and authorization.

Transactions

Many pages of print have been dedicated to Microsoft Transaction Server, but precious few of them address the serious issues related to the new transactional programming model implied by MTS. This chapter offers eight concrete pieces of advice that will help make your MTS-based systems more efficient, scalable, and correct. Topics discussed include the importance of interception, activity-based concurrency management, and the dangers of relying on just-in-time activation as a primary mechanism for enhancing scalability.

Acknowledgments

First and foremost, Chris would like to thank his wife, Melissa, for supporting him in his various extra-circular activities, including this book.

Thanks to J. Carter Shanklin and the Addison Wesley staff for providing the ideal writing environment. I couldn't imagine writing for another publisher.

Thanks to all of the reviewers for their thoughtful (and thorough) feedback.

Thanks to all my students as well as the contributing members of the DCOM and ATL mailing lists. Whatever insight this book provides comes from discussing our mutual problems with COM.

Last but not least, thanks to my fellow authors for their hard work and diligence in seeing this project through to the end. It is truly a pleasure and an honor to be included as an author with professionals of such caliber.

Don would like to thank the three other Boxes that fill up his non-COM lifestyle.

Thanks to my coauthors for sharing the load and waiting patiently for me to finish my bits and pieces (the hunger strike worked, guys).

A tremendous thanks to Scott Meyers for giving us his blessing to leverage[1] his wildly successful format and apply it to a technology that completely butchers his life's work.

Thanks to all of my cohorts at DevelopMentor for tolerating another six months of darkness while I delayed yet another book project.

Thanks to J. Carter Shanklin at Addison Wesley for creating a great and supportive environment.

Thanks to the various DCOM listers who have participated in a long but fun conversation. This book in many ways represents an executive summary of the megabytes of security bugs, MTS mysteries, and challenging IDL puzzles that have been posted by hundreds of folks on the COM front lines.

A special thanks goes to the Microsoft folks who work on COM and Visual C++, for all of the support over the years.

Keith would like to thank his family for putting up with all the late nights. The joy they bring to my life is immeasurable.

Thanks to Don, Tim, and Chris, for thinking enough of me to extend an invitation to participate in this important project.

Thanks to Mike Abercrombie and Don Box at DevelopMentor for fostering a home where independent thought is nourished and the business model is based on honesty and genuine concern for the community.

Thanks to everyone who participates in the often lengthy threads on the DCOM list. That mail reflector has been incredibly useful in establishing a culture among

---

[1] Leverage is a nice-sounding euphemism used in the Windows development world, whose real meaning should be obvious.

COM developers, and from that culture has sprung forth a wealth of ideas, many of which are captured in this book.

Thanks to Saji Abraham and Mike Nelson for their dedication to the COM community.

Thanks, Carter, this book is so much better than it possibly could have been if you had pressed us for a deadline.

And finally, thanks to all the students who have participated in my COM and security classes. Your comments, questions, and challenges never cease to drive me toward a deeper understanding of the truth.

First and foremost, Tim would like to thank his coauthors for undertaking this project and seeing it through to completion. As always, gentlemen, it's been a pleasure.

Also, thanks to friends and colleagues Alan Ewald, Owen Tallman, Fred Tibbitts, Paul Rielly, everyone at DevelopMentor, students, and the participants on the DCOM mailing list for listening to me go on and on about COM—nodding sagely, laughing giddily, or screaming angrily as necessary.

A special thanks to Mike, Don, and Lorrie for suffering through the earliest days of DM to produce an extraordinary environment for thinking.

And, of course, thanks to my family: Sarah for letting me wear a COM ring too, Steve and Kristin for reminding me about the true definition of success, Alan and Chris for allowing me to interrupt endlessly to ask geeky questions, and Nikke and Stephen Downes-Martin for accepting phone calls from any airport I happen to be in.

Finally, thank you J. Carter Shanklin and Addison Wesley for letting us do our own thing.

Chris Sells
Portland, OR
August 1998
`http://www.sellsbrothers.com`

Don Box
Redondo Beach, CA
August 1998
`http://www.develop.com/dbox`

Keith Brown
Rolling Hills Estates, CA
August 1998
`http://www.develop.com/kbrown`

Tim Ewald
Nashua, NH
August 1998
`http://www.develop.com/tjewald`

Shifting from C++ to COM

Moving from pure C++ development to the world of COM can seem especially constraining. Many of the language constructs you have come to know and love are yanked from your arsenal and replaced with a whole new set of language constructs called attributes in a language that looks closer to C than C++. The mindset of a C++ developer is typically focused on implementing objects. It takes a considerable amount of time before one's focus shifts to thinking in terms of components that communicate through request and response messages. This chapter discusses several of the more important attitude shifts that are needed to survive the transition from "100% pure" C++ to the stylized subset we have come to know as the Component Object Model.

1.   Define your interfaces before you define your classes (and do it in IDL).

One of the most basic reflexes of a C++ programmer is to begin the coding phase of a project in a "dot-H" file. It is here that the C++ programmer typically begins defining both the public operations of his or her data types as well as their core internal representations. When working on an exclusively C++-based project, this is a completely reasonable approach. However, when working on a COM-based project, this approach usually leads to pain and suffering.

The most fundamental concept in COM is that of separation of interface from implementation. Although the C++ programming language supports this style of programming, it has very little *explicit* support for defining interfaces as separate entities from the classes that implement them. Without such explicit support for interfaces, it is easy to blur the distinction between interface and implementation.

It is common for novice COM developers to forget that interfaces are intended to be abstract definitions of some functionality. This implies that the definition of a COM interface should not betray implementation details of one particular class that implements the interface. Consider the following C++ class definition:

```
class Person {
   long m_nAge;
   long m_nSalary;
   Person *m_pSpouse;
   list <Person*> m_children;
public:
   Person(void);
   void Marry(Person& rspouse);
   void RaiseSalary(long nAmount);
   void Reproduce(void);
   Person *GetSpouse(void) const;
   long GetAge(void) const;
   long GetSalary(void) const;
   const list<Person*>& GetChildren(void) const;
};
```

This is a completely reasonable class definition; however, if it were used as the starting point for a COM interface definition, the most direct mapping would look like this:

```
DEFINE_GUID(IID_IPerson, 0x30929828, 0x5F86, 0x11d1,
        0xB3, 0x4E, 0x00, 0x60, 0x97, 0x5E, 0x6A, 0x6A);
DECLARE_INTERFACE_(IPerson, IUnknown) {
   STDMETHOD(QueryInterface)(THIS_ REFIID r,void**p)PURE;
   STDMETHOD_(ULONG, AddRef)(THIS) PURE;
   STDMETHOD_(ULONG, Release)(THIS) PURE;
   STDMETHOD_(void, Marry)(THIS_ IPerson *pSpouse) PURE;
   STDMETHOD_(void, RaiseSalary)(THIS_ long nAmt) PURE;
   STDMETHOD_(void, Reproduce)(THIS) PURE;
   STDMETHOD_(IPerson *, GetSpouse)(THIS) PURE;
   STDMETHOD_(long, GetAge)(THIS) PURE;
   STDMETHOD_(long, GetSalary)(THIS) PURE;
   STDMETHOD_(list<IPerson*> *, GetChildren)(THIS) PURE;
};
```

The DECLARE_INTERFACE_ macros are used to emphasize that this interface definition is meant to appear in a C/C++ header file.

The first deficiency of this interface definition is that it uses a standard template library (STL) list to return the collection of children. While this method is reasonable in a closed single-binary system in which all constituent source code will be compiled and linked as an atomic unit, this technique is fatal in COM. Since in COM the component may be built with one compiler and used by client code compiled with a different compiler, it is impossible to guarantee that both the client and the object will agree on the representation of an STL list. Even if both entities are compiled with the same vendor's compiler, it is not guaranteed that the same version of the STL is in use.[1]

A more obvious problem related to returning an STL list is that this interface potentially betrays an implementation detail of the underlying class, namely, that it stores its collection of children using an STL list. For the implementation shown earlier, this is not an issue. However, if other class implementers wish to implement the IPerson interface, they too must store their children in STL lists or create a new list every time the GetChildren method is called. Since STL lists are not the most space-efficient representation for a collection, this constraint imposes an undue burden on all implementations of IPerson.

One last flaw related to data types has to do with the results of each method. The definition of each of the IPerson methods uses the STDMETHOD_ macro that allows the interface designer to indicate the physical result type of the method explicitly. Thus, the following method definition,

```
STDMETHOD_(long, GetAge)(THIS) PURE;
```

will expand as follows once the C preprocessor performs its magic:

```
virtual long __stdcall GetAge(void) = 0;
```

The problem with this method is that it does not return an HRESULT. As detailed in Item 2, COM overloads the physical result of the method to indicate communication failures; since this method does not return an HRESULT, COM has no way to inform the client of any communication errors that may occur.

None of the flaws noted previously would have occurred had the developer defined the interface in COM's Interface Definition Language (IDL). It is tempting to look at IDL and think, Why must I master yet another language? This concern is valid. Most developers older than age 25 have already mastered (at least) one programming language and are reluctant to learn yet another syntax for writing conditionals and loops. This reluctance is understandable, because every decade new programming languages are produced that promise vast increases in programmer productivity but often turn out to be syntactic monstrosities.

---

[1] Many developers eschew their compiler's STL implementation in favor of higher-performance versions available from third-party vendors.

It is important to note that COM's IDL is not a programming language and probably is not all that new to most people. IDL does not have constructs for writing executable statements. IDL is an attribute-based declarative language and only has constructs for defining COM-compatible data types. Also, IDL inherits its syntax from the C programming language, making it familiar to the large number of C, C++, and Java developers working in COM today. IDL syntax is simple enough that developers who work in other languages (e.g., Visual Basic or Object Pascal) can easily master the basics over a weekend. Yes, some future version of COM+ might replace the current IDL compiler with a more integrated solution. However, the attribute-based techniques used by IDL will survive long after MIDL.EXE is in everyone's Recycle Bin. The bottom line is that IDL is here to stay.

IDL directly inherits its syntax for defining enumerations, structures, and unions from C. The following fragment is completely legal IDL:

```
enum COLOR { RED, GREEN, BLUE };
struct ColorPoint {
  enum COLOR color; /* color */
  long x;           /* horiz. coord. */
  long y;           /* vert. coord. */
};
struct NODE {
  struct ColorPoint value; /* value of node */
  struct NODE       *pNext; /* pointer to next node */
};
```

This IDL fragment is also legal C. Note that although it is also legal C++, IDL uses the C (not C++) convention of separating the tag namespace from the type namespace. This means that

```
struct NODE {
  ColorPoint value; // Not legal IDL
  NODE       *pNext; // Not legal IDL
};
```

is *not* legal IDL, because the names `ColorPoint` and `NODE` need to be scoped using the `struct` keyword.

The primary extension that IDL adds to the C language is the capability to define both COM interfaces and COM classes. The following IDL fragment is preferable to the `DECLARE_INTERFACE_`-based definition shown earlier:

```
[ uuid(30929828-5F86-11d1-B34E-0060975E6A6A), object ]
interface IPerson : IUnknown {
```

```
import "unknwn.idl";
void Marry([in] IPerson *pSpouse);
void RaiseSalary([in] long nAmount);
void Reproduce(void);
IPerson * GetSpouse(void);
long GetAge(void);
long GetSalary(void);
list<IPerson*> * GetChildren(void);
}
```

When this interface definition is presented to the IDL compiler, the problems mentioned earlier will cause the IDL compiler to emit error messages informing the interface designer of the error of his or her ways.

For example, since the IDL compiler assumes that the interface will be used across process and host boundaries, it ensures that all methods return HRESULTs. While it is possible to suppress this checking (as well as the generation of remoting code) by using the [local] attribute,

```
[
   uuid(30929828-5F86-11d1-B34E-0060975E6A6A),
   object, local
]
interface IPerson : IUnknown {
   ...
```

it is preferable to simply abide by the rules and conventions of COM and use the [retval] attribute to map physical parameters to logical results:

```
[ uuid(30929828-5F86-11d1-B34E-0060975E6A6A), object ]
interface IPerson : IUnknown {
   import "unknwn.idl";
   HRESULT Marry([in] IPerson *pSpouse);
   HRESULT RaiseSalary([in] long nAmount);
   HRESULT Reproduce(void);
   HRESULT GetSpouse([out, retval] IPerson *pRes);
   HRESULT GetAge([out, retval] long *pRes);
   HRESULT GetSalary([out, retval] long *pRes);
   HRESULT GetChildren([out, retval] list<IPerson*> **p);
}
```

This updated definition now has only one obstacle to successful compilation: the use of STL.

The parameter of the GetChildren method is defined in terms of an STL list. As was mentioned earlier, this technique exposes too much information about one particular implementation of this interface. Even if this didn't bother you, the IDL compiler will not allow STL (or any C++-specific types) to be used. Period. Even if one were to use the C preprocessor to #include the definition of list<>, the IDL compiler would choke on the use of C++-isms (e.g., templates and member function definitions) found in this file. The only reasonable solution is to choose a data type for the result that is compatible with IDL and COM.

If the expected implementation language is C or C++ only, the proper technique (as explained in Item 13) is to use an enumerator to model the resultant collection:

```
// enumerator interface to model collection of children
[ uuid(30929829-5F86-11d1-B34E-0060975E6A6A), object ]
interface IEnumPerson : IUnknown {
  import "unknwn.idl";
  HRESULT Next([in]  ULONG cElems,
      [in, size_is(cElems), length_is(*pcFetched)]
                    IPerson **rgElems,
              [out] ULONG *pcFetched);²
  HRESULT Skip([in] ULONG cElems);
  HRESULT Reset(void);
  HRESULT Clone([out] IEnumPerson **ppEnum);
}
```

With this interface in place, the GetChildren method can be defined as follows:

```
[ uuid(30929828-5F86-11d1-B34E-0060975E6A6A), object ]
interface IPerson : IUnknown {
  ...
  HRESULT GetChildren([out, retval] IEnumPerson **p);
}
```

Since the IEnum convention allows the underlying collection to be stored in any number of different forms (e.g., linked lists, arrays, or something more exotic), this interface does not betray any implementation details of one particular implementation class.

If compatibility with Visual Basic is needed, the resultant collection can be returned as either an automation-compatible collection interface or as a SAFEARRAY of interface pointers. The former would look like this:

```
// enumerator interface to model collection of children
```

```
    uuid(30929829-5F86-11d1-B34E-0060975E6A6A),
    object, dual
]
interface IPeople : IDispatch {
  import "oaidl.idl";
  HRESULT Item([in]  VARIANT varIndex,
               [out, retval] IPerson **ppRes);
  HRESULT Count([out, retval] long *pRes);
// support VB for each syntax via an IEnumVARIANT
  [id(DISPID_NEWENUM)]
  HRESULT _NewEnum([out, retval] IUnknown **ppEnumVar);
}
[
  uuid(30929828-5F86-11d1-B34E-0060975E6A6A),
  object
]
interface IPerson : IUnknown {
  import "oaidl.idl";
  HRESULT GetChildren([out, retval] IPeople **ppRes);
...
```

The latter would look like this:

```
[
  uuid(30929828-5F86-11d1-B34E-0060975E6A6A),
  object
]
interface IPerson : IUnknown {
  import "oaidl.idl";
  HRESULT GetChildren([out] SAFEARRAY(IPerson*) *ppsa);
...
```

The approach using IEnumVARIANT is somewhat more convenient for most Visual Basic programmers, and the approach using SAFEARRAYs will perform better when used across process boundaries due to a reduced number of round-trips. However, both suffer from the fact that the strict type of the interface will be lost as it is stuffed into a VARIANT or SAFEARRAY, which means that the client will need to issue an additional QueryInterface request for each element to regain the IPerson-ness of each object reference.

One remaining factor yet to be addressed is that this interface definition assumes that all implementations of IPerson are employable and that to be an employee, the operations GetSalary and RaiseSalary are correct and valid. Since the operations related to marriage and reproduction are orthogonal (at least in the authors' estimation) to the operations related to having a salary, it is more in line with COM design style to separate the two interfaces:

```
[ uuid(30929828-5F86-11d1-B34E-0060975E6A6A), object ]
interface IPerson : IUnknown {
  import "unknwn.idl";
  HRESULT Marry([in] IPerson *pSpouse);
  HRESULT Reproduce(void);
  HRESULT GetSpouse([out, retval] IPerson *pRes);
  HRESULT GetAge([out, retval] long *pRes);
  HRESULT GetChildren([out, retval] IEnumPerson **ppep);
}
[ uuid(3092982A-5F86-11d1-B34E-0060975E6A6A), object ]
interface ISalariedPerson : IPerson {
  import "unknwn.idl";
  HRESULT RaiseSalary([in] long nAmount);
  HRESULT GetSalary([out, retval] long *pRes);
}
```

The fact that ISalariedPerson derives from IPerson implies that all entities with salaries are also people. If this assumption is not valid (e.g., if animals are allowed to draw a salary), then the interface should derive from IUnknown since drawing a salary would then be orthogonal to being a person.

You may have noticed that we've gotten several pages into the book and haven't yet looked at an executable C++ statement. This is consistent with the COM way. The interface (not the class) dominates COM design style. Simply hacking together some methods and data members won't work any more (sorry).

2.   Design with distribution in mind.

One of the most common mistakes C++ developers make is forgetting that objects may be further away than they actually appear. Consider the following C++ code fragment:

```
// rect.cpp
int Rect::GetLeft() throw() {
  return m_nLeft;
}

// client.cpp
void foo(Rect& rect) {
```

```
    cout << rect.GetLeft();
}
```

As a C++ programmer, it's pretty obvious that the call to GetLeft cannot possibly fail—hence the notation that the function throws no exceptions. Assuming a valid object reference, nothing could possibly go wrong unless the user terminates the process while GetLeft is executing, in which case the calling code (which resides in the same process) won't be around to know the difference.

When designing a COM-based system in which objects potentially reside on different host machines, you cannot be this complacent. Networks can be unreliable, processes can die, and objects can vanish without warning. Therefore, when writing COM code, keep in mind that method calls that would traditionally be trusted to succeed may fail due to circumstances beyond the control of your code. A large dose of paranoia is healthy as you sketch out your design on a whiteboard or write code in your development environment.

To allow clients to detect communication problems, all methods must return an HRESULT. This allows COM's remoting layer to replace the object's return value with an error code that describes the communication failure. In theory, communication errors can be distinguished by checking for FACILITY_RPC via the HRESULT_FACILITY macro defined in winerror.h; however, recent versions of the COM library have begun to use FACILITY_WIN32 error codes as well. To preserve the convenient syntax for languages that support mapping HRESULTs to out-of-band exception mechanisms, use [retval] to specify the logical return value of the function. In most languages, this technique will allow the physical HRESULT return value to be translated automatically into an exception, allowing you to write client code that is easy to read:

```
// rope.idl
interface IRope : public IUnknown {
  HRESULT GetLength([out, retval] long* pnLength);
}
// ropeclient.bas
Sub foo(r As IRope)
  ' failed HRESULT will throw an exception
  ' which can be caught with an On Error statement
  On Error GoTo ExceptionHandler
  MsgBox "The rope is " & r.GetLength() & " ft long"
  Exit Sub
ExceptionHandler:
  MsgBox "Invocation failure."
End Sub
```

Unlike Java and Visual Basic developers, C++ developers must inspect each HRESULT by hand and take the appropriate action. A common approach in this case is to generate wrapper classes that translate failed HRESULTs into C++ exceptions; this allows the C++ developer to take advantage of the [retval] attribute as well. The #import directive provided by Visual C++ is an example of this technique.

Another common approach is to use a C++ class to map failed HRESULTs to C++ exceptions, as shown here:

```
struct HRX {
  HRX(void) { }
  HRX(HRESULT hr) { if (FAILED(hr)) throw hr; }
  HRX& operator=(HRESULT hr)
  { if (FAILED(hr)) throw hr; return *this; }
};
```

This class is convenient because it doesn't rely on compiler-specific extensions and its use looks very much like normal COM code.

```
void foo(IRope* pr) {
  try {
    HRX hrx;
    long    nLength;
    hrx = pr->GetLength(&nLength);
    char    sz[64];
    wsprintf(sz, "The rope is %d feet long", nLength);
    MessageBox(0, sz, 0, 0);
  }
  catch (HRESULT hr) {
    MessageBox(0, "Invocation failure.", "", 0);
  }
}
```

Note that the overloaded operator =() maps failed HRESULTs onto C++ exceptions.

The discussion so far has dealt with objects dying prematurely. It is also possible that a client can die without properly notifying the objects that it is using. This effectively means that any method call could be your last. While COM will eventually release any held object references, no additional action will be taken on behalf of a terminated client. The following is an example of an interface *not* designed with this fact in mind:[3]

---

[3] In fact, putting lock management this close to the client is a bad idea anyway, but it does make for an easy-to-grasp example.

```
[ uuid(31CDF640-E91A-11d1-9277-006008026FEA), object]
interface ISharedObject : IUnknown {
// call prior to calling DoWork
  HRESULT LockExclusive();
// ask object to do work while holding exclusive lock
  HRESULT DoWork();
// release lock held by LockExclusive
  HRESULT UnlockExclusive();
}
```

Given this interface definition, one might expect a client to look like this:

```
// sharedclient.cpp
void DoPrivateWork(ISharedObject *pso) {
  HRESULT hr = pso->LockExclusive();
  if (SUCCEEDED(hr)) {
    for (int i = 0; i < 10 && SUCCEEDED(hr); i++)
      hr = pso->DoWork();
    HRESULT hr2 = pso->UnlockExclusive();
  }
}
```

What happens if the client process terminates prior to reaching the call to
UnlockExclusive? Assuming that the object acquired a lock from the operating system in its implementation of LockExclusive, the lock will never be
released. Granted, the client's outstanding reference will be released automatically
by COM, but assuming that there are other outstanding clients, the object cannot detect that the client that held the lock has just died.

The problem of premature client death can be solved using COM's garbage collector. Since COM will automatically release any held object references when the
client process terminates, the ISharedObject interface could have been
based on having the lock released when an interface pointer was released, rather
than when an explicit method is called. Consider the following modified version
of the interface:

```
[ uuid(31CDF641-E91A-11d1-9277-006008026FEA), object]
interface ISharedObject2 : IUnknown {
// call prior to calling DoWork and release (*ppUnkLock)
// to unlock object
  HRESULT LockExclusive([out] IUnknown **ppUnkLock);
// ask object to do work while holding exclusive lock
  HRESULT DoWork();
}
```

Given this interface definition, it is trivial for the implementation to create a secondary object that will release the lock upon the client's final release. To accommodate this use of a second object identity that represents the lock acquisition, the client would be modified as follows:

```
// sharedclient2.cpp
void DoPrivateWork(ISharedObject2 *pso) {
  IUnknown *pUnkLock = 0;
// acquire lock
  HRESULT hr = pso->LockExclusive(&pUnkLock);
  if (SUCCEEDED(hr)) {
// do work 10 times while holding lock
    for (int i = 0; i < 10 && SUCCEEDED(hr); i++)
      hr = pso->DoWork();
// release lock by releasing "lock" object
    pUnkLock->Release();
  }
}
```

The implementation could then use the secondary object's destructor to fire the unlock operation. The following fragment demonstrates this technique using a Win32 semaphore as the lock:

```
// secondary object that releases lock at final release
class UnlockCookie : public IUnknown {
  HANDLE m_hsem;
  ULONG  m_cRefs;
public:
  UnlockCookie(HANDLE h) : m_hsem(h), m_cRefs(0) {}
  ~UnlockCookie() {
// release lock back to OS at final release
    ReleaseSemaphore(m_hsem, 1, 0);
  }
  // QueryInterface and AddRef omitted for brevity
  // Standard Release() impl. for heap-based object
  STDMETHODOIMP_(ULONG) Release() {
    ULONG cRefs = InterlockedDecrement(&m_cRefs);
    if (0 == cRefs)
      delete this;
    return cRefs;
  }
};
// primary object that holds lock until released
class SharedObject : public ISharedObject2 {
```

```
HANDLE m_hsem; // init'ed in constructor
STDMETHODIMP LockExclusive(IUnknown **ppUnkLock) {
  // acquire lock from OS
  WaitForSingleObject(m_hsem, INFINITE);
  // create and return an intermediate object that
  // will unlock at its final release
  // memory allocation errors ignored for clarity
  (*ppUnkLock = new UnlockCookie(m_hsem))->AddRef();
  return S_OK;
}
:     :      :
};
```

Note that in this example, if the client dies any time after the call to `LockExclusive` succeeds, COM will automatically release the reference to the intermediate object, which will trigger the release of the OS lock.

Although the interface design shown here does not distinguish between the premature death of a client and a client deliberately releasing the lock, this could easily be addressed by the following slight modification:

```
[ uuid(31CDF642-E91A-11d1-9277-006008026FEA), object]
interface IUnlockCookie : IUnknown {
// call to release the underlying lock
  HRESULT UnlockExclusive();
}
[ uuid(31CDF643-E91A-11d1-9277-006008026FEA), object]
interface ISharedObject3 : IUnknown {
// call prior to calling DoWork and call
// ILockCookie::UnlockExclusive to unlock object
  HRESULT LockExclusive([out] IUnlockCookie **ppuc);
// ask object to do work while holding exclusive lock
  HRESULT DoWork();
}
```

Given this interface definition, the object can now distinguish between an explicit unlock or a premature death based on whether the `UnlockExclusive` method is called prior to the intermediate object's final release.

Additional failure modes are only one problem that developers face when moving to distributed object computing. Another common problem is related to the latency that exists when executing a method call. Consider the case of public attributes or properties. When developers first begin building object-oriented (OO) software, they must learn many new concepts, including classes and encapsulation. To this end, most novice developers are told early in their careers that all data members should be private. In order to respect the sensibilities of OO purists, many developers reflexively make all instance data private and then proceed to define individual accessor and mutator functions to expose their members to the public. This technique, known colloquially in some circles as *just enough encapsulation*, in many ways eliminates any potential benefit of encapsulation by exposing implementation details to the outside world. Although this technique is only marginally better than simply using public data members, it is tolerated in the C++ community because it typically has no impact on the performance of member access, since these functions are usually inlined by the compiler.

The real problem with just enough encapsulation arises when it is applied to COM. When designing interfaces for use in a distributed system, you must avoid this technique at all costs. Due to the independent compilation and dynamic binding of method calls inherent in COM, inline implementation is impossible. More important, each call normally implies a round-trip, which may involve a remote procedure call (RPC), depending on the locality of the caller and callee.

As an interface designer, you should always consider the impact of round-trips on both the performance and the semantics of an interface. An interface that requires multiple round-trips to perform a single logical operation is an interface that will subject its users to poor performance and potential race conditions. As an example, consider the following interface:

```
interface IRect : IUnknown {
  HRESULT SetLeft   ([in] long nLeft);
  HRESULT SetTop    ([in] long nTop);
  HRESULT SetRight  ([in] long nRight);
  HRESULT SetBottom ([in] long nBottom);
  HRESULT GetLeft   ([out, retval] long* pnLeft);
  HRESULT GetTop    ([out, retval] long* pnTop);
  HRESULT GetRight  ([out, retval] long* pnRight);
  HRESULT GetBottom ([out, retval] long* pnBottom);
}
```

This interface requires four round-trips to obtain the state of the rectangle. Although IRect is obviously far from optimal in terms of performance, the lack of atomicity is a far more subtle but harmful flaw. While you are busy making round-trips to get the entire state of the rectangle, another client may be changing the state underneath you. Because the entire state of the rectangle cannot be fetched atomically in one round-trip, you cannot be guaranteed a consistent view of the rectangle's state.

With this in mind, you set off to create a better rectangle interface:

```
interface IRect2 : IUnknown {
  HRESULT SetRect( [in] long nLeft,
                   [in] long nTop,
                   [in] long nRight,
                   [in] long nBottom );
  HRESULT GetRect( [out] long* pnLeft,
                   [out] long* pnTop,
                   [out] long* pnRight,
                   [out] long* pnBottom );
}
```

This new and improved interface requires only one round-trip to get or set the state, and thus ensures that you will indeed obtain a consistent view of the rectangle, with much improved performance across apartment boundaries.

Note that IRect2 has lost some of the flexibility of IRect. What if you wanted to set only one coordinate to 100 and leave the other three coordinates as is? This is impossible to do atomically with the current design of IRect2, because it requires two round-trips. One totally acceptable solution is to add an extra parameter to the SetRect function to allow finer-grained control:

```
HRESULT SetRect( [in] long nLeft,
                 [in] long nTop,
                 [in] long nRight,
                 [in] long nBottom,
                 [in] DWORD grfWhichCoords );
typedef enum tagSRWC {
  SRWC_LEFT   = 0x0001,
  SRWC_TOP    = 0x0002,
  SRWC_RIGHT  = 0x0004,
  SRWC_BOTTOM = 0x0008
} SRWC; // SetRectWhichCoords
```

Another solution would be to lump the members of IRect and IRect2 into a single interface; however, this solution would create a somewhat cumbersome interface (as with C++ interfaces, COM interfaces should be minimal and complete). Also, such an interface would not allow setting exactly two or three attributes at a time instead of one or four.

Another common race condition with an interface such as `IRect2` surfaces when you consider offsetting the rectangle by some value, because you must make two round-trips to perform a single logical operation. In this case, you might consider that rectangles are only one species of many that may require translation and, therefore, design a separate interface that eliminates race conditions for many types of two-dimensional (2D) objects:

```
interface I2DObject : IUnknown {
  HRESULT Translate([in] long dx, [in] long dy);
  HRESULT Inflate([in] long dx, [in] long dy);
  HRESULT Rotate([in] double degreesInRadians,
                 [in] long xCenter, [in] long yCenter)
}
```

You may be noticing a common theme here. To avoid race conditions, be sure that each logical operation can be performed by a single round-trip. Unnecessary round-trips are evil: avoid them.

When designing interfaces, it is often an interesting exercise to use a packet sniffer to actually look at what is being sent across the wire,[4] both on a per-method and per-object or client basis. To do this, you must have a client communicating to an object on a remote host, since COM does not use the TCP loopback interface for local communications. One particularly useful technique is to observe the actual size and structure of the marshaled parameters for any given remote call. An afternoon spent with NETMON.EXE or the Network Data Representation (NDR) protocol specification will show that some structures can be more expensive to marshal than you might anticipate.

Developers who anticipate that their interfaces will only be used by in-process (or more specifically, same-apartment) clients often feel that they are exempt from worrying about network failures, round-trips, wire representations, and race conditions. It is important to remember that COM is no different from any other technology in that it is important to design in the future tense. Realize that "in-process" and "out-of-process" are often temporary present-tense implementation details and that most well-designed interfaces can be used effectively in both scenarios. Item 9 discusses a well-known example of the "it will only ever be used in-process" trap.

Finally, remember that one of the big wins of interface-based programming is design reuse. As you spend more of your waking hours poring over the documentation of the hundreds of new interfaces springing up to solve various problems,

---

[4] The Network Monitor that ships with Windows NT Server and Systems Management Server is a reasonable product that parses COM packet traces fairly well, although any DCE RPC- compatible product will do.

you will learn to love the simple, well-designed interfaces (e.g., IUnknown) whose well-known semantics you simply take for granted after a while. When learning a completely new technology exposed via COM interfaces, these well-known interfaces become good friends.

3.   Objects should not have their own user interface.

Model-view-controller. Document-view. Source-sink. These are all different ways of saying the same thing—objects should not have their own user interface (UI). For example, consider an application that has created an object on a remote machine. Assume that the object can calculate pi to any number of digits. Also assume that the object is running on a separate machine in order to leverage remote computational resources. What happens when the client machine requests that the calculation begin but has not yet specified the required precision? Should the pi calculator object (a) fail, (b) pick some default number of digits, (c) perform a callback to the client application to request the number of digits, (d) keep calculating until asked to stop, or (e) ask the end user how many digits to calculate? If you picked anything other than (e), you're right.

On the other hand, if the object were to put up a dialog box and request the number of digits, who would see it? The user is running the client application on a machine other than that of the pi calculator. In all likelihood the two machines are in different rooms, if not different buildings or continents. Perhaps, if the user is lucky, the system administrator happens to be working on the remote machine and the object is running in a context where it can ask him the number of digits. If this is the case, then perhaps somehow the administrator will guess the correct number of digits and will enter them on the user's behalf. Otherwise, the user is out of luck and the calculation will appear to be taking incredibly long to complete while the dialog box sits silently waiting for the warm touch of a human hand.

The argument for decoupling the user interface from an object implementation is hard to refute in the remote case. If you build your user interface into objects that run on remote machines, it's pretty obvious that the intended user is never going to see it. What about objects that live on the same machine or even in the same address space? Isn't it OK for those objects to have their own UIs? No. Here's why. What should the UI of your object look like? Should it be separate and run in its own window? Should it plan to be a part of a larger window hierarchy? Should it be white with black letters? Should it have a 2D look or a more modern 3D look? Who knows? The consumer of your object (the client) certainly doesn't want the end user to think of the pi calculation engine as a different part of the application that has been shoehorned in sideways. Rather, the user should see an integrated whole. The UI for the pi calculation engine should mesh seamlessly into the client's UI, no matter what style of UI the client happens to be using at any given time. One possible approach would be to add a user interface for controlling every conceivable display option and setting. However, this will likely be orthogonal to your object's intended core functionality. Because you will never be able to anticipate every kind of UI with which your object will have to integrate, this approach can only work in the simplest cases. A better approach is to let the object do the real work and consider the UI to be the glue that allows client developers to have a standard disposable mechanism for allowing users to manipulate your object. It is important to isolate the functionality of your low-level components from the UI; otherwise, every UI change is going to ripple through everything. And it's the UI that changes most often, especially in the final phases of development.

This is not to say that some objects shouldn't be user-interface objects. Many UI frameworks further separate their layout into discrete cooperating pieces to form an integrated whole. In COM, UI-only objects are called *controls*. A control basically owns a section of a window that it draws. Since the control exists solely to represent the UI of another object, it should maintain no state that is not directly needed for the local user interface. Any UI-independent state (and functionality) should remain in the actual object that is being represented by the control. This enables users of multiple controls to manipulate and display the same object in different ways, *à la* model-view-controller.

Simply creating distinct UI objects isn't quite enough. You also need to ensure that any nontrivial logic and behavior stays out of the user-interface object hierarchy and stays in the logic and abstraction object hierarchy. A common bad habit that many Microsoft Foundation Classes (MFC) and Visual Basic developers acquire is to use menu-item event handlers as the repository of all application logic. When these developers change their UI, they find themselves moving the logic code around to match the UI *du jour*. This makes it especially difficult to replace the entire UI framework (e.g., MFC) because much of the application logic is tightly coupled to the framework-specific code.

These issues are often addressed by refining the document-view style of architecture to the extreme: multitiered architectures. In a multitiered architecture, every layer of abstraction you add, while it adds communications overhead, offers opportunities for extensibility, maintainability, scalability, and flexibility. One natural artifact of building multitiered architectures is that your core object hierarchy is shielded from the latest UI requirements. This is a fundamental promise of object orientation: not that every object is necessarily self-sufficient but that objects can work together cohesively to perform the required task. When the task changes, the same objects can be reused in a different way without being completely rebuilt.

4.   Beware the COM singleton.

People put a lot of effort into implementing singletons in COM. A *singleton* is an object that is the one and only instance of its class. The patterns movement formalized the concept of a singleton as a technique for allowing multiple clients to acquire references to the same object via a well-known access point.

Singletons are often employed to provide an object-based rendezvous point that can replace class-level methods (e.g., static member functions of a C++ class). The most direct translation of this technique into COM is to expose a custom interface from your class object. However, this requires you to step out of the default behavior of most COM development tools (e.g., ATL, MFC) and therefore is not as common a practice as it perhaps should be. Instead, many developers choose to overload their implementation of `IClass-Factory::CreateInstance` to achieve the same effect:

```
class Dog : public IDog {
// implementation of Dog deleted for clarity
};

// singleton version of CreateInstance
STDMETHODIMP DogClass::CreateInstance(
        IUnknown *pUnkOuter, REFIID riid, void **ppv)
{
// declare a "singleton" object
  static Dog s_Dog;
// disallow aggregation
  if (pUnkOuter)
    return (*ppv = 0), CLASS_E_NOAGGREGATION;
// return a pointer to the "singleton"
  return s_Dog.QueryInterface(riid, ppv);
}
```

The ActiveX Template Library (ATL) uses a variation on this technique when you use the `DECLARE_CLASSFACTORY_SINGLETON` macro in your class definition. Technically, this meets the formal definition of a singleton: every client gets a reference to the same instance of the class Dog through a well-known access point—the Dog class object. However, there are problems with this approach.

First, when you expose singleton objects via CreateInstance trickery, you are violating the semantics of IClassFactory. CreateInstance is documented as *creating* a new, uninitialized object. Clients that expect two calls to CreateInstance to provide two separate objects may be surprised by the behavior of this deviant implementation.

Semantically, it would be better to simply use some other interface to gain access to the singleton. You could define your own custom interface for this purpose or reuse a standard interface that matches your semantic requirements (e.g., IOleItemContainer):

```
// Custom interface implemented by class object
interface ISingletonFactory : IUnknown {
  HRESULT GetSingleInstance([in] REFIID riid,
          [out, iid_is(riid)] void **ppv);
}
// Implementation of GetSingleInstance
HRESULT DogClass::GetSingleInstance(REFIID riid,
                                    void **ppv)
{
  static Dog s_Dog;
  return s_Dog.QueryInterface(riid, ppv);
}
```

Note that this technique is difficult to implement and use in languages that hide the details of class objects (e.g., Visual Basic, Java, and the various scripting languages). You can implement a variation on this theme that works with all languages using a separate Manager class, instances of which can be used to access the singleton.

Maybe you're worried about playing fast and loose with CreateInstance's semantics and maybe you're not. Either way, there's another problem that should cause concern. If your implementation of CreateInstance (or Get-SingleInstance or its equivalent) always returns a reference to the same COM object, it may violate COM's concurrency laws. COM objects live in apartments, and COM requires that you marshal interface pointers if you want to move them across apartment boundaries (see Item 28). If your singleton is being used from multiple apartments in a single process and your class object returns this interface pointer directly, your code violates this rule. This means that if your class is deployed as an in-process server, you must mark it ThreadingModel=Free or leave the ThreadingModel attribute out of the registry. Otherwise, you are subject to the same pitfalls as objects that use the Free-Threaded Marshaler (FTM). (See Item 32 for a detailed description of why apartment-neutral objects require a great deal of attention to implement properly.)

So perhaps you're a tough-as-nails COM developer, and you've mastered all of the threading details of COM. Now you have to think about design. First and foremost, the singleton pattern assumes a naïve association between state and behavior. Even outside the scope of COM, it is commonplace for two or more objects to share state. More often than not, developers use the singleton idiom in COM to achieve a rendezvous point for two or more clients to access shared state. If this is all that is needed, the following singleton-style implementation,

```
class Dog {
  long m_nHairs;
  HRESULT Shed(void) {
    m_nHairs -= 100;
    return S_OK;
  }
};
```

could be replaced by

```
class Dog {
  static long s_nHairs; // shared state
  Dog(void) : m_nHairs(s_nHairs) {}
  long& m_nHairs; // note that a reference is now used
  HRESULT Shed(void) {
    m_nHairs -= 100;
    return S_OK;
  }
};
```

In the former case, some technique is needed to ensure that only one instance of Dog is ever created. In the latter case, there is no restriction on the number of Dogs created, as each dog shares its hair count using a static variable. The advantage of the latter approach is that the implementer can change the state management policy silently in the constructor to implement per-client behavior. This is not possible in a naïve singleton-based approach, as each client gets a reference to one particular object. Additionally, the latter approach is extremely straightforward to implement in any language irrespective of its support for low-level COM plumbing.

It is important to remember that the singleton solution was originally conceived as the remedy for a problem that often arises during the development of *stand-alone* applications. What is the role of a singleton in a *distributed* application that includes multiple processes on multiple machines?

First, what is the singleton's scope? Remember that a COM object can be activated in a client's process, in a separate process on a client's machine, or in a process on some other machine. If you implement your class object to return references to a singleton object, is that singleton unique in its process, on its machine, or across several machines on a network?

When applied to distributed computing, singletons break down fairly rapidly because they limit the implementer's options for load balancing, concurrency management, prioritization, and per-client state management. Consider applying singletons to an airline reservation system. If you represented a particular flight, say United Flight 162 from Boston's Logan Airport to LAX, as a network-wide singleton, you'd create a massive bottleneck. Thousands of users all over the world might need to deal with that one object simultaneously, and that's more than a single COM object should be expected to bear. The singleton mechanism was not designed with this problem in mind.

What's the solution? Realize that singletons are built on the notion of a shared physical identity. In other words, a singleton implies that there is a single COM identity in a single apartment of a single process on a single machine that is the one and only representation of some entity in your distributed system. Discard this idea and instead concentrate on logical identity. Allow multiple COM objects in different apartments of separate processes on more than one machine to represent the same logical entity. To achieve the effects of a singleton, all of these objects, perhaps as many as one per client, simply access the same shared state.

If you follow this path, you open the door to load balancing. If you create a separate COM object per client, you can also cache per-client state in each object. You can detect individual client death based on individual per-client objects being released by COM's garbage collector (see Item 2 for an example of this technique). Assuming each object refers to shared state, you technically are pushing the concurrency issues down one level, which means you (not COM) are on the hook for protecting against concurrent access. Transactions help with this problem immensely (in fact, this is essentially the Microsoft Transaction Server model).

So where are we? If you're a big fan of singletons, that's fine. Just understand where a singleton really helps and where it really hinders. As you build larger and larger distributed systems, realize that network-wide singletons become less and less useful. Also be aware that if you plan on using MTS as part of your infrastructure, singletons are *verboten*.

5. Don't allow C++ exceptions to cross method boundaries.

Exceptions in C++ provide a standard, extensible error handling mechanism that can be used across class libraries built by multiple organizations. Unfortunately, because there is no binary standard for C++ exceptions, their use requires that all of the source code for the application and the libraries be compiled together into a single executable image. This defeats one of the core motivations for using COM. Throwing C++ exceptions between separate executable images simply doesn't work. What that means to you, a COM developer, is that no C++ exception can be thrown from a COM method call.

One fact that developers must realize when shifting to COM from pure C++-based development is that the semantics of C++ exceptions are really twofold. On the one hand, exceptions are simply implicit output parameters of a function. On the other hand, exceptions are used to stop the normal thread of execution and force the caller to react to the exception. It is trivial to handle the former simply by adding additional [out] parameters that can carry information describing exceptional events that might take place during method execution. As for the latter, one could argue that it is not the object's responsibility to mandate alternative execution paths in the client program. This is certainly the philosophy of the COM designers, who felt that it was a client's decision how to deal with application-level errors (after all, not all languages support exceptions). Because of this, COM has no explicit support for C++-style exceptions.

Because it is illegal for a COM method to throw a C++ exception, you must bracket all COM method implementations in a try-catch block if you are using libraries that throw C++ exceptions. Of course, to simulate the expressiveness of C++ exceptions, you may use very specific or even custom error codes:

```
HRESULT CoPenguin::Fly() {
  try {
    return TryToFly();
  }
  // Handle standard C++ out of memory exception
  catch (xalloc& x) {
    return E_OUTOFMEMORY;
```

```
  }
  // Handle custom errors (published in the IDL)
  catch (xbiology& x) {
    return BIRD_E_CHEATEDBYNATURE;
  }
  // Handle everything else
  catch (...) {
    return E_FAIL;
  }
}
```

To define a custom HRESULT, use the standard MAKE_HRESULT macro defined in winerror.h:

```
#define MAKE_HRESULT(sev,fac,code) \
  ((HRESULT) (((unsigned long)(sev)<<31) | \
  ((unsigned long)(fac)<<16) | \
  ((unsigned long)(code))) )
```

Briefly, an HRESULT is broken into a severity bit, a facility code, and an error code. The severity bit describes success or failure, the facility code defines the range of error codes, and the error code itself describes what happened. Custom HRESULTs use the FACILITY_ITF facility. Unfortunately, the OLE group at Microsoft hijacked the first 512 codes in the interface facility for OLE-specific and COM-generic results. When defining an interface-specific HRESULT, remember to start past 0x1ff, as is shown here:

```
#include <winerror.h>
import "objidl.idl";
[ uuid(18FDEA81-1115-11d2-A4B3-006008D1A534), object ]
interface IBird : IUnknown {
  enum BirdResults {
    BIRD_E_CHEATEDBYNATURE =
      MAKE_HRESULT(SEVERITY_ERROR,
                   FACILITY_ITF,
                   0x200),
    BIRD_S_FLYINGHIGH =
      MAKE_HRESULT(SEVERITY_SUCCESS,
                   FACILITY_ITF,
                   0x201)
  };
// IBird methods…
}
```

Unfortunately, a custom HRESULT doesn't capture the expressiveness that is possible using traditional C++ exceptions. For example, an HRESULT can't convey the source of an error or a textual description of the error. Although one can turn a standard HRESULT into a textual description suitable for debugging with the `FormatMessage` function, as shown here,

```
void OutputDebugHresult(HRESULT hr) {
  char szDesc[1024];
  BOOL bRet = FormatMessageA(FORMAT_MESSAGE_FROM_SYSTEM,
                  0, hr, 0, szDesc, sizeof(szDesc), 0);
  if (!bRet)
    lstrcpyA(szDesc, "Unknown Error");
  OutputDebugString(szDesc);
}
```

it is difficult (but not impossible) to extend this technique to retrieve descriptions of custom HRESULTs. Fortunately, there is a much simpler alternative: COM error information objects (often called *COM exceptions*).

Every thread that uses COM has an implicit error information object reference associated with it by COM. At thread initialization time, this reference is NULL, indicating that there is no exception information. When an object wishes to throw an exception to the caller, it associates an error information object with the current thread and then indicates that the method failed by returning a SEVER-ITY_ERROR HRESULT. Clients that wish to catch the exception simply inspect the reference to see if it has been set.

A COM error information object is a COM object that implements at least the `IErrorInfo` interface:

```
interface IErrorInfo : IUnknown {
  HRESULT GetGUID([out] GUID * pGUID);
  HRESULT GetSource([out] BSTR * pBstrSource);
  HRESULT GetDescription([out] BSTR * pBstrDesc);
  HRESULT GetHelpFile([out] BSTR * pBstrHelpFile);
  HRESULT GetHelpContext([out] DWORD * pdwHelpContext);
}
```

Not only does `IErrorInfo` provide a textual description of the error and its source, but it also provides the interface identifier of the method that originated the error. Optionally, it provides a reference into a help file that allows a development environment to provide the developer a great deal of information about an object's errors.

When an error occurs in the course of a COM method call, an error info object can be constructed and returned *even across apartment boundaries*. The error info object interface is marshaled[5] along with the HRESULT back to the caller and can be accessed from any COM client. In this way COM provides the mechanism to throw and catch language-independent exceptions.

While it's possible to implement your own error object that implements IErrorInfo and any custom interfaces you'd like, most clients will only ask for the IErrorInfo interface. Because few clients support anything other than IErrorInfo, it's often convenient to use the COM-provided CreateErrorInfo function, which will create a new default error info object and return the ICreateErrorInfo interface for setting its state:

```
interface ICreateErrorInfo : IUnknown {
  HRESULT SetGUID([in] REFGUID rguid);
  HRESULT SetSource([in] LPOLESTR szSource);
  HRESULT SetDescription([in] LPOLESTR szDesc);
  HRESULT SetHelpFile([in] LPOLESTR szHelpFile);
  HRESULT SetHelpContext([in] DWORD dwHelpContext);
}
```

Once the error info object's state has been set, you can throw it using the SetErrorInfo function. Here's an example:

```
HRESULT ComThrow(LPCOLESTR pszSource, LPCOLESTR pszDesc,
                 REFIID riid) {
  ICreateErrorInfo* pcei = 0;
  HRESULT hr = CreateErrorInfo(&pcei);
  if (SUCCEEDED(hr)) {
    pcei->SetSource(const_cast<OLECHAR*>(pszSource));
    pcei->SetDescription(const_cast<OLECHAR*>(pszDesc));
    pcei->SetGUID(riid);

    IErrorInfo* pei = 0;
    hr = pcei->QueryInterface(IID_IErrorInfo,
                              (void**)&pei);
    if (SUCCEEDED(hr)) {
      hr = SetErrorInfo(0, pei);
      pei->Release();
    }
    pcei->Release();
  }
```

---

[5] To avoid round-trips, error info objects often implement custom marshaling to pass the error information by value. COM's default error info object certainly does this.

```
        return hr;
   }
```

On the client side, you can retrieve the error info object after a failed COM method call using the GetErrorInfo function:

```
void ComCatch() {
   HRESULT       hr;
   IErrorInfo* pei = 0;
   hr = GetErrorInfo(0, &pei);
   if (hr == S_OK) {
      BSTR bstrSource = 0;
      BSTR bstrDesc = 0;

      pei->GetSource(&bstrSource);
      pei->GetDescription(&bstrDesc);

      OLECHAR szErr[1024];
      wsprintfW(szErr, L"%s: %s", bstrSource, bstrDesc);
      OutputDebugStringW(szErr);

      SysFreeString(bstrSource);
      SysFreeString(bstrDesc);
   }
}
```

When using error info objects, the object must implement the ISupport-ErrorInfo interface (this is the equivalent of C++'s throw specification). Well-implemented clients will ask an object for this interface and call its single method, InterfaceSupportsErrorInfo, to guard against unwanted propagation of exceptions.

The discussion so far has ignored the fact that C++ exceptions are typed to allow catching hierarchies of exceptions in a single catch block. If this capability is absolutely critical to your design, you can achieve this kind of typed exception mechanism by mapping typed C++ exceptions as COM output parameters. This means that the following C++ function definition,

```
short LibGetMyShort(void) throw (long, std::wstring);
```

would look like this in IDL:

```
[
   uuid(18FDEA80-1115-11d2-A4B3-006008D1A534),
   object, pointer_default(unique)
```

```
]
interface IFakeExceptions : IUnknown {
  HRESULT GetMyShort([out] long **ppl,
                     [out] LPOLESTR *ppsz,
                     [out, retval] short *pres);
}
```

Given this method definition, objects could then provide the following mapping
of C++ exceptions to [out] parameters:

```
STDMETHODIMP GetMyShort(long **ppl, LPOLESTR *ppsz,
                        short *pres) {
  try {
// null out exception parameters
    *ppl = 0;
    *ppsz = 0;
// call exception-throwing C++ code
    *pres = LibGetMyShort();
    return S_OK;
  }
  catch (long l) { // map exception to [out] param
    *ppl = (long*)CoTaskMemAlloc(sizeof(long));
    **ppl = l;
  }
  catch (const wstring& s) { // map exception to param
    DWORD cb = (s.length() + 1) * sizeof(OLECHAR);
    *ppsz = (OLECHAR*)CoTaskMemAlloc(cb);
    wcscpy(*ppsz, s.c_str());
  }
  catch (...) {
  }
  return E_FAIL;
}
```

Clients wishing to map the explicit [out] parameters back to C++ exceptions
could do so as follows:

```
short CallGetMyShort(IFakeExceptions *pfe)
                                throw (long, std::wstring) {
  long *pl; LPOLESTR pwsz = 0; short s;
  HRESULT hr = pfe->GetMyShort(&pl, &pwsz, &s);
  if (SUCCEEDED(hr))
    return s;
  if (pl) { // a long was thrown
```

```
      assert(pwsz == 0); // only one exception allowed
      long ex = *pl;
      CoTaskMemFree(pl);
      throw ex;
   }
   else if (pwsz) { // a string was thrown
      assert(pl == 0); // only one exception allowed
      std::wstring ex = pwsz;
      CoTaskMemFree(pwsz);
      throw ex;
   }
   else
      unexpected(); // std routine for bad exceptions
}
```

Granted, this technique requires a nontrivial amount of manual conversion from
explicit parameters to exceptions, but the result retains the semantic information
that was originally available using typed exceptions. However, because mapping
C++ exceptions in this manner is extremely tedious, many developers make do
with the utilitarian (if less functional) GetErrorInfo/SetErrorInfo
mechanism.

Interfaces

In COM, the interface is everything. If interfaces are not properly designed, the system is doomed to poor performance at best and unpredictable behavior at worst. A properly designed interface lends itself to natural implementation techniques. Poorly designed interfaces tend to be difficult to implement and to use. In many ways, interfaces represent a significant portion of a component's design. In this spirit, time spent up front getting the interface right will pay off in spades when implementing and testing. While it is possible to implement interfaces using a variety of tools, the authors firmly and unanimously agree that all interfaces should be defined first in the Interface Definition Language (IDL), irrespective of the language in which you choose to implement your components. This deliberate act of transcribing your thoughts and ideas into a nonexecutable form forces you to think outside the constraints of the particular coding problem at hand. This chapter discusses the factors that influence efficiency and ease of use when designing interfaces, focusing on techniques that are likely to work properly in concurrent and distributed scenarios.

6. Interfaces are syntax and loose semantics. Both are immutable.

Prior to the release of COM in 1993, COM interfaces were originally called protocols. The term *protocol* comes from the Greek word *proto-koleon*, which was a sheet glued to the front of a manuscript, bearing an abstract of the contents. If one replaces the word *manuscript* in the previous sentence with *object*, this definition captures the essence of what a COM interface is all about.

COM interfaces describe the abstract requests you can make of an object. This description takes two forms. One form is that of syntax. The IDL definition of an interface completely defines the syntax of each request. The exact form of the call stack can be determined from the IDL description. Assuming that the IDL compiler will be generating the interface marshaler, the exact form of the ORPC request and response messages can be determined as well. Syntactically, the IDL description leaves no room for misinterpretation.

The second form of an interface description is that of semantics. Unfortunately, this form of description is very hard to capture in an IDL file. A well-behaved interface design must also provide clear and concise documentation that describes the purpose of the interface, the semantic meaning of each method, the legal parameter values and results, and any pre- or postconditions that must be fulfilled by all clients and implementations of the interface.

A properly designed (and documented) interface will provide clients with reasonable assurances with respect to how the object will behave, without putting undue restrictions on how object implementers will implement the interface. By leaving some room for interpretation, a properly designed interface will allow a controlled amount of uncertainty to exist on the client's behalf. This controlled uncertainty is the underpinning of polymorphism and is critical to the interface-based programming style used in COM-based systems.

It is possible to be overly specific in an interface definition. For example, consider the following interface for allowing objects to render themselves:

```
[ object, uuid(B286B9F0-6118-11d1-9234-006008026FEA) ]
interface IRenderable : IUnknown {
  HRESULT Draw([in] HDC hdc, [in] const RECT *prcBound);
  HRESULT GetExtent([out] long *pnw, [out] long *pnh);
}
```

Consider hypothetical documentation for the Draw method that contained a phrase such as the following:

All implementations of Draw must display yellow polka dots on a solid green background. There should be one polka dot for each 100 units. Each polka dot should have a diameter of 30 units.

This description leaves no room for interpretation. The semantics of Draw will always be "draw yellow polka dots on a green background" irrespective of the object that implements the interface. In this case, there is virtually no uncertainty in the definition, making polymorphism pointless. Based on this definition, one implementation of IRenderable is as good as any other implementation.

In contrast, consider the semantics of the Draw method when phrased as follows:

All implementations of Draw *must use the* hdc *parameter to render themselves. This device context will only remain valid for the duration of the method call. Storing the* hdc *for later use is not guaranteed to work. The* hdc *provided must already be configured to draw in hi-metric units by the client. No implementation of* Draw *should render outside the* prcBound *rectangle*

This description is vastly superior to the previous description. Note that much more information is provided about the semantics of each parameter. Also, the interface description provides as many guidelines for clients as it does for implementers.

It is often tempting to change the definition after an interface has been published. This is anathema in COM. There are three types of changes developers are known to make: (1) deleting or changing existing method signatures, (2) adding new methods, and (3) changing the semantics of existing methods. All three are equally bad. The reasons why the first type of change is bad should be obvious. Consider the IRenderable interface shown above. If one object implementer were to change the interface definition as follows,

```
[ object, uuid(B286B9F0-6118-11d1-9234-006008026FEA) ]
interface IRenderable : IUnknown {
  HRESULT Draw([in] HDC hdc, [in] const RECT *prcBound);
  HRESULT GetExtent([out] double *pnw,
                    [out] double *pnh);
}
```

to accommodate floating-point numbers for dimensioning, what would happen if the following legacy client were to encounter one of these floating-point-based objects?

```
bool HowBig(IUnknown *pUnk, long& width, long& height) {
  IRenderable *pRend = 0;
  HRESULT hr = pUnk->QueryInterface(IID_IRenderable,
                                    (void**)&pRend);
  if (SUCCEEDED(hr)) {
    hr = pRend->GetExtent(&width, &height);
    pRend->Release();
  }
  return SUCCEEDED(hr);
}
```

Because the same globally unique identifier (GUID) is used, both the client and the object believe they are talking about the same interface, so the QueryInterface request will not fail. However, because both parties have differing views on what IID_IRenderable means, there is an impedance mismatch between the client and the object.

If the object exists in the apartment of the client, then a malformed stack frame would be presented to the object and, in all likelihood, data corruption would occur as the object attempted to write an 8-byte value into a 4-byte memory location. If the object were in a different apartment, then either the client or the object would wind up with a malformed stack frame, depending on which version of the proxy/stub dynamic-link library (DLL) was registered last on the machine. If two machines are involved, then the impedance mismatch will occur at the packet level instead, likely resulting in invalid results but, in this case at least, with no additional side effects.

Consider the case of deleting a method altogether. If the method definition is removed from the IDL file,

```
[ object, uuid(B286B9F0-6118-11d1-9234-006008026FEA) ]
interface IRenderable : IUnknown {
  // deleted Draw method
  HRESULT GetExtent([out] long *pnw, [out] long *pnh);
}
```

far worse things will happen. Because COM method invocation is based on offsets into function pointer vectors, there is now a mismatch between the old offsets and the new offsets. Preexisting clients and objects believe that the Draw method is at offset 3 and that the GetExtent method is at offset 4 (the three IUnknown methods always occupy offsets 0, 1, and 2). Clients and objects compiled against this new interface definition believe that offset 3 now belongs to GetExtent and that offset 4 is not a valid offset. For newly compiled objects, offset 4 in the vtable will contain garbage. The following table shows what happens when old and new interface definitions meet.

Scenario	Client calls Draw	Client calls GetExtent
Old client, old object	Draw invoked	GetExtent invoked
New client, new object	N/A	GetExtent invoked
Old client, new object	GetExtent invoked	Undefined
New client, old object	N/A	Draw invoked

Note that when the versions match, the results are reasonable, but when there is a version mismatch, the results are predictably wrong. This table applies not only to intra-apartment invocation, where the offsets represent an index into an array of function pointers, but also to interapartment invocation, where the same offsets are used as operation numbers in the DCE RPC packet header.

The issue of offset management also comes into play when you try to add new methods to an existing interface. Consider the following modification to `IRenderable`:

```
[ object, uuid(B286B9F0-6118-11d1-9234-006008026FEA) ]
interface IRenderable : IUnknown {
  HRESULT Draw([in] HDC hdc, [in] const RECT *prcBound);
  HRESULT GetExtent([out] long *pnw, [out] long *pnh);
  HRESULT SetExtent([in] long nw, [in] long nh);
}
```

This interface definition now claims that there is a new offset (5) that must be valid in all `IRenderable` vtables. However, the contents of offset 5 in all existing `IRenderable` vtables is undefined, resulting in the following table.

Scenario	Client calls `SetExtent`
Old client, old object	N/A
New client, new object	`SetExtent` invoked
Old client, new object	N/A
New client, old object	Undefined

Here, the hazards of versioning seem less dangerous because only one combination results in bad things happening. However, this one combination may or may not be avoidable, depending on the deployment scenario. Of course, since the interface definition may seep out of one project and into another, completely controlling deployment is probably not an option in most development organizations.

The final type of change that developers are tempted to make to an interface is to change the semantics. Of all possible changes, this one seems the most innocuous, as it does not change the *binary* aspects of the interface. No clients will get undefined vtable offsets. No stack frames or ORPC messages will be malformed. That is what makes this type of change the most dangerous of all.

To understand the damage that can be caused by changing interface semantics, consider the following original definition of GetExtent:

> *The GetExtent method returns the natural width and height of the object's rendering in hi-metric units (100 units per millimeter).*

Suppose one object implementer were to decide that the interface definition should read as follows:

> *The GetExtent method returns the natural width and height of the object's rendering in pixels.*

What happens to all of the existing clients that are calculating layout based on physical units, not device units (pixels)? How can the client know which types of units are being returned by the object? The answer is that it can't. The client program is developed against a static interface definition that cannot be changed. The syntax of the interface cannot change, nor can the semantics of the interface. If interfaces can mutate randomly beneath the feet of the developer, then having a type system is pointless.

7.   Avoid **E_NOTIMPL**.

The type system of COM is based on coarse-grained functionality negotiation. When a client uses QueryInterface, it's really asking the object, "Do you support this broad class of functionality?" If the answer is S_OK, the object has responded "yes." Barring catastrophic failure (see Item 2), a client expects to be able to call the methods of the returned interface and have the object implement them. Unfortunately, there is a back door in COM that destroys this assumption: E_NOTIMPL.

Many of the standard interfaces in COM are documented to allow an object to return E_NOTIMPL to notify the client that this method is not implemented. If an interface is allowed to return this HRESULT, the client's coarse-grained assumptions are no longer valid. The only way to know if an object supports a given functionality is to actually try it and hope for the best. Not only does this make writing client code more difficult, but it also makes notifying the user of an object's functionality impossible. For example, if an object doesn't support an interface, the client may want to disable or remove user interface elements that access this functionality. In the presence of E_NOTIMPL, however, the user interface must be written to assume the presence of method-level functionality and notify the user only after an operation has failed. This tends to upset users, and since they're the ones writing the checks, E_NOTIMPL is to be avoided when implementing objects.

How can it be avoided? Is it the fault of the object when it's forced to implement a standard interface to fit in with existing clients but is not able to sensibly implement all of the methods? The problem lies not in the implementation of the interfaces but rather in their design. For example, imagine the following interface:

```
interface IBird : IUnknown {
   HRESULT Eat();
   HRESULT Sleep();
   HRESULT Fly();
}
```

In the face of fitting into a client interested in birds, what should an object that represents penguins do? What choice does it have but to return E_NOTIMPL as the result of the Fly method? The problem is that the coarse-grained functionality defined by the IBird interface assumes operations not readily implemented by all birds. To detect this problem, interfaces should be implemented by a few representative classes before they are published; test your interfaces before casting them in stone. (For more information about the immutability of interfaces, see Item 6.)

To solve IBird's E_NOTIMPL problem, the required functionality of all birds (i.e., eating and sleeping) should be separated from the optional functionality (i.e., flying). This process is called *interface factoring*. Here's an example of the IBird interface factored into required and optional functionality for birds:

```
interface IBird : IUnknown {
   HRESULT Eat();
   HRESULT Sleep();
}

interface IFlyingBird : IBird {
   HRESULT Fly();
};
```

You now have coarse-grained negotiation back. Clients can ask for birds or flying birds, depending on their needs. IBird implementations can implement flying bird functionality or not, based on their capabilities.

Notice that in the previous example, IFlyingBird derives from IBird. This works out well because flying birds are a specialization of birds (all flying birds are also birds). However, the problem of E_NOTIMPL can also be found in interfaces that derive from bases that provide unrelated or orthogonal functionality. For example, consider the IMoniker interface. Briefly, monikers provide an object location and initialization service. In addition, most monikers are capable of persistence (i.e., monikers typically know how to read and write their state for reactivation). These two capabilities, object lookup and persistence, are orthogonal but are joined together in the IMoniker interface via inheritance, since IMoniker derives from IPersistStream. For a custom moniker not itself capable of persistence, the implementer has no choice but to return E_NOTIMPL for the IPersistStream methods.

The solution to this problem is another form of interface factoring. When designing interfaces, you should not derive an interface from a base interface with orthogonal functionality. In this case, the IMoniker interface should have been factored apart from the IPersistStream interface, thereby allowing clients to regain coarse-grained negotiation. When two interfaces with orthogonal functionality are brought together via inheritance, the negotiation is too coarse-grained and defeats the benefits of interface-based programming.

8. Prefer typed data to opaque data.

COM is a slight variation on the classic remote procedure call (RPC) protocol, which has been proven to be an effective mechanism for distributed computing. Like classic RPC, COM can be mapped onto the Open Systems Interconnection (OSI) reference model:

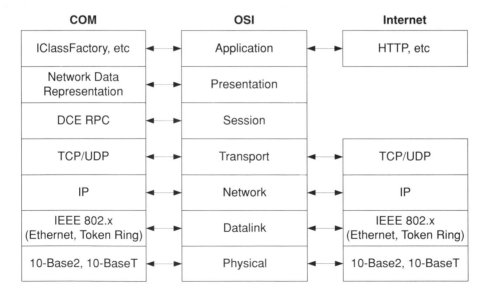

Note that classic Internet-style developers primarily live in the world of sockets and don't really use session, presentation, or application protocols to speak of. While the session layer deals with conversation management (which is usually handled implicitly in most application protocols), for the purposes of this discussion we will focus on the presentation layer, which requires explicit, deliberate support.

The presentation layer is responsible for ensuring that information *presented* by an application can be mapped to a *transmissible* representation that can be decoded on any host platform. In COM, the Microsoft IDL (MIDL)-generated proxies and stubs carry out this mapping. COM proxies and stubs are responsible for translating the presented call stack into Network Data Representation (NDR) prior to transmission. When incoming requests or responses arrive in a process, the proxies and stubs unmarshal the NDR payload into the native format of the destination machine.

Sockets programmers are used to implementing this layer by hand, flattening data structures into a stream to be sent across the wire and then rehydrating the data structures on the other end. They have to deal with platform dependency issues such as byte ordering, Unicode/multibyte strings, character sets, floating-point formats, alignment, and so forth.

COM programmers never need to write this code. Simply describe all data types in IDL (see Item 1), and the IDL compiler happily generates the proxy/stub code that can be compiled and linked into a proxy/stub DLL. In case you're wondering, the NDR format is incredibly efficient—a multicanonical format, it uses the optimistic assumption that the remote host will have the same native data format as the local host, in many cases avoiding the overhead of conversion altogether.[1] COM's presentation layer is truly a big win for cross-platform compatibility as well as rapid application development. It is silly to duplicate this effort. Additionally, the MIDL-generated proxies and stubs are incredibly efficient (especially when compiled with the /Oicf option). It is unlikely you can do better with a hand-crafted implementation.

Because the first versions of COM (namely, 16-bit COM) did not provide an IDL compiler, many old-time COM developers have fallen prey to seductive interfaces such as IDataObject, which was designed for out-of-process rendering. IDataObject supports transferring blobs of data that represent a bitmap or metafile rendering of an out-of-process object. The keyword you should note here is *blob*. Blobs are opaque data structures that must be marshaled manually (i.e., you must flatten your data structure manually in order to expose it to clients

---

[1] Of course, in the case of a heterogeneous pairing of host machines, the NDR unmarshaler will handle the differences in data representations quite happily.

via `IDataObject`). This works fine for local use in OLE document-style applications, where platform independence is not an issue (traditional OLE document apps run on the same machine) and where OLE's default handler provides built-in support for extracting and caching metafile renderings via `IDataObject`. However, `IDataObject` is clearly inappropriate as a generic means of interprocess communication when the IDL compiler is available.

To take full advantage of COM, define your data types in IDL and let the IDL compiler generate the marshaling code. High-level languages such as Visual Basic (VB) know nothing about how to deal with opaque data, whereas they are perfectly happy (within limits) dealing with data structures defined in IDL. Here's an example of a design that hasn't come to grips with modern COM:

```
interface IJukeBox : IUnknown {
  HRESULT GetDiskInfo(
    [in] long nDiskNumber,
    [out, retval] IDataObject** ppDataObject );
  //...
}
```

The designer of this jukebox interface determined that `IDataObject` was a flexible way to provide data about each disk. The client can ask for any clipboard format and get data about the musician who recorded the tracks, the track titles, the actual music on the tracks, and so on. All for the price of a single interface!

Now imagine that you are presented with this interface and asked to develop the front-end controller for the jukebox (imagine the old 1950s-style controls at each seat in a diner). One obvious task is to simply list the titles that are available in the jukebox, along with the recording musician. So you look at the documentation and find a list of all the supported clipboard formats and the associated data types. Then you start coding . . .

```
#include <jukebox.h>
const UINT CF_JUKEBOX_TITLE_INFO =
  RegisterClipboardFormat( "JukeboxTitleInfo" );

void DisplayItems(IJukeBox* pjb, ostream& os) {
  IDataObject* pdo = 0;
  for ( long i = 0;
        SUCCEEDED(pjb->GetDiskInfo(i, &pdo));
        i++ ) {
    FORMATETC fe = {CF_JUKEBOX_TITLE_INFO, 0,
                    DVASPECT_CONTENT, -1,
                    TYMED_HGLOBAL};
```

```
            STGMEDIUM stgm; ZeroMemory(&stgm, sizeof stgm);
            if (SUCCEEDED(pdo->GetData(&fe, &stgm))) {
              JUKEBOX_TITLE_INFO* pInfo =
                  (JUKEBOX_TITLE_INFO*) GlobalLock(stgm.hGlobal);
              os << pInfo->Author << ": "
                  << pInfo->Title  << endl;

              GlobalUnlock(stgm.hGlobal);
              ReleaseStgMedium(&stgm);
            }
            pdo->Release();
        }
    }
```

IDataObject is clearly being used in this case as a substitute for QueryInterface. Note the reliance on clipboard formats (which is hacked up to work across machines, by the way) to determine the supported data types. You may also need to call IDataObject::QueryGetData (or even worse, IDataObject::EnumFormatEtc) to allow the extensibility mechanism of IDataObject to kick in (unnecessary round-trips are evil—see Item 2). Yet another problem is that you are typically left guessing which types of media (TYMED_XXX) the data object supports. All this leads to code that is difficult to read and maintain. And once again, keep in mind that you will not be able to use this interface from high-level languages such as VB.

Here is a better solution:

```
interface IJukeBox : IUnknown {
  HRESULT GetDiskInfo(
    [in] long nDiskNumber,
    [out, retval] IDiskInfo ** ppInfo);
  //...
}
```

This solution allows the simple use of COM interfaces to obtain information about the disks:

```
interface IDiskInfo : IUnknown {
  HRESULT GetTitleInfo(
    [out] BSTR * pbstrTitle,
    [out] BSTR * pbstrAuthor );
  //...
}
```

With the `IDiskInfo` interface, we once again achieve language and platform independence, and the client code becomes much more readable:

```
#include <jukebox.h>
void DisplayItems(IJukeBox* pjb, ostream& os) {
  IDiskInfo* pdi = 0;
  for ( long i = 0;
        SUCCEEDED(pjb->GetDiskInfo(i, &pdi));
        i++ ) {
    BSTR bstrTitle = 0;
    BSTR bstrAuthor = 0;
    if (SUCCEEDED(pdi->GetTitleInfo(&bstrTitle,
                                    &bstrAuthor))) {
      os << bstrTitle  << ": "
         << bstrAuthor << endl;
      SysFreeString( bstrTitle );
      SysFreeString( bstrAuthor );
    }
    pdi->Release();
  }
}
```

If you wanted, you could even decouple `IJukeBox` from `IDiskInfo` by using the `[iid_is]` IDL attribute (see Item 9 for more details).

Judge for yourself. The modern version spends time dealing with jukeboxes and disks rather than interpreting blobs of data. If the extra round-trip to get the two strings from the intermediate `IDiskInfo` interface is unacceptable, the object implementer could elect to use marshal-by-value on the intermediate object to avoid the second round-trip. Or better yet, just use a structure.

Another common interface that was used for intertask communication in 16-bit COM was `IStream`. As its name suggests, `IStream` represents an unstructured opaque stream of bytes that can be read or written sequentially. This interface is often [ab]used to perform client-side flow control (see Item 13 for a better way). Note that `IStream` may make sense in cases where truly opaque byte streams are required (for instance, transmitting large medical images), but it could be argued that simply dropping down to sockets for transferring this type of data would be preferable anyway. There is nothing wrong with using COM to transmit a dynamic TCP endpoint to set up a transient connection for purposes like this.

You may wonder what direction to take when confronted with an existing application that needs to become distributed via COM. The resounding answer is described in Item 1. Start your project by designing and writing IDL. Use `QueryInterface` to discover types at runtime. Redefine your data structures in IDL. Follow the example of Win32—see `wtypes.idl`. Like retrofitting `const` correctness into a C++ class hierarchy, retrofitting IDL is a big job, but the benefits are enormous.

9. Avoid connection points.

A common misconception among COM programmers is that connection points enable bidirectional communication between clients and objects. They don't. What connection points provide is a standard mechanism for establishing bidirectional communication. Bidirectional communication is enabled when the client has an interface pointer to the object and vice versa. While you can use connection points to establish this bidirectional communication channel, you shouldn't for one important reason: round-trips (see Item 2). It takes five round-trips to establish bidirectional communication using connection points and four round-trips to tear it down, when it really should take only one.

It can be hard to resist the siren song of connection points. The tools (MFC, ATL, VB) support both implementing connection points and using them. IDL even has a special connection point syntax for declaring the difference between an incoming interface that an object will implement and an outgoing interface that an object is willing to call back on. For example, imagine a Worker object willing to notify all concerned when its work is completed or delayed:

```
library WorkerLib {
  // Outgoing interfaces are often dispinterfaces
  // to support late-binding clients, e.g. IE
  dispinterface DWorkerEvents {
  properties:
  methods:
    [id(1)] void OnWorkCompleted();
    [id(2)] void OnWorkDelayed();
  }
  interface IWorker : IUnknown {
    HRESULT StartWork();
  }
  coclass Worker {
    interface IWorker; // incoming
```

```
      [source] dispinterface DWorkerEvents; // outgoing
   }
}
```

Notice that the `Worker` class declares its willingness to call back on client implementations of the `DWorkerEvents` interface using the `source` attribute. This implies that the object will support the `IConnectionPointContainer` interface to allow clients to begin the negotiation process for bidirectional communication:

```
interface IConnectionPointContainer : IUnknown {
   HRESULT EnumConnectionPoints(
            [out] IEnumConnectionPoints ** ppEnum);
   HRESULT FindConnectionPoint(
            [in]  REFIID riid,
            [out] IConnectionPoint ** ppCP);
}
```

To obtain this interface, the client uses `QueryInterface` to request the `IConnectionPointContainer` interface from the object (round-trip #1). The client then calls `FindConnectionPoint`, passing in the interface identifier (IID) for the interface that the client has implemented (e.g., `DIID_DworkerEvents`) (round-trip #2). If this succeeds, the object has expressed its ability to notify clients of the requested events and will return an `IConnectionPoint` interface to allow the client to attach its event sink:

```
interface IConnectionPoint : IUnknown {
   HRESULT GetConnectionInterface([out] IID * piid);
   HRESULT GetConnectionPointContainer(
            [out] IConnectionPointContainer ** ppCPC);
   HRESULT Advise([in]  IUnknown *pUnkSink,
                  [out] DWORD *pdwCookie);
   HRESULT Unadvise([in] DWORD dwCookie);
   HRESULT EnumConnections([out] IEnumConnections ** pp);
}
```

The object's implementation of `IConnectionPoint` will maintain a list of clients interested in receiving notifications. For the client to add itself to the list, it calls the `Advise` method, passing in an interface pointer for the event interface that it has implemented (round-trip #3). Notice that even though the client may pass a specifically typed interface as the event sink parameter, the object (and the underlying remoting layer) can only assume that the parameter is an `IUnknown` reference. Therefore, to cache the event interface it wants, the object must call `QueryInterface` against the sink's `IUnknown` interface to acquire the typed event interface (round-trip #4). This last round-trip could have been avoided had the designer of connection points looked at Item 14. Finally, because the implementation of IConnectionPoint is often a distinct COM identity, when the client subsequently releases it, COM will perform one final round-trip (round-trip #5) to tell the subobject that it has been released.

In general, it's obvious that connection points were designed for in-process objects, in which round-trips are not as important as in the distributed case (see Item 2). In fact, they are required to establish bidirectional communication with an ActiveX control container or current ActiveX script engines. If you're going to build components that integrate with these environments, you're going to have to live with connection points. Otherwise, you should replace them with another mechanism for establishing bidirectional communications.

IViewObject is a perfect example. The IViewObject interface is implemented by an object that is willing to render itself in the client area of a container's window. It does this by defining a Draw method. To notify the container that its rendered state has changed and that it would like to be redrawn, it holds an implementation of the client's IAdviseSink interface. If the client is interested in this notification from the self-rendering object, it can pass its IAdviseSink interface to the object via the IViewObject method SetAdvise. If the client is already holding the object's IViewObject interface (the most common case for a container), it is a single round-trip to establish bidirectional communication between the client and the object. In case you missed it, this is four times faster than the protocol required for connection points. In addition, when calling SetAdvise, the client passes flags that the object can use for filtering events (i.e., only sending the events that the client is interested in), further reducing round-trips. Another downside of connection points is that there is no mechanism for filtering or prioritizing events. Every client gets all events whether they're interested or not.

At this point, you might think that all objects should be shoehorning their bidirectional communications through IViewObject and IAdviseSink. This is definitely not the case. IAdviseSink is an event interface that has been paired with IViewObject for events specific to self-rendering objects. The concept of having domain-specific protocols such as these is a good idea. However, unless you are building rendering plumbing, you have no business using IAdviseSink or IViewObject. When one of your custom interfaces implies events, add a pair of methods for managing interested clients. Where appropriate, include flags to filter or prioritize events to further reduce

round-trips. For example, consider an augmented `IWorker` interface and another events interface:

```
// We're not supporting late-binding clients
// (which tend to require connection points)
// so this doesn't need to be a dispinterface
interface IWorkerEvents : IUnknown {
  HRESULT OnWorkCompleted([in] IWorker *pWorker);
  HRESULT OnWorkDelayed([in] IWorker *pWorker);
}

interface IWorker : IUnknown {
  enum WorkerAdviseFlags {
    WAF_COMPLETED = 0x1,
    WAF_DELAYED   = 0x2,
    WAF_ALL       = 0x3
  };
  HRESULT StartWork();
  HRESULT WorkerAdvise(
    [in]   IWorkerEvents* pEvents,
    [in]   enum WorkerAdviseFlags flags,
    [out]  long * pnCookie);
  HRESULT WorkerUnadvise([in] long dwCookie);
  }
```

For a client interested in Worker events, it is a single round-trip to add itself to
the list for the specific events in which it's interested.

There are a few things worth mentioning about the design of these two interfaces. First, notice that the `IWorkerEvents` methods pass in an interface
pointer for the object sending the event. This makes building a client holding
multiple instances of a class more convenient. Now the client can have one implementation of `IWorkerEvents` instead of one implementation per held object. Since the client-side proxy has already cached the `IWorker` interface, this
represents no additional marshaling requirements.

Second, notice that the name of the `Advise` and `Unadvise` methods are pre-
fixed with the word `Worker`. If an object implements several interfaces that
imply events, it's often more convenient to implement them if they have different
names.

Third, notice that the flags and the cookie arguments are signed longs instead of
the more intuitive unsigned longs (`DWORD`s). Certain clients (notably the current
implementation of Visual Basic) do not support unsigned types. While signed

types aren't quite what we mean, they work and they allow more restricted clients to use this mechanism. Since we're explicitly supporting VB, here's an example of establishing a bidirectional communications channel between a Worker object and a VB client:

```
' Event interface implementation
Implements IWorkerEvents

Dim g_worker As IWorker
Dim g_cookie As Long

Private Sub Form_Load()
    Set g_worker = New Worker
    ' Set up communication for a subset of events
    g_cookie = g_worker.WorkerAdvise(Me, WAF_COMPLETED)
End Sub

' Handle the events we're interested in
Private Sub _
IWorkerEvents_OnWorkCompleted(ByVal IWorker src)
    MsgBox "Work Completed"
    g_worker.WorkerUnadvise g_cookie
End Sub
Private Sub _
IWorkerEvents_OnWorkDelayed(ByVal IWorker src)
    ' this will never be called since WorkerAdvise
    ' was called with WAF_COMPLETED only
End Sub
```

If an object supports events independent of any specific interface, it's often necessary to factor the methods for setting up and tearing down the communication into a separate interface (see Item 7). If you do this, it's convenient to be able to support multiple event interfaces via a single `Advise` method. The `iid_is` technique described in Item 14 can be used for this.

10. Don't provide more than one implementation of the same interface on a single object.

COM authorities love to talk and write about per-interface reference counting. They also are known to expound on the virtues of defining all interfaces as dual interfaces. Both of these techniques are interesting, but both are in conflict with the basic tenets of `QueryInterface`.

The COM specification is fairly clear about the rules of `QueryInterface`. It states that the set of interfaces an object exports is static for the lifetime of the object. It also states that the set of interfaces that an object exports can be thought of as a collection of fully connected nodes; that is, one can acquire any available interface from any other interface and in any order. These rules form the notion of COM identity and must be followed for the COM remoting architecture to work properly.

Most discussions of COM identity frame the traversal of interface pointers on an object in terms of yes/no answers; that is, do you support the interface or don't you? In general, this is a reasonable level of detail except with respect to the case of `QueryInterface(IID_IUnknown)`, which has special significance. However, in glossing over what it means to hand out an interface pointer from `QueryInterface`, a subtle problem that bites most COM developers is often overlooked.

As Item 6 stated, an interface is an immutable contract that implies concrete syntax and loose, abstract semantics. When a client requests an interface from an actual object, it can safely assume that the object implementer was aware of this contract and will provide a pointer (vptr) to a vtable chock full of interface-compliant code. The COM specification explicitly provides a loophole that allows implementers to dynamically allocate these vptrs on an as-needed basis, potentially returning different physical results for identical `QueryInterface` requests. This technique is often referred to as a *tearoff*, because a new vptr is "torn off" on demand. What is not explicitly stated in the COM specification is that trouble will ensue when you give out different *logical* results for identical `QueryInterface` requests.

To grasp the problem of returning different logical results from `QueryInterface`, consider the following code fragment that asks a cat to bark like a dog:

```
HRESULT BarkLikeADogYouCat(ICat *pCat) {
  IDog *pDog = 0;
  HRESULT hr = pCat->QueryInterface(IID_IDog,
                                    (void**)&pDog);
  if (SUCCEEDED(hr)) {
    hr = pDog->Bark();
    pDog->Release();
  }
  return hr;
}
```

If the following function were also available that asked a bird to bark like a dog,

```
HRESULT BarkLikeADogYouBird(IBird *pBird) {
  IDog *pDog = 0;
  HRESULT hr = pBird->QueryInterface(IID_IDog,
                                     (void**)&pDog);
  if (SUCCEEDED(hr)) {
    hr = pDog->Bark();
    pDog->Release();
  }
  return hr;
}
```

it would be strange to say the least if the following code resulted in two different barks:

```
HRESULT CreateAndBarkTwice(void) {
// create a DogCatBird
  ICat *pCat = 0;
  HRESULT hr = CoCreateInstance(CLSID_DogCatBird, 0,
                    CLSCTX_ALL, IID_ICat, (void**)&pCat);
    IBird *pBird = 0;
    hr = pCat->QueryInterface(IID_IBird,(void**)&pBird);
    if (SUCCEEDED(hr)) {
// ask object to bark via two different interfaces
      hr = BarkLikeADogYouCat(pCat);
      if (SUCCEEDED(hr))
        hr = BarkLikeADogYouBird(pBird);
      pBird->Release();
    }
    pCat->Release();
  }
}
```

Since the `ICat` and `IBird` interface pointers both point to the same object identity, it is obvious that either both `QueryInterface(IID_IDog)` requests will succeed or both requests will fail.

The subtlety of this code surrounds what happens when the `Bark` method is called from each of the helper functions. The call will always be dispatched to the same object identity; however, due to the loophole in the COM specification, it is possible that the object implementer has given out two different *physical* results from `QueryInterface(IID_IDog)`. Because there may be two different physical results, there also may be two different *logical* results; that is, the vtable referenced by the result of

```
pBird->QueryInterface(IID_IDog, (void**)&pDog1);
```

may be different from that referenced by

```
pCat->QueryInterface(IID_IDog, (void**)&pDog2);
```

This means that the actual code that is executed via

```
pDog1->Bark();
```

may be different from the code executed via

```
pDog2->Bark();
```

While technically this can still be considered legal COM, it flies in the face of a basic tenet of QueryInterface, namely, that the order in which you acquire interfaces doesn't matter. In this example, the code that will execute when you ask the object to bark will differ depending on the order in which you acquired the IDog interface.

You may be saying to yourself that this seems like a largely academic discussion and that your objects are probably exempt from this semantic brouhaha. As long as your objects follow the letter of the COM specification, you just want to be left alone. If your objects will only be used within a single apartment, you may be able to get away with this assumption. However, once your object is accessed across apartment boundaries, your main physical client is now the COM remoting layer, and the architects of the COM remoting layer read a lot into the COM specification that you may not have.[2]

To understand the issue at hand, it is useful to reexamine the top-level client code shown earlier:

```
HRESULT CreateAndBarkTwice(void) {
// create a DogCatBird
  ICat *pCat = 0;
  HRESULT hr = CoCreateInstance(CLSID_DogCatBird, 0,
                    CLSCTX_ALL, IID_ICat, (void**)&pCat);
    IBird *pBird = 0;
    hr = pCat->QueryInterface(IID_IBird,(void**)&pBird);
    if (SUCCEEDED(hr)) {
// ask object to bark via two different interfaces
      hr = BarkLikeADogYouCat(pCat);
      if (SUCCEEDED(hr))
```

---

[2] Actually, the architects of the COM remoting layer *wrote* the COM specification, but that isn't important for this discussion.

```
        hr = BarkLikeADogYouBird(pBird);
      pBird->Release();
    }
    pCat->Release();
  }
}
```

Assume that the DogCatBird object will reside in a distinct apartment from the caller (e.g., the server is remote or out-of-process or the class identifier [CLSID] is marked with an incompatible `ThreadingModel` attribute). The call to `CoCreateInstance` will cause a stub manager to be created in the apartment of the object, and because the resultant pointer is of type `ICat`, an `ICat` interface stub will be created as well. The stub manager will hold an `IUnknown` reference to the actual object, and the interface stub will hold an `ICat` reference that will be used to dispatch the incoming `ICat` requests. The client will receive a pointer to an `ICat` interface proxy that has been bound to a new proxy manager that represents the identity of the object in the client's apartment.

When the call to `QueryInterface(IID_IBird)` is made, the proxy manager notes that it does not yet have an `IBird` interface proxy, so it forwards the request to the object's apartment, where an `IBird` interface stub is bound to the object (the new interface stub will hold an `IBird` reference to the object). When the remote `QueryInterface` request returns, a new `IBird` interface proxy will be dynamically aggregated into the proxy manager so that the overall proxy will appear to implement both `ICat` and `IBird`.

The interesting problem arises when the two helper functions call `QueryInterface(IID_IDog, ...)`. The first request for `IDog` will go through the same steps as the request for `IBird`; that is, a new interface stub will be created, as will a new interface proxy. It is at the second request for `IDog` that the fireworks begin. Since the proxy manager has already aggregated an `IDog` interface proxy in the call to `BarkLikeADogYouCat`, the second `QueryInterface` request will be satisfied by returning a pointer to the cached interface proxy. The good news is that there will be no second round-trip to the object, improving performance. The bad news is that there will be no second round-trip to the object, which robs the object of the chance to return the second implementation of `IDog`.

The moral of the story is that when your object is accessed remotely, the first implementation of an interface that is returned is the one you are stuck with for the lifetime of the object. COM doesn't tear down the interface stub until the last proxy manager releases its connection to the object. If you had designed your object around having two or more distinct logical implementations of an interface, your code will break once proxies are used. Item 11 shows a very common situation where this occurs (in particular, trying to expose more than one dual/dispatch interface per identity). As a corollary, if you designed your object around being notified of individual interfaces being released, your code will break once proxies are used. This means that techniques such as per-interface reference counting or tearoff interfaces are largely useless in scenarios where more than one apartment is involved.

11. Typeless languages lose the benefits of COM.

The power and expressiveness of the COM programming model is based on one simple idea: program against abstract interfaces, not concrete implementations. To determine which interfaces an implementation supports, the client must ask explicitly via calls to QueryInterface. This coarse-grained negotiation is the foundation of the COM type system. It provides encapsulation, abstraction, and polymorphism (all the good points of object orientation), while avoiding the problems related to versioning and coupling that often occur in classic object orientation. Unfortunately, typeless languages such as JavaScript or Visual Basic Script throw these additional benefits of COM away in favor of increased simplicity.

To support the use of COM objects, typeless languages currently expect all objects to support the IDispatch interface. IDispatch provides the functionality of a mini-interpreter to the runtime system used by these languages. When invoking methods or accessing properties on an object, the language runtime will ask the object via IDispatch::GetIDsOfNames if it supports a given named operation. If the answer is yes, the runtime will package the parameters into a self-describing stack frame for interpretation by the object via IDispatch::Invoke. It is the object's job to unpack the parameters and perform the operation. For example, consider a dispatch interface defined in IDL:

```
dispinterface IDog {
properties:
methods:
  void Bark([in] long nVolume);
};
```

The IDog interface has one logical method, Bark. An object that supports this interface must implement IDispatch to allow clients to physically access this operation. However, because typeless languages do not allow the programmer to associate type or interface names with variables, the language runtime will not be able to distinguish IDog from any other dispatch interface on the object. In this way, typeless languages limit objects to a single interface.

It is not completely impossible to support interface-based programming from typeless languages. Consider the following IDL:

```
[object,dual,uuid(92284211-9221-2412-11d1-552124391232)]
interface ICat : IDispatch {
  [id(1)] HRESULT Meow([in] long nVolume);
}
[object,dual,uuid(92284212-9221-2412-11d1-552124391232)]
interface IDog : IDispatch {
  [id(1)] HRESULT Bark([in] long nVolume);
}
[uuid(92284213-9221-2412-11d1-552124391232)]
coclass DogCat {
    interface ICat;
    [default] interface IDog;
}
```

If the client is written in a typed language (e.g., C++, Visual Basic, Java), the following code will work as expected:

```
Sub MeowAndBark( )
  Dim dog as IDog
  Dim cat as ICat
  Set dog = new Dog
  Set cat = dog
  cat.Meow 100
  dog.Bark 200
End Sub
```

If, however, the client is written in a typeless language (e.g., Visual Basic Script, JavaScript), variables cannot be typed, making it impossible to bind two different IDispatch-based references to the same object identity.[3]

Object implementers who wish to allow typeless languages to use their objects in an interface-based model often resort to adding properties to each interface to allow the typeless client to call QueryInterface indirectly via a property access. The following modified IDL illustrates this technique:

```
interface IDog; // ICat requires this fwd. declaration

[object,dual,uuid(92284211-9221-2412-11d1-552124391232)]
```

---

[3] See http://www.sellsbrothers.com/tools/multidisp/index.htm for possible solutions to this problem.

```
interface ICat : IDispatch {
  [id(1)] HRESULT Meow([in] long nVolume);
  [id(2),propget] HRESULT AsDog([out, retval] IDog **p);
}

[object,dual,uuid(92284212-9221-2412-11d1-552124391232)]
interface IDog : IDispatch {
  [id(1)] HRESULT Bark([in] long nVolume);
  [id(2),propget] HRESULT AsCat([out, retval] ICat **p);
}
```

In theory, this allows the typeless client to write the following:

```
Sub MeowAndBark( )
  Dim cat ' typeless language, so everything is variant
  Dim dog ' typeless language, so everything is variant
  Set dog = CreateObject("DogCat")
  Set cat = dog.AsCat ' pseudo QueryInterface
  dog.Bark 100
  cat.Meow 200
End Sub
```

This code assumes that the object implementer wrote the property accessors as
follows:

```
STDMETHODIMP DogCat::get_AsDog(IDog **ppDog) {
  (*ppDog = static_cast<IDog*>(this))->AddRef();
  return S_OK;
}
STDMETHODIMP DogCat::get_AsCat(ICat **ppCat) {
  (*ppCat = static_cast<ICat*>(this))->AddRef();
  return S_OK;
}
```

Ignoring the problems related to having tight coupling between two otherwise
unrelated interfaces, this technique basically works provided that the object
resides in the same apartment as the client (that is, there is no proxy or stub).
However, once the object resides in a distinct apartment, all access is via
proxy/stub connections. Because the results of IDispatch::Invoke must
be marshaled through VARIANTs, the IDog-ness or ICat-ness of the result
is lost. Instead, the client will always get the first IDispatch pointer that
has been marshaled from the object. In the case of the previous Visual Basic
Script fragment, this means that all references to the object will be of type IDog
simply because the initial interface pointer was acquired via a call to

QueryInterface(IID_IDispatch). Again, refer to the discussion about objects' not providing multiple implementations of the same interface in Item 10.

Instead of relying on objects with multiple interfaces, typeless languages typically access multiple functionalities via multiple distinct COM objects. These objects are typically exposed via relationship hierarchies called *object models*. An object model is simply a set of related objects, typically traversed via a top-level object (often called the *application object* in classic automation hierarchies) and a set of lower-level objects that provide various finer-grained services. Consider the following automation-style model for Dogs and Cats:

```
[ uuid(E4244920-3DA0-11d1-A84F-0080C7667ABF) ]
library AnimalLib {
  dispinterface _PetStore; dispinterface _Animal;
  dispinterface _Dog;      dispinterface _Cat;

  // Top-level object
  [ uuid(E4244921-3DA0-11d1-A84F-0080C7667ABF) ]
  dispinterface _PetStore {
  properties:
    [id(1), readonly] _Animal Youngest;
    [id(2), readonly] _Animal Cutest;
  methods:
    [id(3)] _Animal GetAnimal([in] BSTR bstrName);
    [id(4)] void PutAnimal([in] _Animal a);
  }


  [ uuid(E4244922-3DA0-11d1-A84F-0080C7667ABF) ]
  dispinterface _Animal {
  properties:
    [id(1), readonly] _PetStore PetStore;
    [id(2), readonly] _Dog Dogness;
    [id(3), readonly] _Cat Catness;
  methods:
    [id(4)] void Eat();
  }


  [ uuid(E4244923-3DA0-11d1-A84F-0080C7667ABF) ]
  dispinterface _Dog {
  properties:
    [id(1), readonly] _Animal Animalness;
  methods:
```

```
        [id(2)] void Bark();
    }
    [ uuid(E4244924-3DA0-11d1-A84F-0080C7667ABF) ]
    dispinterface _Cat {
    properties:
        [id(1), readonly] _Animal Animalness;
    methods:
        [id(2)] void Meow();
    }
    [uuid(E4244925-3DA0-11d1-A84F-0080C7667ABF),appobject]
    coclass PetStore {
        [hidden, default] dispinterface _PetStore;
    }
    [uuid(E4244926-3DA0-11d1-A84F-0080C7667ABF)]
    coclass Animal {
        [hidden, default] dispinterface _Animal;
    }
    [uuid(E4244927-3DA0-11d1-A84F-0080C7667ABF),
        noncreatable]
    coclass Dog {
        [hidden, default] dispinterface _Dog;
    }
    [uuid(E4244928-3DA0-11d1-A84F-0080C7667ABF),
        noncreatable]
    coclass Cat {
        [hidden, default] dispinterface _Cat;
    }
}
```

Object models are designed and implemented in a class-oriented style (i.e., each object has a single public interface). This makes the model simple to understand. However, this design style also leads to versioning problems. If management requests a new feature for this object hierarchy, you're in trouble because each object can only support a single implementation of IDispatch (see Item 10). However, because we're using dynamic invocation instead of vtable-based invocation, you might suspect we have a bit more flexibility. If we were to add a new method or property to one of the interfaces, new clients would have access to that functionality via GetIDsOfNames and Invoke. If, on the other hand, a new client gets hold of an old implementation of the revised interface expecting that the new functionality will be there . . . whammo! It's not going to be there and that's a runtime error.

Why does this happen? It's true that `GetIDsOfNames` is basically a fine-grained `QueryInterface` (i.e., it checks if the object supports a named method or property). However, for simplicity, most scripting environments bundle `GetIDsOfNames` and `Invoke` into a single operation. No typeless languages that are currently available allow the client application to ask for the availability of an operation before calling it.

One way to support evolution of objects and object hierarchies for typeless clients is to fall back on version management. That's why all type libraries are tagged with a major and minor version number. Unfortunately, most typeless clients don't have direct access to the object's type library or its version number. To allow typeless clients to check the version number, the top-level object should support a `CheckVersion` method:

```
HRESULT PetStore::CheckVersion(
    short          major,
    short          minor,
    VARIANT_BOOL* pbCompatible)
{
  if (!pbCompatible) return E_POINTER;
  if (major == MAJOR_VERSION && minor <= MINOR_VERSION)
    *pbCompatible = VARIANT_TRUE;
  else
    *pbCompatible = VARIANT_FALSE;
  return S_OK;
}
```

Unfortunately, many existing object hierarchies do not have this method. Rather, they expect typeless clients to deal with the runtime errors. That sort of manual version management technique is not for the faint of heart, though, and should be avoided.

12. Dual interfaces are a hack. Don't require people to implement them.

Today's COM interfaces fall into one of three categories: (1) pure vtable interfaces, which are usable from most typed languages, (2) pure dispatch interfaces, or dispinterfaces, which are usable from most untyped languages, and (3) dual interfaces, which are hybrids of vtable and dispatch interfaces. Dual interfaces are part of the Visual Basic architecture and were introduced with the release of Visual Basic 4.0. Dual interfaces are the only type of interface that can be defined within the Visual Basic environment (although Visual Basic programmers can implement externally defined pure vtable and pure dispatch interfaces). In theory, dual interfaces combine the best aspects of both vtable and dispatch interfaces. That's the theory at least.

Most COM-aware development environments make it easy to implement dual interfaces to allow your object to be accessed from both typed and untyped languages. For this purpose, dual interfaces are an adequate solution given the nature of COM's circa-1998 dynamic invocation. However, it is a common mistake to define callback interfaces as dual interfaces, which ultimately makes no sense. Consider the following pure vtable-based interface hierarchy:

```
[ uuid(18FDEA82-1115-11d2-A4B3-006008D1A534), object ]
interface IStopWatchEvents : IUnknown {
  HRESULT OnStart();
  HRESULT OnTicking();
  HRESULT OnStop();
}
[ uuid(18FDEA83-1115-11d2-A4B3-006008D1A534), object ]
interface IStopWatch : IUnknown {
  HRESULT Advise([in] IStopWatchEvents *pswe);
  HRESULT Start();
  HRESULT Stop();
}
```

This hierarchy allows IStopWatch clients to register an event sink interface to be notified when certain temporal events happen in a Stopwatch object. Given this interface hierarchy, the IStopWatch::Stop method might look something like this:

```
STDMETHODIMP Stop() {
// stop running stopwatch
  this->InternalStopTimer();
// notify event sink (attached in Advise method)
  if (m_pStopWatchEvent)
    m_pStopWatchEvent->OnStop();
  return S_OK;
}
```

It is often common practice to define callback interfaces as pure dispatch interfaces:

```
[ uuid(18FDEA84-1115-11d2-A4B3-006008D1A534)]
dispinterface IStopWatchEvents {
properties:
methods:
  [id(1)] void OnStart();
```

```
    [id(2)] void OnTicking();
    [id(3)] void OnStop();
}
```

Had this been the case with IStopWatchEvents, the event would then be
fired by calling IDispatch::Invoke:

```
STDMETHODIMP Stop() {
// stop running stopwatch
  this->InternalStopTimer();
// notify event sink (attached in Advise method)
  if (m_pStopWatchEvent) {
    DISPPARAMS params = { 0, 0, 0, 0 };
    m_pStopWatchEvent->Invoke(3, IID_NULL, 0,
                  DISPATCH_METHOD, &params, 0, 0, 0);
  }
  return S_OK;
}
```

In either case, the Stopwatch object knows either to call through a direct vtable
entry or through the IDispatch mechanism.

Now, consider the case in which IStopWatchEvents is defined as a dual
interface:

```
[uuid(18FDEA85-1115-11d2-A4B3-006008D1A534),object,dual]
interface IStopWatchEvents : IDispatch {
  HRESULT OnStart();
  HRESULT OnTicking();
  HRESULT OnStop();
}
```

Given this interface, how should the implementation of IStop-
Watch::Stop notify the event sink? If you say it should use
IDispatch::Invoke, then what purpose was there in defining the interface
as dual instead of a pure dispinterface? If you say it should use the OnStop
vtable entry directly, then what purpose was there in not just defining the interface as a pure vtable interface? Granted, most tools make implementing dual interfaces trivial; however, in this situation, there are two equally legal mechanisms
for invoking the methods, with no clear guideline as to which one is preferred.

For an example of what can happen when a dual interface is used as a callback interface, consider what happens when you define the event sink of a control as
dual and then deploy it in Internet Explorer 4.0. Yes, Internet Explorer will
gladly give you an implementation of your dual callback interface at initialization

time. And yes, Internet Explorer will fail miserably when you try to fire an event using a vtable entry. The bottom line is that dual interfaces were designed to solve a problem that never should have affected COM programmers. One hopes that a future version of COM will render them completely obsolete.

13. Choose the right array type (avoid open and varying arrays).

All arrays have two interesting characteristics: a maximum capacity, or *conformance*, and a current content, or *variance*. For example, an array that *can* hold 100 elements but *does* hold 12 elements has a conformance of 100 and a variance of 12. You can define four types of arrays in IDL: fixed, conformant, varying, and open. The type of array you use to transfer data determines how much runtime control you have over its conformance and variance.

A fixed array's conformance is defined at IDL compile time. A conformant array's conformance is specified dynamically at runtime by some other data sent as part of the call stack. The arrays are defined using standard array and pointer syntax, respectively.

```
// An inbound fixed array
HRESULT Method1([in] short rgs[256]);
// An inbound conformant array
HRESULT Method2([in] short cMax,
                [in, size_is(cMax)] short *prgs);
```

The [size_is] attribute is used with a conformant array to specify the current conformance. Both the proxy/stub code and an object implementing Method2 use this information to determine how many elements prgs really points to.

The variance of both fixed and conformant arrays is the same as the conformance. In other words, when you send a fixed or conformant array as an argument to a method, all the data in the array is sent. The wire representation for fixed arrays is simply the content of the array itself (with any embedded pointers dereferenced, of course). For conformant arrays, the array capacity is also sent, since it can change from call to call.

Like fixed and conformant arrays, varying and open arrays have their conformance defined at compile time and runtime, respectively. However, the variance for both varying and open arrays is specified dynamically at runtime. Both these array types are typically defined using standard C-style syntax:

```
// An inbound varying array
HRESULT Method3([in] short cActual,
               [in,
                length_is(cActual)] short rgs[256]);
// An inbound open array
HRESULT Method4([in] short cMax,
               [in] short cActual,
               [in,
                size_is(cMax),
                length_is(cActual)] short *prgs);
```

The [length_is] attribute is used with either a varying or an open array to specify the current variance. Again, both the proxy/stub code and an object implementing either Method3 or Method4 use this information to determine how many of the maximum possible elements of rgs or prgs are valid.

You can think of an array's variance as a window onto its entire content. When you use a varying or open array as an argument to a method, you are sending only what is visible through the window. The wire representation for both types of arrays includes just that subset of the elements, along with the size of the current variance, since that can change from call to call. The wire representation for open arrays also includes conformance since that is set dynamically at runtime as well.

By default, the window defined by [length_is] is aligned with the beginning of the array. In other words, the first element in the window is at array index 0. You can change this default with the [first_is] attribute.

```
// An inbound varying array
HRESULT Method5([in] short nFirst,
               [in] short cActual,
               [in,
                first_is(nFirst),
                length_is(cActual)] short rgs[256]);
// An inbound open array
HRESULT Method6([in] short cMax,
               [in] short nFirst,
               [in] short cActual,
               [in,
                size_is(cMax),
                first_is(nFirst),
                length_is(cActual)] short *prgs);
```

Using [first_is] allows you to slide the window defined by [length_is] along the array. When you use [first_is], the offset value is sent along as part of the wire representation of the array to which it's applied.

You may look at the list of array options and wonder when to use which type. At first this seems daunting. Here are some guidelines:

1. Use fixed arrays when you have *a priori* knowledge of the exact (and constant) number of elements. For instance, a fixed array would be great for representing a U.S. social security number as an array of characters because there will always be nine digits.

2. Use a conformant array when you don't know the maximum number of elements at interface design time. Arbitrary strings and other variable-length collections of elements are easily handled this way.

3. Avoid using varying or open arrays as [in] parameters.

Why give up two perfectly good array types, one of which (the open array) seems incredibly flexible? Here's why.

Varying and open arrays are inefficient as [in] parameters. Remember that both types allow you to explicitly control variance, thereby sending some subset of the entire contents. There are hidden expenses here. First, there's the increased size of the wire representation, which now has to include the current variance. Second, and much more important, there is the extra work that has to be done by a stub whenever it receives either a varying or an open array as an argument. The proxy and stub collaborate to replicate a call stack from one apartment to another. It's easy for a stub to reproduce the image of either a fixed or conformant array because the data in the incoming RPC packet is identical to the argument the client passed to the proxy. A pointer into the midst of the RPC packet can be handed directly to the object expecting the array. It's hard for a stub to reproduce the image of either a varying or an open array because the data in the incoming RPC packet is *not* identical to the argument the client passed to the proxy. The stub has to create a separate buffer, copy the packet's contents into it, and then hand the object a pointer to the copy. This extra copying takes time *and* space.

The extra copy can be avoided if you always use conformant arrays. You aren't giving up much flexibility when you chose a conformant array over an open array, because a client can always treat a subset of an array it holds as a conformant array in its own right.

```
// An array client
short rgs[] = { 0, 1, 2, 3, 4, 5, 6, 7, 8, 9 };

// Send subset of rgs as open array to Method6
pObj->Method6(10, 2, 3, rgs);

// Send same subset of rgs as conformant array to
// Method2
pObj->Method2(3, rgs + 2);
```

From the object's point of view, these two invocations are identical if it doesn't care about the difference between the original array's conformance and variance (i.e., `size_is` minus `length_is`) or the offset of the variance into the array (i.e., `first_is`). The stub's handling of the latter invocation avoids extra `memcpy`-ing.

Varying and open arrays are also inefficient as out parameters. It is often the case that a client wants to retrieve "all the elements" an object has to send. At first glance, both varying and open arrays seem perfect for this, since the variance can be set to reflect the current content when the object fills in the array to hand back to the client.

```
// An explicitly sized outbound varying array
HRESULT Method7([out] short *pcActual,
               [out,
                length_is(*pcActual)] short rgs[256]);
// A client-sized outbound open array
HRESULT Method8([in] short cMax,
               [out] short *pcActual,
               [out,
                size_is(cMax),
                length_is(*pcActual)] short *prgs);
```

`Method7` and `Method8` use a varying and an open array as out parameters, respectively.

The problem with both these methods is that the client has to know in advance what the conformance of the outbound array is. It is specified explicitly in `Method7`, and if the object holds more than 256 elements, there is a problem. This problem is solved by `Method8`, which allows the conformance to be set explicitly. Unfortunately, if the client has to allocate a buffer large enough to hold "all the elements" an object has to send, it has to first ask the object how many that is. This requires an extra, and expensive, round-trip. It also means the client has to be prepared for the object's state to change in between the call to request the buffer size and the call to fetch the data.

You can solve this problem by having the object allocate and fill a buffer during a single method invocation:

```
// An object-sized outbound open array
HRESULT Method9([out] short *pcMax,
                [out] short *pcActual,
                [out,
                 size_is(,*pcMax),
                 length_is(,*pcActual)] short **pprgs);
```

Method9 uses this technique, but is inefficient. If the object is going to allocate the buffer to hold all the data it wants to return, there is no need to use an open array because the array's conformance and variance will always be the same. If the method were defined using a conformant array, no extra information about variance would have to be sent over the wire.

```
// An object-sized outbound conformant array
HRESULT Method10([out] short *pcMax,
                 [out,
                  size_is(,*pcMax)] short **pprgs);
```

Method10 is equivalent to Method9, but the code is easier to write and you don't have to send the variance over the wire.[4]

Is there ever a time when varying or open arrays are useful? They make sense as [in] parameters only when the object receiving the array needs to know either the difference between its conformance and variance or the offset of the variance into the array. They make sense as output parameters only when the client knows (or wants to control) the necessary conformance in advance. The standard enumerator interfaces (e.g., IEnumUnknown) provide an example of this latter case. The enumerator model's Next method uses a client-sized outbound open array (like Method8) to allow client-side flow control. This technique sprang from a realization that asking an object for "all the elements" it has in a collection can take a long time and potentially exhaust client-side resources if "all" is a very large number.

---

[4] Note that both Method9 and Method10 use an odd syntax when they specify the argument to size_is. The extra comma forces the size_is argument, *pcMax, to control the dimension of the second level of indirection. With the comma, pprgs is a pointer to a pointer to an array of *pcMax shorts. Without the comma, pprgs would be a pointer to an array of *pcMax pointers to individual shorts.

By the way, if you are wondering why this discussion doesn't consider the array types as [in, out] parameters, then see Item 15.

14. Avoid passing IUnknown as a statically typed object reference (use iid_is).

Imagine you are designing a system that is composed of a hierarchy of objects. Your clients might want to traverse the hierarchy for a variety of reasons: to obtain type information about each object, to render each object, or to make each object persistent. These three orthogonal functionalities can be expressed using standard COM interfaces: IProvideClassInfo for exposing type information, IViewObject/IDataObject for rendering, and IPersistStream/IPersistPropertyBag for persistence. If the standard interfaces don't cut it, you can, of course, roll your own.

Now you decide to implement a custom interface to represent the hierarchy:

```
interface IContainer : IUnknown {
  HRESULT GetObject(
    [in, string] const OLECHAR* pszName,
    [out, retval] IUnknown** ppUnk );
}
```

Fantastic! you exclaim. By using IUnknown, you've clearly expressed your desire to live the COM lifestyle and program with multiple interfaces. Clients enumerating the hierarchy can query for whatever interface is appropriate. So you write some client code:

```
void SaveObject(IStream *pStm, IContainer* pContainer,
                const OLECHAR* pszName) {
  IUnknown* pUnk = 0;
  HRESULT hr = pContainer->GetObject(pszName, &pUnk);
  if (SUCCEEDED(hr)) {
    IPersistStream* pPS = 0;
    hr = pUnk->QueryInterface( IID_IPersistStream,
                               (void**)&pPS );
    if (SUCCEEDED(hr)) {
      // perform the save...
      hr = pPS->Save(pStm, FALSE);
      pPS->Release();
    }
    pUnk->Release();
  }
```

After writing several pieces of client code like this, you realize that having to write code to call QueryInterface every time you retrieve an object is silly. Worse yet, your design requires two round-trips to obtain an object with a specific interface. So, you redesign your interface to allow the client to specify the type of interface desired:

```
HRESULT GetObject([in, string] const OLECHAR* pszName,
                  [in] REFIID riid,
                  [out, retval] IUnknown** ppUnk);
```

In fact, you've seen something similar to this many times (e.g., IClassFactory::CreateInstance or IMoniker::BindToObject), but since void** doesn't seem to please the compiler (at least not with the attributes shown here), you stick with the IUnknown** signature. Now your client code is much simpler, and only one round-trip seems to be required:

```
IPersistStream* pPS = 0;
HRESULT hr = pContainer->GetObject(pszName,
    IID_IPersistStream, (IUnknown**)&pPS);
```

Your implementation of GetObject simply leverages QueryInterface to implement the dynamically typed result:

```
STDMETHODIMP Cntr::GetObject(const OLECHAR *pszName,
                REFIID riid, IUnknown **ppItf) {
  IUnknown *pUnkObject = this->Lookup(pszName);
  HRESULT hr = pUnkObject->QueryInterface(riid,
                                (void**)ppItf);
  pUnkObject->Release();
  return hr;
}
```

Once these changes are in place, everything works great, *provided* pContainer *doesn't refer to a proxy.*

In the case of a proxy, the code that uses the IPersistStream pointer blows up with an access violation. Hmm . . . What could be happening? Your implementation of GetObject is certainly returning the correct pointer. The problem is that the interface stub for IContainer believes the interface being returned is always IID_IUnknown (based on the signature of the method in IDL) and creates an OBJREF (via CoMarshalInterface) based on this information. Back on the client side, the interface proxy creates a new object proxy from the OBJREF in the client's apartment (via CoUnmarshalInterface). This proxy represents the new COM identity being returned to the client, and since the interface that was marshaled was `IID_IUnknown`, this is actually the only interface implemented by the proxy at this time. The client's downcast is therefore unsafe.

What you need is a way to let the interface stub know the dynamic type of the interface so it can call `CoMarshalInterface` with the correct IID. A mechanism was provided for just this situation: the `iid_is` attribute. Here is the correct method definition:

```
HRESULT GetObject(
   [in, string] const OLECHAR* pszName,
   [in] REFIID riid,
   [out, retval, iid_is(riid)] void** ppv);
```

In fact, an existing interface for navigating object hierarchies is `IOleItem-Container`, and its `GetObject` method is defined using `iid_is` for exactly this reason.

Note that `iid_is` comes in handy in other types of situations as well. Recall the less-than-optimal design of `IConnectionPoint::Advise` (see Item 9), whose `[in]` parameter is statically typed to `IUnknown`. A much better design would have been

```
HRESULT Advise( [in] REFIID riid,
                [in, iid_is(riid)] IUnknown* pUnk,
                [out] DWORD* pdwCookie );
```

Due to the proliferation of designs that support interface-challenged clients (read: scripting clients), there is a growing tendency to forget that COM allows multiple interfaces per object. Scripting clients typically rely on `IDispatch`, and the lure of dual interfaces leads many to design object hierarchies with a single interface per object for all clients (see Item 11). Newcomers to COM see many existing dual-interface-based designs that use statically typed interfaces as out parameters when navigating instance hierarchies:

```
interface IDBProvider : IDispatch {
  HRESULT OpenDatabase( [in] BSTR bstr,
                        [out, retval] IDatabase** p );
}
interface IDatabase : IDispatch {
  HRESULT OpenRecordset( [in] BSTR bstr,
                         [out, retval] IRecordset** p);
}
interface IRecordset : IDispatch {
  HRESULT GetField( [in] BSTR bstr,
```

```
                        [out, retval] IField** p );
    }
```

Although this is somewhat better (performance-wise) than statically typing parameters to `IUnknown`, this type of design blurs the distinction between objects and interfaces. Another problem is that versioning a single interface now creates a dramatic ripple effect throughout the other interfaces because of the tight coupling introduced by static typing. Suppose `IField` were modified in some way and changed to `IField2`. This would ripple throughout the other interfaces:

```
    interface IDBProvider2 : IDispatch {
      HRESULT OpenDatabase( [in] BSTR bstr,
                            [out, retval] IDatabase2** p );
    }
    interface IDatabase2 : IDispatch {
      HRESULT OpenRecordset( [in] BSTR bstr,
                             [out, retval] IRecordset2** p);
    }
    interface IRecordset2 : IDispatch {
      HRESULT GetField( [in] BSTR bstr,
                        [out, retval] IField2** p );
    }
```

Bottom line: distinguish between objects and interfaces. Leverage the power of interface-based programming. Make use of `iid_is` so this happens safely.

15. Avoid [in, out] parameters that contain pointers.

Imagine designing an interface that represents an associative array of strings. You might choose to provide a lookup method that overloads a single parameter for specifying the key (on the way in) and the value (on the way out):

```
    interface IStringMap : IUnknown {
      // S_OK == successful lookup
      // S_FALSE == key not found
      HRESULT Lookup( [in, out, string] OLECHAR** ppsz );

      //...
    }
```

Implementing `Lookup` would be pretty easy:

```
    STDMETHODIMP StringMap::Lookup(OLECHAR** ppsz) {
      if (!ppsz || !*ppsz )
```

```
      return E_INVALIDARG;
    const wchar_t* pszFound = InternalLookup(*ppsz);
    if (pszFound) {
      DWORD cb = (wcslen(pszFound)+1) * sizeof(OLECHAR);
      CoTaskMemFree(*ppsz);
      *ppsz = (OLECHAR*)CoTaskMemAlloc(cb);
      if (!*ppsz)
        return E_OUTOFMEMORY;
      CopyMemory(*ppsz, pszFound, cb);
    }
    return pszFound ? S_OK : S_FALSE;
  }
```

Using Lookup also seems pretty straightforward:

```
  bool PrintUserAddress(const wchar_t* pszUser) {
    DWORD cb = (wcslen(pszUser)+1) * sizeof(wchar_t);
    OLECHAR* psz = (OLECHAR*)CoTaskMemAlloc(cb);
    if (!psz) throw OutOfMemoryException; // or whatever
    CopyMemory(psz, pszUser, cb);
    HRESULT hr = g_pStringMap->Lookup(&psz);
    bool bResult = false;
    if (SUCCEEDED(hr)) {
      if (S_OK == hr)
          wcout << psz << endl;
      else wcout << L"User not found" << endl;
      if (psz)
        CoTaskMemFree(psz);
    }
    else {
      // hmm...
    }
    return bResult;
  }
```

If all goes well and you get a success code (either S_OK or S_FALSE), you should have no problem determining whether you are responsible for freeing the resulting string. The rules for this are straightforward: you allocate a resource on the way in (in this case a string), and the server either leaves your resource as is or releases your resource and replaces it with a newly allocated resource. In either case, you are required to release the resource after the call.

Dealing with [in,out] pointer parameters in failure modes is not nearly as straightforward. Here is the section of the COM spec that deals with resource management of [in,out] parameters in failure modes:

> *In error returns, all in-out parameters must either be left alone by the callee (and thus remaining at the value to which it was initialized by the caller; if the caller didn't initialize it, then it's an out parameter, not an in-out parameter) or be explicitly set as in the out parameter error return case.*

This rule implies that even in the case of an error, you must check the [in,out] parameter to determine whether the resource it points to needs to be freed (e.g., it's nonzero). Recall that failure codes come from two places in COM: the callee or the RPC runtime and stub code. Generally speaking, it is not a good idea to depend on the contents of [out] parameters after receiving a failure code, so why should [in,out] parameters be any different? Recall that failure modes tend to be the least-tested path through any code, so even if someone assures you that you can rely on the value of [in,out] parameters in this case, you should be somewhat skeptical. Taking this view, you would find it impossible to determine whether to free the resource or not.

Consider a different interface design:

```
interface IStringMap2 {
   // S_OK == successful lookup
   // S_FALSE == key not found
   HRESULT Lookup( [in, string] const OLECHAR* pszKey,
                   [out, string] OLECHAR** ppszValue );


   //...
}
```

This new interface uses two separate parameters to specify the key and value, thus eliminating any resource management ambiguity. Recall from the basic rules of COM that you are responsible for resources (obtained via [out] parameters) when a method returns a success code. Note that since the direction of the parameter limits data transmission to either the request or response packet, the marshaling code will be just as efficient as the previous version. The new version is also easier to use, since the caller does not have to allocate pszKey on the free store.

But wait, you say. This is so obvious—who in their right mind would ever design an interface like IStringMap in the first place? Ahh, but consider a much more common example—pointers embedded in structures. Structures are often passed as [in, out] parameters. Structures commonly contain pointers. Keep this issue in mind when designing interfaces that pass structures as parameters.

Another interesting issue with [in, out] pointer parameters occurs when dealing with conformant arrays. Consider the following interface:

```
interface ICalvinCalculator : IUnknown {
  HRESULT Transmogrify(
    [in,out] long* pcItems,
    [in,out,size_is(*pcItems)] long* prgItems );
}
```

This particular interface apparently takes a conformant array and operates on it in some way (potentially changing the size of the array) before returning to the client.

Recall that the caller manages memory for top-level pointer parameters; therefore, this interface is somewhat dangerous, especially if you consider the following implementation:

```
STDMETHODIMP
CCalvinCalculator::Transmogrify(long* pcItems,
                               long* prgItems) {
  // leave original items in array
  // append squares of items to end of array
  for (int i = 0; i < *pcItems; ++i)
    prgItems[*pcItems+i] = prgItems[i] * prgItems[i];
  *pcItems *= 2;
  return S_OK;
}
```

This code is obviously wrong, since it overwrites the end of the array.

By splitting up [in, out] pointer parameters, you'll have a much better interface:

```
[pointer_default(unique), ...]
interface IHobbesCalculator : IUnknown {
  HRESULT Transmogrify(
    [in] long cItems,
    [in, size_is(cItems)] const long* prgItems,
    [out] long* pcItems,
    [out, size_is(,*pcItems)] long** pprgItemsOut );
}
```

This new interface is efficient and easy to use, and the output array can be any size the callee desires. Check out Item 13 for more details on passing arrays as parameters (including the `size_is(,n)` syntax).

16. Be conscious of cyclic references (and the problems they cause).

Reference counting works great when multiple clients hold references to some transient entity. This is the way most modern operating systems work with respect to file descriptors, handles, or other cookies into the kernel. Many clients (processes) can hold open references (handles) to kernel resources (files, semaphores). Once the last reference goes away, the kernel is free to reclaim any held resources. Although clients must explicitly release their references by making a system call (e.g., `CloseHandle`), the OS is smart enough to clean up after prematurely terminated processes that don't get a chance to explicitly release their references.

Like kernel objects, COM objects fall into the category of transient entities held by multiple clients. Clients deal in handles (object references) that refer to resources (COM objects). As is the case with kernel objects, COM clients must explicitly notify the object when they are done using it (by calling `IUnknown::Release` instead of `CloseHandle`). Like kernel objects, COM cleans up any leaked references at process termination time. All of these analogies are good news to the average COM developer who is used to making system calls against the Win32 or UNIX APIs.

The one fundamental problem with reference counting in COM is *not* the fact that the C++ programmer must manually manage the reference counts. This aspect of COM programming is no different from any other resource acquisition problem that C++ programmers face. Either programmers do it instinctively or they rely on runtime test harnesses that find leaked resources, or they simply move over to Java, where resource reclamation is hidden from the programmer (sometimes by simply never reclaiming resources). The fundamental problem with reference counting in COM is that unlike many kernel objects, COM objects can hold references to each other, potentially creating cycles.

A reference-counting cycle can occur when two or more objects need to collaborate beyond the scope of a single method call. Consider the three objects A, B, and C shown in the following figure:

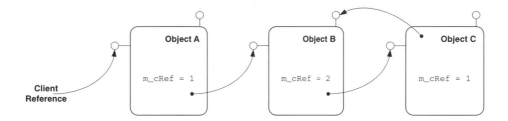

Note that since B uses the services of C, it holds a reference to C. But because C needs to call into B to get its work done, B holds a reference to C. Even after A releases its reference to B, C will still hold its reference. Assuming a naïve implementation, C will not release its reference until it is destroyed, which of course will not happen until B releases its reference to C. Assuming that B holds its reference to C until its destruction, we now have a reference-counting cycle.

There are three techniques that COM programmers have at their disposal: weak references, out-of-band methods, and split identity. All three have their pitfalls. Unfortunately, only one (split identity) is suitable for building distributed systems.

The weak reference technique is simple: one of the objects in the cycle caches an interface but doesn't add to the other object's reference count (i.e., it doesn't call `AddRef`). Here is an example applied to the simple ABC object hierarchy shown previously:

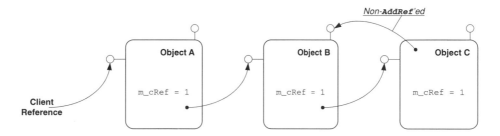

Since C does not hold an `AddRef`'ed reference to B, B will now destroy itself when its client (A) releases its reference. This technique can only work when the holder of the non-`AddRef`'ed object reference will not live longer than the referenced object. A common example of this occurs in COM aggregation, where an aggregated controlled inner caches the controlling outer's `IUnknown*` without adding a reference. This is legal because the inner knows that its lifetime is completely subsumed within that of the outer. There is no way for the outer to go away without taking the inner with it, and therefore the weak reference will not cause any problems.

On the other hand, imagine a less intimate relationship between objects that can't guarantee the same lifetime. Consider the scenario in which object C holds a weak reference to object B. If C has other parties holding references to it, it's possible for B to go away while C still lives, leaving C with a dangling pointer to B. One hopes that C doesn't share an apartment with B, so that when the dangling reference is used, the proxy will handle the error without crashing. If, on the other hand, the two objects *do* share the same apartment, C is holding a one-way ticket to nowhere and even a call to `IUnknown::Release` will likely cause an exception.

The previous paragraph implied that if B and C were in two different apartments, the proxy would at least keep C's process from crashing when it released its dangling reference to B. This implication ignored the fact that weak references cannot be used across apartment boundaries. Consider the case in which objects B and C live in different apartments. Since C's reference to B is actually a reference to a proxy, C does not have the option of not `AddRef`'ing the object reference. Suppose C were to try to hold the reference it received to B without calling `AddRef`:

```
STDMETHODIMP C::HeresB(/* [in] */ IB *pb) {
// hold onto pointer in a data member
  m_pb = pb;
// do not call AddRef, but just return
  return S_OK;
}
```

The held reference to the proxy will be invalid, since the proxy is not aware of the weak reference relationship between B and C. When the method is complete, COM will tear down the proxy, which will send a disconnect message to the stub, which will release its reference to B.

A common reaction to the problems with weak references is to use an application-specific shutdown method to break the cycle. This method would be "out-of-band" from the normal `AddRef/Release` life cycle used in COM. In the simple ABC object hierarchy, this would mean that A would need to call some explicit method on B to signal that it is time for B to shut down. In response to this method request from A, B would then release its reference to C:

```
STDMETHODIMP B::ImDone(void) {
// the client is done with me, so release C (which
```

```
// will then release us when it destroys itself)
  m_pc->Release(); m_pc = 0;
  return S_OK;
}
```

This out-of-band technique works well provided there is only one client. If multiple clients are possible, then B would need to keep a second reference count. Only when B received the appropriate number of `ImDone` calls would it then do the shutdown. Of course, this is reference counting, and if it is possible that B were to hold a reference to A, then we have another cycle—this time based on the second reference count used by B's `ImDone` method.

Even in the case of one client, the out-of-band method approach suffers from the fact that A must remember to call the `ImDone` method. As discussed in Item 2, any call could be your last, which means it is possible that A's process might crash before getting a chance to call B's `ImDone` method. In such a case, A would go away and its `IUnknown::Release` call would be issued by COM's garbage collector, but B would remain alive indefinitely, since C still holds a reference and no one will be calling `ImDone`. This makes the out-of-band solution unreliable and inappropriate for long-running applications.

So, if weak references and out-of-band methods don't work in the general case, what's left? The answer is buried in the definition of a COM object. A COM object is a collection of vptrs in an apartment that follows the identity rules of `QueryInterface`. Although this defines a *COM* object, your *logical* object may actually span two or more physical COM objects or identities. Consider the cycle that exists between B and C. This cycle occurs because B cannot distinguish between A's and C's references. As far as B is concerned, there are two outstanding references, and to be safe, B must remain alive as long as both A and C are alive. B really wants to distinguish between A's *necessary* reference and C's *advisory* reference. To do this, B should give C a distinct COM identity to call back through. Here is an example of this split-identity technique applied to the ABC object hierarchy:

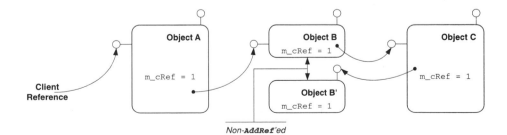

Note that B is now composed of two COM identities. The primary identity is the one that A uses to make requests on B. This is the identity that actually controls the lifetime of B. C, on the other hand, holds a reference to a secondary identity. The COM life cycle of this identity is distinct from that of the primary identity. The secondary identity's implementation simply operates on the state that is shared between the two internal identities of B.

Here's why the use of split identity breaks the reference-counting cycle: when A releases B either via an explicit call to `IUnknown::Release` or through process termination, the primary identity will shut down. This will trigger an `IUnknown::Release` call to C. When C shuts down, it will release the reference to the secondary identity of B, cleaning up any remaining resources.

You may be asking yourself why this discussion is in the interfaces chapter and not the implementations chapter. This is a reasonable question. The motivation for talking about cycles here is that it is imperative that methods document whether or not the object may hold onto a reference beyond the scope of an individual method call. Consider the following IDL:

```
HRESULT Advise([in] IB *pb, [out] DWORD *pdwCookie);
```

Although the method name implies that the object will hold a reference, the documentation should explicitly state this fact so that the caller knows that a cycle may be possible. Otherwise, it is easy to wind up with islands of leaked objects due to unexpected cycles.

17. Avoid `wire_marshal`, `transmit_as`, `call_as`, and `cpp_quote`.

Because you have taken Item 1 to heart, you define all of your COM interfaces in IDL, which you compile to generate language bindings and proxy/stub pairs for marshaling and remoting. Language bindings define the *presented types* with which your clients and objects deal. The proxy/stub code takes care of mapping those types to *transmissible types* that get sent between apartments during a remote call. The mapping is defined by the Network Data Representation standard originally defined by Distributed Computing Environment (DCE) RPC.

IDL allows you to define custom type mappings using the `[wire_marshal]` and `[transmit_as]` attributes. Both allow you to specify an arbitrary relationship between a presented type and a transmitted type, and you get to write the code that translates back and forth. This sort of aliasing is most useful when you want your client and object to deal with a legacy data type that is impossible to marshal.

The HWND type is a great example. One might expect that HWND would be a bad parameter type because it is defined as an opaque pointer in the system header file. However, the definition of HWND in wtypes.idl uses the [wire _marshal] attribute to alias the type to RemotableHandle*.

```
// RemotableHandle type
typedef union _RemotableHandle switch(long fContext) u
{
   case WDT_INPROC_CALL:   long    hInproc;
   case WDT_REMOTE_CALL:   long    hRemote;
} RemotableHandle;

// wireHWND is a pointer to a RemotableHandle
typedef [unique] RemotableHandle * wireHWND;

// HWND is presented as a void* but marshaled as a
// wireHWND
typedef [wire_marshal(wireHWND)] void* HWND;
```

The use of [wire_marshal] enables the client and object codes to deal with the native HWND type, while the proxy/stub pair will translate the presented HWND to a RemotableHandle* as needed, using conversion code provided in this case by the RPC runtime libraries.

The problem with this approach is that it doesn't work with type libraries. When you compile IDL that uses HWND,

```
[ uuid(CCD6A420-338A-11d1-867A-00A024A9F22B), object ]
interface IUseHWNDs : IUnknown
{
   HRESULT SendAnHWND([in] HWND hwndIn);
   HRESULT ReceiveAnHWND([out] HWND *phwndOut);
}

[ uuid(CCD6A420-338A-11d1-867A-00A024A9F22B) ]
library UseHWNDsLib
{
   importlib("stdole32.tlb");
   interface IUseHWNDs;
}
```

the generated header file for the C++ language mapping includes the correct presented type,

```
// Signatures use presented type, HWND
virtual HRESULT STDMETHODCALLTYPE SendAnHWND(
            /* [in] */ HWND hwndIn) = 0;
virtual HRESULT STDMETHODCALLTYPE ReceiveAnHWND
            /* [out] */ HWND __RPC_FAR *phwndOut) = 0;
```

but the generated type library includes the *transmissible* type. The code below was regenerated from a type library.

```
typedef union tag__MIDL_IWinTypes_0009 {
  long hInproc;
  long hRemote;
} __MIDL_IWinTypes_0009;

typedef struct tag_RemotableHandle {
  long fContext;
  __MIDL_IWinTypes_0009 u;
} _RemotableHandle;

typedef [public] _RemotableHandle* wireHWND;

// Signatures use transmitted type!!!
[ uuid(CCD6A420-338A-11d1-867A-00A024A9F22B), object ]
interface IUseHWNDs : IUnknown {
  HRESULT _stdcall SendAnHWND(
                        [in] wireHWND hwndIn);
  HRESULT _stdcall ReceiveAnHWND(
                        [out] wireHWND* phwndOut);
};
```

This is a shortcoming in the current MIDL compiler.

The [call_as] attribute and cpp_quote present similar problems. The [call_as] mechanism aliases methods instead of types, and type libraries always carry the remotable method's signature (not the callable version, which would be correct). The cpp_quote statement inserts code directly into the generated C++ header, and type mappings defined this way don't appear in type libraries at all.

This limitation makes it impossible to use aliased data types if you depend on a type library for any reason. If you are using a language binding that interprets a type library directly (e.g., Visual Basic) or indirectly (e.g., Java, or `#import` from Visual C++), your clients have a corrupted view of your interfaces. Even if they can deal with the transmitted type directly (which may not be the case), they can't pass it as an argument. The object they are invoking (or its proxy, if it is in another apartment) is expecting to see the presented type, and a mismatched type on the stack will invariably result in an access violation.

If the type library accurately reflected your presented type, clients would build the right call stack and invocations would succeed. But there is a larger problem lurking. Once you use aliased types, the interface definition you write in IDL is no longer enough to create a proxy/stub pair. You need to provide the conversion code that implements your custom presentation/translation type mapping. Your translation code must be linked into every proxy/stub pair that uses your aliased type.

Future versions of COM may no longer support compiled proxy/stub pairs. Instead, they may generate proxy/stub implementations dynamically based on type information (just as the Universal Marshaler does for a subset of interfaces today). At that point, having accurate signatures in your type libraries isn't enough, and since it may not be possible to use a compiled proxy/stub DLL, you may have painted yourself into a corner. This doesn't mean there won't be a way to do custom type mappings—such a feature may exist. It does mean that it probably won't work the way it works today using `[wire_marshal]`, `[transmit_as]`, `[call_as]`, or `cpp_quote` in IDL.

So, if you have legacy data types that aren't remotable, your best bet is to replace them with types that are. If that is an expensive proposition, map between the two types directly in your client and object codes. In any case, avoid IDL's explicit support for aliasing.

Implementations

In COM, the implementation is where the assumptions made in Interface Definition Language (IDL) are tested against the physical laws of nature. Sometimes the assumptions are sound, making implementation fairly straightforward. Sometimes the assumptions are completely Martian, making the developer curse the immutability of interfaces. In either case, implementing COM classes in C++ requires as much attention to detail as any other C++ coding task, if not more. The dynamic nature of COM-based systems makes implementation much trickier, as one never knows in exactly what client context a given piece of code will find itself. To this end, many of the guidelines in this chapter address defensive coding practices, although a fair amount of attention is paid to techniques to improve the runtime efficiency of a component.

18. Code defensively.

Writing code in the pre-COM era was a lot simpler. You basically had three entities you needed to worry about with respect to bad code: your own code, any libraries you were using, and the underlying operating system. All three of these entities were predictably buggy. The defects in an operating system are usually fairly well known and reasonably documented, due to the large numbers of developers that may be writing code against it. Commercial source code libraries also benefit from a potentially large number of developers finding and reporting bugs. For most developers, the primary source of defects is in their own code. In an ideal world, you were targeting a final release of the operating system using final releases of any source code libraries in use. This meant that, theoretically, you were building your software on a solid, predictable, and *tested* foundation. This type of development can be compared to driving a car in the Mojave Desert. There are no other drivers who can make a mistake and cause your car to crash.

The landscape is fairly static and not apt to hurl debris at your vehicle. As long as you are a reasonably competent driver, the odds of a mishap are fairly low.

Writing code in the post-COM era can be compared to driving a motorcycle on the Los Angeles freeway system. While the terrain is fairly static except for periodic tremors, mudslides, and fires, there are lots of other motorists of dubious qualifications that at best are simply trying to stay out of your way and at worst are doing everything short of homicide to prevent you from reaching your destination.

COM-based systems often are composed of objects implemented by developers from multiple organizations. Depending on the target platform and domain, much of the operating system and supporting technologies are exposed via COM interfaces. Your code may utilize commercial COM-based libraries or controls. Your code might also have been designed for extensibility via COM-based plugins. Because COM-based systems are dynamically composed at runtime, it is often impossible to predict exactly whose code you will be working with. To this end, it makes sense to assume the worst to avoid unpleasant surprises.

One common mistake made by inexperienced COM programmers is forgetting to set [out] parameters to NULL on failure (see Item 19 for why these programmers can't get away with this for long). This means that the HRESULT should be your primary indicator of whether a method succeeded or not. The following code,

```
void f(IClassFactory *pcf) {
  IUnknown *pUnkInstance = 0;
  pcf->CreateInstance(0, IID_IUnknown,
                         (void**)&pUnkInstance);
  if (pUnkInstance) {
    UseObject(pUnkInstance);
    pUnkInstance->Release();
  }
}
```

is considerably less robust than this version, which uses the HRESULT to determine the outcome of the method:

```
void f(IClassFactory *pcf) {
  IUnknown *pUnkInstance = 0;
  HRESULT hr = pcf->CreateInstance(0, IID_IUnknown,
                                      (void**)&pUnkInstance);
  if (SUCCEEDED(hr)) {
    UseObject(pUnkInstance);
```

```
        pUnkInstance->Release();
    }
}
```

Notice that this version does not check the validity of the resultant object reference. Unfortunately, to code defensively, simply testing against NULL is insufficient, as NULL is but one of many invalid pointer values.

The safest solution to this problem would be to take a lesson from the MIDL-generated interface stubs. Standard interface stubs wrap method invocation around a Win32 structured exception handler to catch potential access violations before they crash the process. The following version of the function demonstrates this technique:

```
void f(IClassFactory *pcf) {
  __try {
  IUnknown *pUnkInstance = 0;
  HRESULT hr = pcf->CreateInstance(0, IID_IUnknown,
                         (void**)&pUnkInstance);
  if (SUCCEEDED(hr)) {
    UseObject(pUnkInstance);
    pUnkInstance->Release();
  }
  } __except(EXCEPTION_EXECUTE_HANDLER) {
  // handle error here (but don't crash the process)
  }
}
```

Depending on your compiler, you may also be able to use a C++ exception handler for the same purpose.[1] This technique may seem drastic, but if you have a critical process that must not crash and you are foolish enough to load in-process code written by arbitrary third parties, this technique is not as far-fetched as it may seem.

Another classic error is related to COM enumerators. The Next method on COM enumerators has two very strange exceptions to normal COM practices. First, it uses S_FALSE. In general, S_FALSE is a dangerous HRESULT to mandate in an interface. This is because COM programmers become so accustomed to using the SUCCEEDED macro to check method results that it is easy to forget to perform the special-case test for this result. Second, the IEnum protocol has a strange relationship between the HRESULT and the third parameter. Consider the definition of IEnumUnknown::Next:

---

[1] The Microsoft C++ compiler will allow you to do this, provided that no structured exception translator has been installed. Consult your compiler documentation for more information.

```
[local] HRESULT Next([in] ULONG cElems,
                     [out] IUnknown **prgpElems,
                     [out] ULONG *pcFetched);
```

The documentation for all enumerator interfaces states that if the number of elements returned is less than the number requested, the result of the method should be S_FALSE, and *pcFetched will contain the actual number of elements returned. If the enumerator was able to return the requested number of elements, then S_OK should be returned. The oddity of this method is that the third parameter is allowed to be NULL *provided* that the first parameter indicates that only one element is needed. This rule is to accommodate the following usage:

```
void f(IEnumUnknown *peu) {
  IUnknown *pUnk = 0;
  HRESULT hr = peu->Next(1, &pUnk, 0);
  if (hr == S_OK) { // note, SUCCEEDED not used
    UseObject(pUnk);
    pUnk->Release();
  }
}
```

Note that if the enumerator were at the end of its collection, it would have returned S_FALSE, indicating that less than the requested number of elements was returned (and since only one element was requested, this means zero elements was returned).

Potential problems can arise due to this strange intermixing of HRESULT and output parameters. One common error is for the implementer of the enumerator to forget to set the pcFetched parameter when returning the requested number of elements (that is, cElems elements). A defensive user must therefore write the following code to properly handle this forgotten detail:

```
void f(IEnumUnknown *peu) {
  IUnknown * rgpUnk[100] = { 0 };
  HRESULT hr = S_OK;
  do {
    ULONG cFetched;
    hr = peu->Next(100, rgpUnk, &cFetched);
    if (hr == S_OK) // ensure cFetched is correct
      cFetched = 100;
    for (ULONG i = 0; i < cFetched; i++) {
      UseObject(rgpUnk[i]);
      rgpUnk[i]->Release();
```

```
      }
   } while (hr == S_OK);
}
```

On the implementation side, you must also be prepared to handle the case in which the caller provides a NULL pointer for pcFetched but asks for more than one element:

```
STDMETHODIMP MyEnum::Next(ULONG cElems,
                 IUnknown **prgpUnk, ULONG *pcFetched)
   if (prgpUnk == 0)
      return E_POINTER;
   if (pcFetched == 0 && cElems != 1) {
   // clear [out] params and return
      ZeroMemory(prgpUnk, sizeof(*prgpUnk) * cElems);
      return E_INVALIDARG;
   }
// else do normal processing
}
```

It is unfortunate that one must be this paranoid, but as long as arbitrary code can be loaded into your process, you don't have much of an alternative.

One lesson to take away from this discussion is to think about the robustness ramifications on both clients and implementers when designing COM interfaces. If it looks like everyone will need to use extreme (and unnatural) techniques such as the ones we just discussed, consider changing the protocol of the interface to simplify the assumptions that both the caller and the callee can make.

19. Always initialize [out] parameters.

In intra-apartment method calls, it is a courtesy for an object to clear pointers to [out] parameters. For example, in the event that an interface is not supported by an object, implementations of QueryInterface are required to set the second parameter to zero like so:

```
STDMETHODIMP
CoPenguin::QueryInterface(REFIID riid, void** ppv) {
   if( riid == IID_IUnknown || riid == IID_IBird )
      *ppv = static_cast<IBird*>(this);
   else {
      *ppv = 0;
```

```
    return E_NOINTERFACE;
  }
  reinterpret_cast<IUnknown*>(*ppv)->AddRef();
  return S_OK;
}
```

For the client, this is a convenience because it does not have to bother to set its
invalid interface pointer to zero in the event of a failed query:

```
IFlyingBird* pFlyingBird;
HRESULT      hr;
hr = pBird->QueryInterface(IID_IFlyingBird,
                           (void**)&pFlyingBird));
if( SUCCEEDED(hr) ) // Use and release pFlyingBird
else pFlyingBird = 0; // No need for this code
```

However, initializing all [out] parameters (even in the face of errors) is far
more than a convenience; it is a requirement. The reason for this is that the stub
does not check the HRESULT for failure when deciding which [out] parameters to marshal back to the client. Recall the syntax for IUnknown:

```
interface IUnknown {
  HRESULT QueryInterface([in] REFIID riid,
          [out, iid_is(riid)] void** ppv);
  ULONG AddRef();
  ULONG Release();
}
```

Notice that the first parameter of QueryInterface, the interface identifier
(IID), is an [in] parameter and that the second parameter, a pointer to the returned interface pointer, is an [out] parameter. When any method is called on
an interface that has been marshaled across apartment boundaries, the client is
actually talking to a proxy. It becomes the proxy's job to take all [in] parameters that are on the stack and serialize them into a request message that is sent to
the stub. The stub, in turn, deserializes the parameters from the request message
onto the stack and calls the object's implementation of the method. When the
object method call returns, it packages up the [out] parameters and the HRE-
SULT into the response message that it then sends back to the proxy, which in
turn deserializes them back onto the stack prior to returning control to the client.
In this process, the stub *never checks the HRESULT*. As far as the stub is concerned, the HRESULT is just another [out] parameter to send back to the
proxy. Even if the HRESULT is a SEVERITY_ERROR value, the stub derefer-
ences all nonzero pointers to send the data back to the proxy. What does this

mean? It means that you are on the hook for putting output parameters in a reasonable state, even when you're returning an error as an HRESULT.

Acknowledging this requirement, most COM developers make it a practice to always clear all [out] parameters at the beginning of their method implementations before any real code is executed. Unfortunately, clearing [out] parameters is not always easy. For example, in the intra-apartment case (i.e., no proxy and stub) the client may send in NULL pointers. Blindly dereferencing them would be a bad idea. On the other hand, in the event of a remotable interface, a NULL pointer is an error (designated via E_POINTER), which will be caught by COM's remoting layer). In the event of multiple [out] parameters, any of them could be NULL in the intra-apartment case, but all non-NULL pointers will need to be cleared before returning. Properly checking and clearing [out] parameters dictates code like the following:

```
// bird.idl
interface IBirdInfo : IUnknown {
  HRESULT GetBirdInfo([out] LPOLESTR *ppszGenus,
                      [out] LPOLESTR *ppszPhilum
                      [out] LPOLESTR *ppszSpecies);
}

// bird.cpp
HRESULT CoBird::GetBirdInfo(
  LPOLESTR *ppszGenus,
  LPOLESTR *ppszPhilum,
  LPOLESTR *ppszSpecies)
{
  HRESULT hr = S_OK;
  if (ppszGenus) *ppszGenus = 0;
  else hr = E_POINTER;

  if (ppszPhilum) *ppszPhilum = 0;
  else hr = E_POINTER;

  if (ppszSpecies) *ppszSpecies = 0;
  else hr = E_POINTER;

  if (FAILED(hr)) return hr;

  // If we get this far, all out params are properly
  // cleared and none of the pointers is null
  hr = S_OK;
```

```
    // Set genus, philum, and species...
    return hr;
}
```

Notice how this sample must check every [out] parameter for NULL separately before clearing it. If any of the pointers is NULL, the function returns the appropriate error, after clearing the non-NULL pointers to avoid marshaling garbage.

To simplify this kind of repetitive code, you could use macros such as these:

```
#define BEGIN_OUT_PARAMS() \
   { HRESULT _hr = S_OK;
#define OUT_PARAM(p) \
   if (p) *p = 0; else _hr = E_POINTER;
#define END_OUT_PARAMS() \
   if (FAILED(_hr)) return _hr; }
```

When used at the beginning of a function, these macros will properly clear any non-NULL pointers and return in the event of an error before any real code is executed. Using these macros, the [out] parameter clearing and checking code can now be significantly simplified:

```
HRESULT GetBirdInfo(
   LPOLESTR *ppszGenus,
   LPOLESTR *ppszPhilum,
   LPOLESTR *ppszSpecies)
{
   BEGIN_OUT_PARAMS()
     OUT_PARAM(ppszGenus)
     OUT_PARAM(ppszPhilum)
     OUT_PARAM(ppszSpecies)
   END_OUT_PARAMS()

   // If we get this far, all out params are properly
   // cleared and none of the pointers is null
   HRESULT hr = S_OK;

   // Set genus, philum and species…
   return hr;
}
```

These macros are helpful, but we're not done yet. In the event that resources have been allocated but the method fails for some other reason, those resources must be deallocated and the [out] parameters cleared to avoid leaks. Here's an example of a method implementation to fully avoid leaks:

```
// Utility function to duplicate an OLE string
HRESULT TaskStrDup(OLECHAR** ppsz, const OLECHAR* psz) {
  HRESULT hr = S_OK;
  *ppsz = 0;
  if (!psz)
    hr = E_INVALIDARG;
  else {
    DWORD cb = (wcslen(psz)+1)*sizeof(OLECHAR);
    *ppsz = CoTaskMemAlloc(cb);
    if (*ppsz)
      wcscpy(*ppsz, psz);
    else
      hr = E_OUTOFMEMORY;
  }
  return hr;
}


HRESULT GetBirdInfo(LPOLESTR *ppszGenus,
                    LPOLESTR *ppszPhilum,
                    LPOLESTR *ppszSpecies)
{
  BEGIN_OUT_PARAMS()
    OUT_PARAM(ppszGenus)
    OUT_PARAM(ppszPhilum)
    OUT_PARAM(ppszSpecies)
  END_OUT_PARAMS()

  HRESULT hr;

  // Set genus, philum and species…
  if (FAILED(hr = TaskStrDup(ppszGenus, m_pszG)) ||
      FAILED(hr = TaskStrDup(ppszPhilum, m_pszP)) ||
      FAILED(hr = TaskStrDup(ppszSpecies, m_pszS))) {
    CoTaskMemFree(*ppszGenus); *ppszGenus = 0;
    CoTaskMemFree(*ppszPhilum); *ppszPhilum = 0;
    CoTaskMemFree(*ppszSpecies); *ppszSpecies = 0;
  }
  return hr;
}
```

Before widely applying the techniques in this item, you need to be aware that they will not work for `[in,out]` parameters. Checking and clearing `[in,out]` parameters are just two of the complications of their use. To learn more about the dangers of `[in,out]` parameters, see Item 15.

20. Don't use interface pointers that have not been `AddRef`'ed

Wow, you may be wondering. How could this item possibly apply to me? How could I ever get hold of an interface pointer that has not been `AddRef`'ed? Isn't that against the rules of COM? Well, there are at least four cases where you could end up with interface pointers on which you have no reference counts to speak of. And you should never use these interface pointers. Ever.

The most obvious case (but one that bites many novice COM developers) is simply using an interface pointer that has been released. For example, consider the following code:

```
IUnknown* pUnk = 0;
if (SUCCEEDED(GetObject(&pUnk))) {
  UseObject(pUnk);
  pUnk->Release();

  UseObject(pUnk); // whoops!
}
```

The above code has a glaring error. Using an interface pointer after all `AddRef`s have been balanced by calls to `Release` results in undefined behavior. Assuming `GetObject` follows normal COM rules and calls `AddRef` through the interface pointer after copying it into the caller's pointer variable, the second call to `UseObject` results in undefined behavior. Undefined behavior manifests itself via the "it works great on my machine" syndrome. In fact, certain laws of computer science guarantee that this code will fail quietly during all test suites until the code ships, at which time it will begin to fail quite dramatically. The failure (when it finally raises its ugly head) is guaranteed to occur in a seemingly unrelated piece of code written by the person responsible for your next performance review.

The simplest way to avoid this particular breed of nastiness is to get into the habit of resetting pointers after they become invalid. The way to enforce this behavior is to create a simple inline function to do it for you:

```
template <typename InterfacePtr>
inline void ReleaseAndNull(InterfacePtr& rp) {
  if (rp) {
    rp->Release();
    rp = 0;
  }
}
```

Using this mechanism will ensure that you avoid embarrassing bugs:

```
IUnknown* pUnk = 0;
if (SUCCEEDED(GetObject(&pUnk))) {
  UseObject(pUnk);
  ReleaseAndNull(pUnk);

  UseObject(pUnk); // 0xC0000005 Access Violation!!!
}
```

Another mechanism that solves this problem (but may compound it if you're not careful) is the smart pointer, but this issue alone is not sufficient reason to warrant its use (see Item 22).

The second case you should be aware of arises during construction of new instances of COM objects. Consider the following code:

```
interface IDog : IUnknown {
  HRESULT CreatePuppy( [in] REFIID iid,
                       [out, iid_is(iid)] void** ppv );
  //...
}
interface IPuppy : IUnknown {
  //...
}


STDMETHODIMP CDog::CreatePuppy(REFIID iid, void** ppv) {
  IPuppy* pPuppy = new CPuppy;
  if (!pPuppy)
    return (*ppv = 0), E_OUTOFMEMORY;
  return pPuppy->QueryInterface(iid, ppv);
}
```

This code has a subtle bug. The CreatePuppy method was obviously designed by someone concerned with extensibility, since it makes use of the polymorphic result (see Item 14). The code leaks memory when the caller asks

for an interface not supported by the Puppy and the call to QueryInterface
fails.

So to fix this, you simply add some special-case code to remove the memory leak:

```
STDMETHODIMP CDog::CreatePuppy(REFIID iid, void** ppv) {
  IPuppy* pPuppy = new CPuppy;
  if (!pPuppy)
    return (*ppv = 0), E_OUTOFMEMORY;
  HRESULT hr = pPuppy->QueryInterface(iid, ppv);
  if ((FAILED(hr))
    delete pPuppy;
  return hr;
}
```

This code still has a serious bug. Can you see it? COM interfaces do not have virtual destructors. The call to operator delete *through the IPuppy pointer* happily
frees the memory associated with the Puppy, but it does not invoke any destructors other than the empty inline destructors provided by the compiler for
IPuppy and IUnknown.

So you change the implementation once more to use a CPuppy pointer instead
of an IPuppy pointer:

```
CPuppy* pPuppy = new CPuppy;
```

Now the destructor for CPuppy will be correctly invoked. One final problem
that lurks here is the fact that we create an instance and destroy it without transi-
tioning through the normal AddRef/Release pair. Why might this be a
problem? Consider the following (correct) implementation of AddRef and
Release:

```
STDMETHODIMP_(ULONG) CPuppy::AddRef() {
  if (InterlockedIncrement(&m_cRef) == 1)
    ModuleLock();
  return m_cRef;
}
STDMETHODIMP_(ULONG) CPuppy::Release() {
  LONG res = InterlockedDecrement(&m_cRef);
  if (res == 0) {
    delete this;
    ModuleUnlock();
  }
  return res;
}
```

Imagine you were implementing IClassFactory::CreateInstance in an out-of-process server and that you implemented ModuleUnlock in the traditional way, such that it shut the server down when the lock count transitioned to zero. Imagine that the following client code launches the server process:

```
HRESULT CreateAndUsePugPuppy() {
  IPug* pPug = 0;
  HRESULT hr = CoCreateInstance(CLSID_Puppy,
                        0, CLSCTX_ALL,
                        IID_IPug, (void**)&pPug);
  if (SUCCEEDED(hr)) {
    hr = pPug->Slobber();
    pPug->Release();
  }
  return hr;
}
```

If the Puppy does not support the IPug interface, the server will never shut down, because it has not been driven through an AddRef/Release transition, and ModuleUnlock will never be called.

The solution to the problem is to immediately place a reference on any new interface pointer you manufacture and plan to expose to COM:

```
STDMETHODIMP CDog::CreatePuppy(REFIID iid, void** ppv) {
  CPuppy* pPuppy = new CPuppy;
  if (!pPuppy)
    return (*ppv = 0), E_OUTOFMEMORY;
  pPuppy->AddRef(); // stabilize the interface pointer
  HRESULT hr = pPuppy->QueryInterface(iid, ppv);
  pPuppy->Release(); // then destabilize - avoids leaks
  return hr;
}
```

Note how this implementation guarantees that the instance is always driven through an AddRef/Release transition, thus ensuring that the instance will not be leaked (if QueryInterface fails, the call to Release will clean up the object). This is simply another case of not using interface pointers until they have been AddRef'ed.

Some popular frameworks adjust the server lock count in the construction and destruction of objects rather than explicitly watching for AddRef/Release transitions. Although it solves this particular problem of server shutdown, this practice deviates somewhat from the implementation suggested in the COM spec and creates its own share of problems.

The third case occurs when implementing COM aggregation. One of the idiosyncrasies of COM aggregation is that the inner object passes an interface pointer to the outer object, but that interface pointer does not have a reference count associated with it. This is done to avoid a circular reference between the two objects, since the outer object always holds a reference to the inner object. (See Item 16 to understand why using weak references in this way is not a good general practice.)

It is often a good idea to be lazy about aggregating objects (e.g., wait until an interface is requested before aggregating), but many frameworks encourage the simpler approach of creating aggregates during construction of the outer object. This introduces some interesting reference-counting issues. Consider the class CPuppy that exposes the following interface by aggregating the class NamedObject:

```
interface INamedObject : IUnknown {
  HRESULT SetName( [in, string] const OLECHAR* psz );
  HRESULT GetName( [out, string] OLECHAR** ppsz );
}
coclass NamedObject { interface INamedObject; }
```

It is not uncommon for an object that aggregates an implementation of an interface to want to collaborate with the implementation of the inner object:

```
CPuppy::CPuppy() : m_cRef(0), m_pInner(0) {
  HRESULT hr = CoCreateInstance(CLSID_NamedObject,
                    static_cast<IPuppy*>(this),
                    CLSCTX_INPROC_SERVER,
                    IID_IUnknown, (void**)&m_pInner);
  if (SUCCEEDED(hr)) {
    INamedObject* pno = 0;
    hr = m_pInner->QueryInterface(IID_INamedObject,
                          (void**)&pno);
    if (SUCCEEDED(hr)) {
      hr = pno->SetName(OLESTR("Fido"));// collaboration
      pno->Release(); // whoops!!!
    }
  if (FAILED(hr)) throw hr;
}
```

Note that when aggregating, you pass an interface pointer to the inner object so it can delegate the client's IUnknown requests back to you, thus maintaining the illusion of a single COM identity. The problem is that the interface pointer handed to the inner object points to an object with a reference count of zero. Stabilizing the pointer using AddRef and Release doesn't work in this case, since you never want to trigger a destructor call from within a constructor.

So, you ask, what's the big deal? Recall that correct implementations of QueryInterface always call AddRef through the physical interface pointer being handed to the caller, which in this case is an INamedObject interface pointer. INamedObject is not the special "nondelegating" unknown (which we tucked away in m_pInner), so the call to AddRef will be delegated to the outer object. So after the call to QueryInterface, the outer object's reference count is one. The call to Release is also delegated back to the outer object, which transitions the reference count to zero, deleting the object before it even leaves the constructor! This is an incredibly bad idea and not what the programmer had in mind.

All of this happens because the outer object has chosen to use an interface pointer that has no references on it (pno). Consider also that COM aggregation can occur at many levels (e.g., the inner object in this case might aggregate another object under it, *ad infinitum*). This is a problem that must be dealt with by the outermost object (the one to which all inner objects delegate their identity). We must stabilize the outer object, but we cannot do it via calls to AddRef and Release because we want to safely leave the constructor with a reference count of zero. The solution to this dilemma is to manually stabilize the reference count without calling AddRef or Release, thus constructing the COM object in its entirety before performing the normal stabilization used when actually exposing the object to COM:

```cpp
CPuppy::CPuppy() : m_cRef(0), m_pInner(0) {
  ++m_cRef; // stabilize object, rc == 1
  HRESULT hr = CoCreateInstance(CLSID_NamedObject,
                  static_cast<IPuppy*>(this),
                  CLSCTX_INPROC_SERVER,
                  IID_IUnknown, (void**)&m_pInner);
  if (SUCCEEDED(hr)) {
    INamedObject* pno = 0;
    hr = m_pInner->QueryInterface(IID_INamedObject,
                        (void**)&pno);
    if (SUCCEEDED(hr)) {
      hr = pno->SetName(L"Fido"); // collaboration
```

```
        pno->Release(); // OK, ref count drops to one
    }
  if (FAILED(hr)) throw hr;
  --m_cRef; // destabilize object, rc == 0
}
```

Due to the potential nesting of aggregates, you should *always* stabilize your reference count in this way whenever creating aggregates in a constructor, regardless of whether you are actually the one collaborating. The ActiveX Template Library (ATL) framework provides an optional macro that implements this manual stabilization for safety during COM aggregation: DECLARE_PRO-TECT_FINAL_CONSTRUCT.

The fourth and final case occurs frequently with objects collaborating via simple bidirectional communication. Consider a pizza store that delivers:

```
interface IPizza; // use your imagination...
interface IWaitForPizza : IUnknown {
  HRESULT ItsDone( [in] IPizza* pPizza );
}
interface IPizzaPalace : IUnknown {
  HRESULT OrderPizza(
    [in] long nSize,
    [in, string] const OLECHAR* pszToppings,
    [in, string] const OLECHAR* pszCustomerName,
    [in] IWaitForPizza* pSink );
  HRESULT WhatsTakingSoLong(
    [in, string] const OLECHAR* pszCustomerName );
}
```

With this architecture, when ordering a pizza you must provide a simple sink object that implements IWaitForPizza. When the pizza is done, the pizza store will call you back. Of course, until the pizza is actually delivered, you'll want to occasionally remind the store that you really do want that pizza by calling WhatsTakingSoLong. This requires that you hold a pointer to the IPizzaPalace interface. Simple bidirectional communication. What could be easier?

To see the potential problems, consider the implementation of your sink:

```
STDMETHODIMP
CWaitForPizza::ItsDone(IPizza* pPizza) {
  m_pPizza = pPizza;
  m_pPizza->AddRef();
```

```
    m_pPizzaPalace->Release();// done with the store!
    m_pPizzaPalace = 0;
    SetEvent(m_hEventPizzaReady);
    return S_OK;
}
```

Note that once the pizza has been delivered, there is no reason to hold a reference back to the store. (You were only holding that pointer so you could bug the manager via WhatsTakingSoLong, remember?) With this in mind, let's take a look at the code for the pizza store:

```
STDMETHODIMP
CPizzaPalace::OrderPizza(
    long nSize, const OLECHAR* pszToppings,
    const OLECHAR* pszName,
    IWaitForPizza* pWaitForPizza )
{
    m_OrderQueue.Enqueue( nSize, pszToppings,
                          pszName, pWaitForPizza );
    return S_OK;
}
```

The order process is simple—just place the order into a queue and return to the caller. Several workers would be processing the orders in the kitchen:

```
DWORD CPizzaPalace::KitchenThreadProc(void* pv)
{
    CPizzaPalace* pThis = (CPizzaPalace*)pv;
    IWaitForPizza* pwfp = 0;
    while (pThis->m_OrderQueue.Dequeue(..., &pwfp)) {
        // if only making a pizza were this easy
        IPizza* pPizza = new CPizza( ... );
        pPizza->AddRef();
        pwfp->ItsDone( pPizza ); // hmmm...
        pPizza->Release();
        pwfp->Release();
    }
    return 0;
}
```

What would happen if you were the only customer holding an outstanding reference to the Pizza Palace, and when your pizza was delivered (via a synchronous call to ItsDone), you released your reference? This final release would be synchronously propagated back to the Pizza Palace, which (for the sake of argument) chooses to shut down. By the time `ItsDone` returns, `pThis` has been deleted, and the call to `Dequeue` causes an access violation. This is yet another instance of having a client (in this case the kitchen worker) hold a pointer without a reference count. (The fact that the pointer is in a different thread is interesting but irrelevant to this point—see Item 30 for more details on threading and reference counts.)

The solution here would be to stabilize the pointer. The kitchen worker should `AddRef` the Pizza Palace and `Release` just before exiting the thread procedure.

So be aware of reference counts, stabilize pointers whenever you are concerned about the issues discussed above, and watch out when aggregating. Use the `ReleaseAndNull` mechanism, smart pointers, or just be very disciplined about resetting pointers.

21. Use `static_cast` when bridging between the C++ type system and the COM type system.

It is ironic that although COM is an extremely type-conscious programming model, the C++ language mapping for COM provides multiple opportunities for type-related programming errors. Easily the most susceptible area for type-related defects is `QueryInterface`. Consider the IDL definition of `QueryInterface` as it appears in the system IDL file, UNKNWN.IDL:

```
HRESULT QueryInterface([in] REFIID riid,
                       [out, iid_is(riid)] void **ppv);
```

The `[iid_is]` attribute indicates that `ppv` is a dynamically typed interface pointer whose type is specified at runtime by the `riid` parameter. This attributes binds the specified parameter (in this case, `riid`) as the type of interface that is being requested. This means that it is imperative that the two parameters are treated as a unit when writing code.

Unfortunately, your C++ compiler is completely unaware of the relationship implied by `[iid_is]` and is perfectly happy to allow you to specify the wrong interface type. The following code is completely legal C++:

```
HRESULT BarkLikeADog(IUnknown *pUnk) {
  IDog *pDog = 0;
  HRESULT hr = pUnk->QueryInterface(IID_IBird,
                                    (void**)&pDog);
  if (SUCCEEDED(hr)) {
    hr = pDog->Bark();
```

```
      pDog->Release();
   }
   return hr;
}
```

Note that the IID passed to `QueryInterface (IID_IBird)` does not match the variable that will hold the resultant pointer (a pointer to an `IDog` interface). Another common error is to forget the address-of operator:

```
IDog *pDog = 0;
hr = pUnk->QueryInterface(IID_IDog, (void**)pDog);
```

Unfortunately, the `(void**)` cast completely disables the compiler from catching either of these two programming errors.

A safer version of the previous example could use `static_cast` to ensure that the type relationships are enforced by the compiler:

```
HRESULT BarkLikeADog(IUnknown *pUnk) {
   IDog *pDog = 0;
   HRESULT hr = pUnk->QueryInterface(IID_IBird,
reinterpret_cast<void**>(static_cast<IBird**>(&pDog)));
   if (SUCCEEDED(hr)) {
     hr = pDog->Bark();
     pDog->Release();
   }
   return hr;
}
```

The use of `static_cast` informs the compiler of your intention and gives the compiler the opportunity to remind you that your actions are not consistent with your intent. This technique would catch both the mismatched IID error as well as the missing address-of operator error.

Given the fact that the MIDL compiler emits IID names that are easily derived from the name of the interface, one could write the following macro that encapsulates the binding of IID to C++ typename:

```
#define IID_PPV_ARG(Type, Expr) IID_##Type, \
   reinterpret_cast<void**>(static_cast<Type**>(Expr))
```

Given this macro, one would then write the following:

```
IDog *pDog = 0;
hr = pUnk->QueryInterface(IID_PPV_ARG(IDog, &pDog));
```

If you can assume that Microsoft C++'s Direct-to-COM functionality is available, you can write a simpler version of this macro that leverages the __uuidof keyword:

```
#define IID_PPV_DTC(Expr) __uuidof(*(Expr)), \
                    reinterpret_cast<void**>(Expr)
```

With this macro in place, one would then write the following:

```
IDog *pDog = 0;
hr = pUnk->QueryInterface(IID_PPV_DTC(&pDog));
```

In fact, to accommodate this usage, newer versions of the system headers include the following additional method definition within IUnknown:

```
template <typename Itf>
HRESULT QueryInterface(Itf **ppItf) {
   return QueryInterface(__uuidof(Itf), (void**)ppItf);
}
```

While this addition to IUnknown is a great technique for catching QueryInterface-related errors, it does not help for all of the other places where the [iid_is] attribute is in use (e.g., CoCreateInstance). For these cases, the IID_PPV_XXX macros are more appropriate.

The use of static_cast is not restricted to clients. It is also useful for object implementers. The most common application of static_cast is in the implementation of QueryInterface. Consider the following buggy implementation that does not use static_cast:

```
class DogCat : public IDog {
  STDMETHODIMP QueryInterface(REFIID riid, void**ppv) {
    if (riid == IID_ICat)
      *ppv = (ICat*)this; // note, ICat is not a base
      :    :    :
```

Because the C-style cast syntax is in use, the compiler first tries to convert the cast to a static_cast. However, if this conversion would cause an error, the compiler silently demotes the cast to a reinterpret_cast (which was the only kind of cast available in C). Unfortunately, a reinterpret_cast in this situation will yield unpredictable results. Had the implementer used static_cast explicitly,

```
class DogCat : public IDog {
  STDMETHODIMP QueryInterface(REFIID riid, void**ppv) {
    if (riid == IID_ICat)
```

```
        *ppv = static_cast<ICat*>(this);
    :        :        :
```

the compiler would have known the programmer's intent and would flag the malformed line with a compile-time error.

One additional place where `static_cast` comes in handy is when an interface pointer must be passed as a `void*`. This usually occurs in low-level plumbing interfaces and APIs (such as the first parameter to `IType-Info::Invoke`). Consider the following potentially buggy implementation of `IDispatch::Invoke`:

```
STDMETHODIMP MyClass::Invoke(DISPID id, ... ) {
  return s_pTypeInfo->Invoke(this, id, ...);
}
```

This code fragment assumes that the object layout begins with the expected interface. This is highly compiler- and class-definition sensitive and is often not the case. However, since the first parameter to `ITypeInfo::Invoke` is a `void*`, the compiler cannot catch the potential error. If, however, the programmer had made his or her intentions clear via a `static_cast`,

```
STDMETHODIMP MyClass::Invoke(DISPID id, ... ) {
  return
    s_pTypeInfo->Invoke(static_cast<IMyInterface*>(this),
                        id, ...);
}
```

the compiler will ensure that the appropriate subset of the object is passed as the parameter.

22. Smart interface pointers add *at least* as much complexity as they remove.

If you use C++ exception handling, you are going to have to make sure that acquired interfaces are properly released. In the event of an exception, the current code path will stop executing and the stack will be unwound until a catch statement is found. Along the way, all objects whose names are going out of scope will be properly destroyed. Unfortunately, an interface pointer is not an object but rather a reference to an object. The C++ runtime does nothing to clean up an interface pointer in the event of an exception.

For example, in the following code, the `Leak` function may cause the `IBird` interface to be acquired but not released:

```
void TryToEat(IBird* pBird) {
  if(FAILED(pBird->Eat()))
    throw "spilled";
}

void Leak(IUnknown* punk) {
  HRESULT hr;
  IBird*  pBird;
  hr = punk->QueryInterface(IID_IBird, (void**)&pBird);
  if (SUCCEEDED(hr)) {
    TryToEat(pBird); // May throw an exception
    pBird->Release();
  }
}
```

To properly release the interface in the face of exceptions, you could use an explicit `try-catch` block:

```
void DontLeak(IUnknown* punk) {
  HRESULT hr;
  IBird*  pBird;
  hr = punk->QueryInterface(IID_IBird, (void**)&pBird);
  if (SUCCEEDED(hr)) {
    try {
      TryToEat(pBird); // May throw an exception
      pBird->Release();
    }
    catch (...) {
      pBird->Release();
      throw;
    }
  }
}
```

While this technique avoids the leak, it is not the most elegant code in the world.

This would be a good place to leverage the automatic destruction of objects as the stack is unwound. Since objects are destroyed, why not build an object whose job it is to release the interface pointer? When the object goes out of scope, either via the normal code path or because of an exception, the object will release the interface pointer. For example:

```
class InterfaceHolder {
public:
  InterfaceHolder(IUnknown* punk) : m_punk(punk) {}
  ~InterfaceHolder() { if (m_punk) m_punk->Release(); }
private:
  IUnknown* m_punk;
};
```

Now the client code can be written like this:

```
void DontLeak(IUnknown* punk) {
  HRESULT hr;
  IBird*  pBird;
  hr = punk->QueryInterface(IID_IBird, (void**)&pBird);
  if (SUCCEEDED(hr)) {
    InterfaceHolder ih(pBird);
    TryToEat(pBird); // May throw an exception
  }
}
```

In this case, the client no longer has to catch exceptions—the Interface-
Holder will release the interface when it is destroyed. As an additional convenience, the client no longer has to call Release on the interface at all. The
InterfaceHolder object will be destroyed even if no exception is thrown,
thereby causing the interface to be released.

The InterfaceHolder may seem like an elegant solution, but it has a couple of problems. First, the InterfaceHolder doesn't do an AddRef on the
interface it holds, even though it caches it for later Release. This is necessary
for it to function properly, but it clearly violates the lifetime rules of COM.
Second, any reader of the code who is not familiar with the implementation of
the InterfaceHolder may think that pBird is not being released. In an
attempt to fix what appears to be incorrect code, the well-meaning coder may
add a line to release pBird after the call to TryToEat. After all, according to
the rules of COM, if the InterfaceHolder object cached the reference, it is
responsible to AddRef it. Of course, the compiler would be perfectly happy
with this, but at runtime it will lead to duplicate releases. The reason we have this
problem is that we're trying to manage a single interface reference but we're splitting the calls to AddRef and Release between two interface references. In an
attempt to improve our code, we've made it worse. We've traded code maintainability for a quick fix.

Instead of augmenting the interface pointer with a C++ object, one could replace
the interface pointer with a C++ object that *acts* like an interface pointer. These

types of objects are commonly called *smart pointers*. Unlike raw pointers, smart pointers are C++ objects that have destructors that will be called when the smart pointer goes out of scope. What gives it pointer-like behavior is that it overloads a few of the operators (notably the -> operator) so that it can be used like a pointer. Microsoft Foundation Classes (MFC), ATL, and the Direct-to-COM support in Visual C++ each come with complicated smart interface pointer implementations, but a simple one would look like this:

```
template <typename I>
class SI {
public:
    SI(I* pitf = 0) : m_pitf(pitf)
    { if( m_pitf ) m_pitf->AddRef(); }

    ~SI()
    { if( m_pitf ) m_pitf->Release(); }

    I* operator->()
    { return m_pitf; }

    void** GetPPV() {
      if( m_pitf ) m_pitf->Release(), m_pitf = 0;
      return (void**)&m_pitf;
    }

    operator I*()
    { return m_pitf; }

private:
    I*  m_pitf;
};
```

Using the smart pointer class, the client code can be written like this:

```
void DontLeak(IUnknown* punk) {
  HRESULT hr;
  SI<IBird>  spBird;
  hr = punk->QueryInterface(IID_IBird,
                            spBird.GetPPV());
  if (SUCCEEDED(hr)) {
    // Use operator->
    hr = spBird->Sleep();

    if (SUCCEEDED(hr)) {
```

```
        // Use operator IBird*
        TryToEat(spBird); // May throw an exception
    }
  }
}
```

A smart interface pointer may seem like a convenient thing to have. Notice the lack of any calls to `AddRef` or `Release`. Also notice that the operator `->` and the operator `I*` allow the smart interface pointer object to be used like a pointer. Finally, notice that object destruction causes the underlying interface pointer to be properly released in both the normal and the exceptional execution paths. All this convenience is unfortunate because it lulls the unwary user of a smart interface pointer into a false sense of security. What's the use of remembering the rules of `AddRef` and `Release` when you have a smart pointer taking care of it for you? Resist this feeling.

There are quite a few problems with the simple `SI` class shown earlier. One problem is identical to that of the `InterfaceHolder`. `SI` allows access to both `AddRef` and `Release` via the `->` operator. For example, code such as this will compile but will cause a double release when `spBird` goes out of scope:

```
void DoubleRelease(IUnknown *punk) {
  HRESULT    hr;
  SI<IBird> spBird;
  hr = punk->QueryInterface(IID_IBird,
                            spBird.GetPPV());
  spBird->Release();
}
```

This turns out to be a particularly nasty problem when new COM programmers first learn of smart interface pointers, hastily port their code, and forget to remove the redundant calls to `AddRef` and `Release`. While it is possible to make the compiler flag calls to `AddRef` and `Release` on a smart interface pointer as an error, at the time of this writing, few or no commercial smart interface pointers do this.[2]

Here's another problem with the `SI` smart pointer class. In the implementation of `GetPPV`, if `m_pitf` holds a valid interface pointer, it is released. This makes it convenient for using `SI` with `QueryInterface` or `CoCreate-Instance`, but the following innocent code will cause a potentially unexpected side effect:

---

[2] Shortly before this book went to press, ATL 3.0 was released with a fix for this problem.

```
SI<IBird> spBird;
hr = punk->QueryInterface(IID_IBird, spBird.GetPPV());
if (SUCCEEDED(hr)) {
  // Simple assignment releases interface
  void** ppv = spBird.GetPPV();
  // Dereference null pointer — kaboom
  spBird->Sleep();
}
```

Clearly GetPPV isn't meant to be used this way, but without being extremely familiar with the implementation details of SI, the side effects of GetPPV are not likely to be readily apparent. Unfortunately, learning how SI works isn't enough, because all smart interface pointers work differently. Even if you only use one, you'll have to make yourself familiar with its implementation details to avoid misuse.

If you ignore the last two errors as readily fixable or SI-specific, there is another common problem with smart interface pointers. The implementations of the type coercion operators don't have enough context to be properly implemented. For example, the interface pointer type coercion operator allows an SI object to be passed as an input parameter. To enable this kind of usage, SI doesn't AddRef the interface pointer. However, what about using the same operator as an [out] parameter?

```
HRESULT CoZoo::GetBird(IBird **ppBird) {
  *ppBird = m_spBird; // Missing AddRef
  return S_OK;
}
```

In the assignment of m_spBird to the output parameter ppBird, the developer assumed that since a smart interface pointer was being used, it would handle any required AddRefs. Of course, because of the other usage, the implementation of SI doesn't work that way. This is another case where you might have been hoping to forget AddRef and Release altogether, but you can't. One solution to this problem is to remove the type coercion operator altogether and replace it with a pair of functions so that the user can supply the context (e.g., GetAddRefedItf and GetNonAddRefedItf). While this makes for more maintainable and more readable (if not more writable) code, it still does not excuse you from understanding the rules of AddRef and Release, because you still have to know which function to call.

In short, smart pointers are very useful for handling exceptions, and they offer some seductive notational convenience. However, to use smart interface pointers correctly, not only do you have to know and use the rules of COM lifetime reference counting, but also you and everyone who reads your code must know the implementation details of your smart pointer(s) of choice.

23. Don't hand-optimize reference counting.

Item 20 talked a lot about interface pointer stabilization via calls to AddRef and Release. You might be starting to worry that these techniques lead to unnecessary round-trips (which are evil and should be avoided—see Item 2). Stop worrying. COM already does a fantastic job of optimizing the mechanics of reference counting. For instance, when you call AddRef through an interface pointer to a proxy, network packets are *never* sent across the wire.[3] Similarly, when you call Release, network packets are only sent if it is the final release for the object identity.

How is this possible? It's a very natural optimization. The proxy manager is simply a COM object, and like most heap-based COM objects, it has an internal reference count. When this reference count drops to zero (on the final release), the proxy sends a message to the stub decrementing the stub's reference count appropriately. This is a simple case of caching state in the proxy to avoid round-trips, and it works incredibly well. In fact, if you examine a MEOW packet (the wire format for a marshaled interface pointer), you'll notice that it contains a field (cPublicRefs) representing the count of references that the packet represents on the stub. This means that the proxy can be marshaled several times before needing to go back to the stub to get more references. (Each proxy needs to represent at least one reference on the stub; otherwise, the stub would disappear prematurely.) If a proxy is marshaled with five references on the stub[4] and is released before giving away any of its five references, it can still release all five references in one round-trip, since proxies and stubs communicate reference-counting information via the IRemUnknown interface. Some of these optimizations are lost if secure references are enabled, but still, calls to AddRef are never remoted.

The bottom line is that the designers of COM realized that reference counting could potentially cause unnecessary network traffic and addressed the problem so you don't have to worry about it. This means you have no reason to be extra careful about redundant calls to AddRef and Release. When in doubt about lifetimes, simply add another pair.

---

[3] This assumes standard marshaling, but even with custom marshaling, it would not be useful to make network round-trips in response to AddRef.

[4] Five references is the default for normal marshals as of this writing.

Here's an example where you might be tempted to optimize:

```
class Child {
  IUnknown* m_pUnk;
public:
  Child(IUnknown* pUnk) : m_pUnk(pUnk) {}
  ~Child() {}
  //...
};
class Parent {
  IUnknown* m_pUnk;
  Child     m_child;
public:
  Parent(IUnknown* pUnk)
    : m_pUnk(pUnk), m_child(pUnk)
    { if (m_pUnk) m_pUnk->AddRef(); }
  ~Parent()
    { if (m_pUnk) m_pUnk->Release(); }
  //...
};
```

You could argue that since the Child object's lifetime is completely encapsulated within the lifetime of the parent, the child does not need to AddRef the shared resource. Well, in this case, you probably just saved a few clock cycles. However, suppose that someone else, unaware of your grand micro-optimization scheme, comes along and unwittingly assumes that the Child class follows the basic principles of COM reference counts; that is, always AddRef when you copy an interface pointer:

```
Child* YourBossesCode() {
  Child* pChild = 0;
  IUnknown* pUnk = 0;
  if (SUCCEEDED(CoCreateInstance(CLSID_FooBar, 0,
    CLSCTX_ALL, IID_IUnknown, (void**)&pUnk)) {
    // your boss assumes you followed the rules
    pChild = new Child(pUnk);
    pUnk->Release(); // whoops!
  }
  return pChild;
}
```

The Child object does not have its own reference count. If you're lucky, the code will fail immediately and loudly as opposed to other, more insidious failure modes.

The solution here is to have the Child object keep its own reference count:

```
class Child {
  IUnknown* m_pUnk;
  Child(IUnknown* pUnk) : m_pUnk(pUnk)
    { if (m_pUnk) m_pUnk->AddRef(); }
  ~Child() { if (m_pUnk) m_pUnk->Release(); }
  //...
};
```

Keep in mind that optimizing away redundant pairs of `AddRef`/`Release` calls is a micro-optimization 99 percent of the time. There are very few cases in which localized optimization can yield noticeable performance benefits, and you should use a profiling tool to find them. Write correct code first, then apply optimizations if necessary.

24. Implement enumerators using lazy evaluation.

The standard mechanism for flow-controlled data transfer in COM is the enumeration interface. An enumerator is a custom interface defined in terms of a generic enumeration prototype. Enumeration interfaces could easily be described if IDL only had templates:

```
template <typename T>
interface IEnum : IUnknown {
  HRESULT Next([in] ULONG cItems,
[out, size_is(cItems), length_is(*pcFetched)] T *rg,
                 [out] ULONG *pcFetched);
  HRESULT Skip([in] ULONG cItems);
  HRESULT Reset();
  HRESULT Clone([out] IEnum<T> **ppEnum);
};
```

An enumerator allows the receiver to decide how many items from a collection it is willing to consume at once. This is handy for a couple of reasons. First, the receiver is allowed to balance round-trips with memory consumption. Second, the receiver can ask for smaller chunks of data if responsiveness is important. The more the receiver asks for, the fewer the round-trips but the longer the receiver must wait for the results to be transmitted by the sender. For example, imagine an interface to enumerate a string of letters:

```
interface IEnumLetters : IUnknown {
  HRESULT Next([in] ULONG cItems,
   [out, size_is(cItems), length_is(*pcFetched)]
```

```
                 OLECHAR *rg,
                 [out] ULONG* pcFetched);
    HRESULT Skip([in] ULONG cItems);
    HRESULT Reset();
    HRESULT Clone([out] IEnumLetters **ppEnum);
};
```

Given this interface definition, the client could enumerate over the string using code like this:

```
void OutputLetters(IEnumLetters* pEnum) {
  const ULONG CHUNKSIZE = 10;
  OLECHAR rgLetters[CHUNKSIZE+2];
  HRESULT hr = S_OK;
  do {
    ULONG cFetched = 0;
    hr = pEnum->Next(CHUNKSIZE, rgLetters, &cFetched);
    if (SUCCEEDED(hr)) {
      if (hr == S_OK)
        cFetched = CHUNKSIZE;
      rgLetters[cFetched] = L'\n';
      rgLetters[cFetched+1] = 0;
      OutputDebugString(rgLetters);
    }
  } while (hr == S_OK);
}
```

Enumerators are commonly implemented using a fixed-size collection (e.g., an array or a list). Here's an example of implementing the enumeration interface using a fixed-sized array:

```
class CoEnumLetters : public IEnumLetters {
public:
  CoEnumLetters(const OLECHAR* rgLetters,
                ULONG nLetters, ULONG nIndex = 0)
  : m_cRef(0), m_rgLetters(rgLetters),
    m_nLetters(nLetters), m_nIndex(nIndex)
  {}

// IEnumLetters methods
  STDMETHODIMP Next(ULONG cItems, OLECHAR *rg,
                    ULONG *pcFetched) {
    if (!rg)
      return E_POINTER;
```

```
        ULONG cFetched = 0;
        while (cFetched < cItems && m_nIndex < m_nLetters)
          rg[cFetched++] = m_rgLetters[m_nIndex++];
        if (pcFetched)
          *pcFetched = cFetched;
        return (cFetched == cItems ? S_OK : S_FALSE);
      }
      STDMETHODIMP Skip(ULONG cItems) {
        if (m_nIndex + cItems < m_nLetters ) {
          m_nIndex += cItems;
          return S_OK;
        }
        m_nIndex = m_nLetters;
        return S_FALSE;
      }
      STDMETHODIMP Reset() {
        m_nIndex = 0;
        return S_OK;
      }
      STDMETHODIMP Clone(IEnumLetters **ppEnum) {
        if( !ppEnum )
          return E_POINTER;
        *ppEnum = new CoEnumLetters(m_rgLetters,
                                    m_nLetters,
                                    m_nIndex);
        if( *ppEnum ) {
          (*ppEnum)->AddRef();
          return S_OK;
        }
        return E_OUTOFMEMORY;
      }

private:
  ULONG           m_cRef;
  const OLECHAR*  m_rgLetters;
  ULONG           m_nLetters;
  ULONG           m_nIndex;
};
```

While an enumerator over a precalculated collection can sometimes be useful, this technique has problems in less restrictive situations. For example, if the collection to which the enumerator has a reference changes in size, the enumerator must be notified or it could easily walk off the end or fail to return all of the items in the collection. To avoid this problem, enumerator implementations often make a copy of their collection, adding to the overhead. Plus, if the client decides it doesn't really want all of the items, the results have been calculated and never used.

For these reasons, it is often a good idea to avoid wrapping an enumeration around a precalculated set of data. Instead, implement enumerators using lazy evaluation, waiting until a call to Next to calculate the data. This style of lazy evaluation is very similar to the way in which Standard Template Library (STL) iterators work and can improve performance considerably, as the sender can start sending earlier and doesn't need to keep buffer space in memory for the entire collection. Instead of retrieving all of the rows from a database query and wrapping an enumeration around the results, design the enumeration to pull the rows as required. Similarly, if the underlying collection resides in a file, don't read the entire contents of the file. Instead, the enumeration should simply hold a file handle and read the contents as required.

Applying lazy evaluation to our character enumeration, we would replace the cached string of letters and modify Next to calculate the letters on demand:

```
STDMETHODIMP CoEnumLetters::Next(
  ULONG    cItems,
  OLECHAR *rg,
  ULONG   *pcFetched)
{
  if (!rg) return E_POINTER;
  ULONG cFetched = 0;
  while (cFetched < cItems && m_nIndex < m_nLetters)
    rg[cFetched++] = m_chFirstLetter + m_nIndex++;
  if (pcFetched) *pcFetched = cFetched;
  return (cFetched == cItems ? S_OK : S_FALSE);
}
```

As far as the client is concerned, the interface behaves in the same way, but instead of accessing precalculated results, it's accessing results calculated on demand. If some of the results aren't needed, they're not calculated.

25. Use flyweights where appropriate.

It is very common for developers to fall in love with COM. It's that kind of a technology. Sometimes these developers love COM so much that they decide that *everything* in their system must be a COM object. From Button to String to

List to Employee (or whatever problem-domain-specific classes they need), every C++ class will ultimately derive from IUnknown. As their systems grow, these developers discover that their impassioned "some is good so more is better," approach causes problems. COM exacts a price for the magic it works, and it is paid in bytes on a per-object basis. For developers who casually render everything in COM, the price can become unacceptably high.

If you are using COM objects within your own apartment, the price of COM is a reference count and/or vptrs. If the object uses reference counting to manage its lifetime (not all COM objects do), that takes 4 bytes. For each new interface an object supports, a 4-byte vptr is required as well. The only exception to this is for interfaces related by inheritance, which can share a single vptr. For example, implementing IBear, which derives from IAnimal, which derives from IUnknown, requires a single vptr. Its vtable would start with the methods of IUnknown, progress through IAnimal's, and end with IBear's.

This doesn't seem like a lot—what's the occasional 4-byte vptr among friends? But consider the formula that describes this overhead: $4n + 4$, where n is the number of separate interfaces (again discounting interfaces related by inheritance) and the extra 4 is for a reference count. When n is 10, the extra overhead is 44 bytes for each object. If you have 10,000 objects, that's around half a megabyte of reference counts and vptrs alone. (If you think 10 interfaces are an extreme example, take a look at the set of interfaces that a typical ActiveX control supports. If you think 10,000 objects is an extreme example, examine some of the information systems your fellow developers are working on.) Implementing interfaces using tearoffs is one way to lessen the burden, but they often introduce more problems than they solve—see Item 26.

If your objects are being accessed from other apartments, the overhead is significantly higher. Every object accessed from outside its apartment requires a stub manager, one or more stubs, and related bookkeeping data structures (IPID table entries, etc.). The price for these pieces starts at approximately 400 bytes and goes up as the stub is widened in response to QueryInterface calls.[5] This space is held as long as outstanding proxies exist (or as long as the stub is locked using CoLockObjectExternal).

So how do you reduce the impact of this overhead? Simple: don't make every single entity in your project a COM object. Remember that, like every other technology, COM is *not* a silver bullet. Use COM only when the benefits outweigh the costs. This way you pay for only the overhead of COM infrastructure where you really need it.

---

[5] These numbers come from the current implementation of COM (NT 4, Service Pack 3).

COM's focus on interfaces makes it the right technology for crossing boundaries in your system: distribution boundaries (apartments, processes, and hosts), language boundaries, product boundaries (including third-party products), and logical boundaries encapsulating subsystems and their extensibility points. If you have objects that will never be accessed across at least one of these boundaries, there is no need to implement them using COM.

But what if your system requires lots of objects that *do* need to be accessed across a significant boundary? How do you avoid the overhead then? You can see a solution in the architecture of COM itself. The COM remoting layer creates stubs as necessary to make objects accessible from other execution contexts. In essence, COM is dynamically expanding your object's functionality to support remote access. The stub defers acquiring resources until the last possible moment and holds them no longer than necessary. Why not take a similar approach with an object's vptrs and reference count? Instead of implementing all your objects as COM objects, implement them as C++ objects and add a COM wrapper only when necessary. COM objects instantiated for this purpose are called *flyweights*. Like a stub, a flyweight dynamically expands the behavior of an object. Flyweights, however, add all of the object's COM functionality: its reference count and all its vptrs. The flyweight in turn relies on the stub for remote accessibility just as any COM object would. This is exactly the approach used by the Java Virtual Machine when Java objects are exported as COM objects.

It's up to you to create flyweights when you need them; the COM remoting layer can't help, as it does with stubs. In general, make a new flyweight whenever you need to send out a COM-based reference to a C++ object that has not yet been wrapped. You may want to track the inverse relationship from a C++ object to its flyweight using a back pointer, a map structure, or some other device to avoid wrapping the same object more than once. On the other hand, wrapping the same object multiple times may be useful if you want to use the separate flyweights themselves to track aspects of the object's use. For example, you might allocate a different flyweight for each client accessing the object so you can keep track of per-client details. To get even more exotic, you might create multiple flyweights of different types to provide clients with different functionality.

You can extend this idea even further. Instead of just adding COM behavior, a flyweight could provide *all* of an object's behavior, again only when it is absolutely necessary to manipulate the object's state. The state of the object would always be there, maybe in memory or maybe in some other storage (e.g., a database). For some reason, this notion often runs against the grain because it appears that the object's state and behavior have been decoupled, something sure to send many a naïve object theorist into a tizzy. If it bothers you, think of the flyweight as an object's in-memory representation and the creation of a flyweight as simply the rehydration of the object's persistent image. This view is apt to make you more comfortable. The key to remember is that this is just a very powerful implementation technique designed to facilitate systems that need to make use of very large numbers of objects without exposing the details of the space-saving shell game to clients.

If you are building a system that requires lots of COM-accessible objects, consider flyweights. They can cut the overhead of using COM significantly. With imagination, they have other interesting benefits as well. Additionally, flyweights on top of other COM objects can be a great way to implement split identity to break reference-counting cycles. Finally, be aware that the Microsoft Transaction Server essentially mandates the use of flyweights for architectures built upon it.

26. Avoid using tearoffs across apartment boundaries.

Tearoffs were first introduced as a technique for implementing COM objects in Crispin Goswell's excellent whitepaper, *The COM Programmer's Cookbook*. A tearoff is a C++ class that implements one or more COM interfaces that are either rarely used or used only transiently. Tearoffs are mixed into standard COM implementation classes dynamically at runtime.

The purpose of tearoffs is to avoid vptr bloat. Consider a class that implements 20 separate interfaces, such as an ActiveX control. If those interfaces are all implemented using multiple inheritance, each instance of the class carries 80 bytes worth of vptrs in addition to whatever problem-domain-specific state is required. If some of those interfaces are rarely used, why not allocate the resources to support them (i.e., the vptrs) only when absolutely necessary?

This sounds very appealing from an efficiency point of view and can be implemented without too much trouble. Tearoffs are implemented as a separate C++ class. For instance, a COM class `Dog` could implement `IDog` directly but provide support for `INamedObject` via a tearoff, since not all dogs have names.

```
// Tearoff implementation of INamedObject
class NamedTearoff : public INamedObject
{
  Dog *m_pThis; // Back pointer to identity
  long m_cRef; // Tearoff has a separate ref count
public:
  NamedTearoff(Dog *pThis) : m_pThis(pThis)
```

```
      { m_pThis->AddRef(); }
    virtual ~NamedTearoff() { m_pThis->Release(); }
    STDMETHODIMP QueryInterface(REFIID riid, void **ppv)
    {
      // Identity-related calls delegated to m_pThis
      // Note that you could check for IID_INamedObject
      // here and return this tearoff's vptr
      return m_pThis->QueryInterface(riid, ppv);
    }
    // Other methods removed for clarity
};

// COM object that uses a tearoff
class Dog : public IDog
{
  long m_cRef; // Main ref count
  std::wstring m_strName; // State is kept with identity
public:
  STDMETHODIMP QueryInterface(REFIID riid, void **ppv)
  {
    *ppv = 0;
    if (riid == IID_IDog || riid == IID_IUnknown)
      *ppv = static_cast<IDog*>(this);
    else if (riid == IID_INamedObject)
      *ppv = static_cast<INamedObject*>(
                        new NamedTearoff(this));
    if (*ppv)
      reinterpret_cast<IUnknown*>(*ppv)->AddRef();
    return *ppv ? S_OK : E_NOINTERFACE;
  }
  ... // Other methods removed for clarity
};
```

The only tricky part of implementing tearoffs is ensuring that the COM identity rules are followed. You accomplish this by forwarding calls to Query-Interface up to the main object, which implements IUnknown and is therefore the identity. AddRef and Release do not have to be forwarded; the tearoff implements them normally to control its own lifetime. In its constructor and destructor, the tearoff maintains m_pThis, a reference to the identity that ensures the main object lives at least as long as the tearoff exists.

At first glance, tearoffs look appealing. The Dog implementation saves 4 bytes when INamedObject is not in use. In return for these savings, the tearoff implementation costs more when `INamedObject` is in use. If a client holds an `INamedObject` pointer, an instance of `NamedTearoff` exists, consuming at least 12 bytes for its vptr, back pointer (`m_pThis`), and reference count (`m_cRef`).[6] This is reasonable given the intended use of tearoffs—implementing interfaces that are rarely or transiently used.

At second glance, tearoffs look even more appealing—tearoffs could be used to track per-client state. In other words, any number of clients could use the same object, but each one could be handed a different tearoff. Each tearoff could maintain data for a separate client. For instance, `NamedTearoff` could track how many times each client had asked to get or set the dog's name. Handing out multiple tearoffs is perfectly legal under the identity laws of COM and solves a common design problem. So why not use tearoffs right and left?

Tearoffs depend on per-interface reference counting to work their magic. This means that tearoffs only work as expected when the client and object *share the same apartment*. As soon as an object is accessed across apartment boundaries, a proxy and a stub enter the picture. Proxies and stubs don't respect per-interface reference counting in the name of efficiency. A stub will hold all the interface pointers to its object until the last proxy goes away; then it will release all of the pointers *en masse*. You can work around this for an object used across apartments in a single process by using the Free-Threaded Marshaler (FTM), but there is nothing you can do to make tearoffs work properly across process or host boundaries.

If you use tearoffs across apartment boundaries, the tearoff interface(s) will be held for the lifetime of the stub (which is typically also the lifetime of the object). A 4-byte vptr is replaced with a 12+-byte tearoff that never goes away; all efficiency gains are lost. There is, however, a useful but esoteric application of tearoffs in this case. Imagine you were implementing a component that supports multiple versions of the same interface. If you knew that any given client would use one and only one of those interfaces, you could dynamically allocate the one that that client needs as a tearoff. In other words, if your component supports `IVersion1`, `IVersion2`, and `IVersion3` through `IVersion20`, and a particular client only needs one of the 20, you could implement all of them as tearoffs and mix in the appropriate one when a client requests it. In this case, the fact that the tearoff exists for the lifetime of the object doesn't matter; transience is not the intention. Here, tearoffs are used to eliminate redundant (mutually exclusive) vptrs. This effect will still work across apartment boundaries and, in the case of 20 distinct interfaces, will save roughly 64 bytes worth of unused vptrs per object.

---

[6] Each instance of `NamedTearoff` consumes at least 12 bytes, but is more likely to consume 16 bytes, due to the alignment behavior of most generic memory allocators.

So, if you are considering or already using tearoffs in a design, be aware that their typical usage model doesn't work across apartment boundaries. Even if you use the (FTM) to fix that, the tearoff mechanism doesn't work as expected across process boundaries. Tearoffs are likely to be a bad choice for out-of-process objects unless you have a component that needs to support one of a large number of mutually exclusive interfaces for the lifetime of the object. If the prospect of using tearoffs for tracking per-client state seemed exciting and you're depressed that it won't work outside an apartment, consider using multiple COM identities to do the same thing (see Item 4 for a discussion of the relevance of physical identity).

27. Be especially careful with BSTRs.

BSTR stands for Basic String. Like any COM string, it is a NULL-terminated array of Unicode characters. To make certain operations (such as marshaling) more efficient, a BSTR is also length-prefixed. In memory, you can imagine a BSTR as a structure such as this:

```
struct BSTR {
    DWORD     cbCharacters;
    OLECHAR pszString[(cbCharacters)/sizeof(OLECHAR) + 1];
};
```

However, in C++, a BSTR is not a structure but rather an alias to OLECHAR*:

```
typedef [wire_marshal(wireBSTR)] OLECHAR *  BSTR;
```

For convenience, a BSTR points past the length prefix to the array of characters. This frees the C++ programmer from performing the following cast for every use of a BSTR:

```
OLECHAR* psz = (OLECHAR*)((BYTE*)bstr + sizeof(DWORD));
```

Arguably, this convenience is the worst thing that could have been done. Because a BSTR looks like an OLECHAR*, the compiler is perfectly happy to take one where the other is meant. For example, consider the following IDL:

```
interface IUseStrings : IUnknown {
    HRESULT GetAString([out] BSTR* pbstr);
    HRESULT SendAString([in] BSTR bstr);
};
```

When programming against this interface, a client could, with the blessings of the compiler, write and execute this code:

```
void GetAndDumpAString(IUseStrings* pus) {
  HRESULT hr;
  OLECHAR* psz = 0; // Danger, Will Robinson!
  hr = pus->GetAString(&psz);
  if (SUCCEEDED(hr)) {
    OutputDebugStringW(psz);
    CoTaskMemFree(psz); // Danger! Danger!
  }
}
```

Because we're working with callee-allocated data, we correctly remember to request that the COM task-memory allocator release the data. For an OLECHAR*, CoTaskMemFree is exactly the right thing to use. Unfortunately, the data is actually a BSTR, and so the data must be deallocated using SysFreeString.

Unfortunately, [in] parameters are no better. Consider this intuitive, compiler-endorsed code:

```
void SendAString(IUseStrings* pus) {
  pus->SendAString(OLESTR("A String"));
}
```

In the unfortunate event that this string is being marshaled, the proxy will take the pointer to the string, back it up 4 bytes looking for the length prefix, and will have only a one in four billion chance of finding the right value. Otherwise, the proxy will most likely try to marshal far too much data. The problem is that the Unicode string passed in is not properly laid out in memory as a BSTR. Instead, the client would need to use the SysXxxString family of functions for managing BSTRs:

```
void SendAString(IUseStrings* pus) {
  BSTR bstr = SysAllocString(OLESTR("A String"));
  pus->SendAString(bstr);
  SysFreeString(bstr); // Don't forget this!
}
```

Even in the intra-apartment case where there is no proxy involved, the object implementation may depend on the length prefix (objects implemented in Visual Basic often do). Again, because the compiler was duped into thinking that BSTRs and OLECHAR* were the same thing, it could not stop us from firing into a helpless crowd of data. Be especially careful when using BSTRs. The compiler cannot help you.

28. COM aggregation and COM containment are for identity tricks, not code reuse.

COM supports interface inheritance; it does not support implementation inheritance.[7] Interface inheritance, or subtyping, enables polymorphism, the ability to treat an object of some specific type as if it were an object of some less specific type (e.g., to treat an Apple as a Fruit). From a client's point of view, this is the only type of inheritance that is important. Implementation inheritance, or subclassing, is simply a way to avoid rewriting code. Unfortunately, a bad thing happened when COM debuted (underneath OLE) in 1993. At that time, most developers didn't distinguish between the two types of inheritance (partly because most of them worked in C++, which blurs the distinction). Worse, most developers saw implementation inheritance as the preferred way to reuse objects. Since reuse was one of the basic benefits the industry was hoping to derive from objects, the lack of implementation inheritance (and by illogical extension, the lack of object reuse) in COM was seen by many as a major weakness.

In an attempt to overcome this obstacle, many early COM proponents legitimately criticized the tendency of implementation inheritance to introduce overly tight coupling between base and derived classes (the infamous fragile base class problem). Unfortunately, they also evangelized two alternative reuse techniques, *COM aggregation* and *COM containment*. These techniques allow a COM object to expose interfaces whose implementation is shunted directly (aggregation) or indirectly (containment) to one or more collaborating COM objects.

Both these mechanisms were criticized as poor replacements for real implementation inheritance, and the result was a long, harrowing, and tedious debate among the object intelligentsia and their partisan backers about the validity of COM as an object-oriented technology. All of this furor could have been avoided if someone had just pointed out that object reuse is not synonymous with implementation inheritance and can be easily achieved through other means.

Consider the task of modeling a bicycle with objects. Assume that you have two existing classes, `Handlebar` and `Wheel`, that you'd like to reuse. Here is one way to do it:

```
class Handlebar; // defined elsewhere
class Wheel;
class Bicycle : public Handlebar, public Wheel {
    ...
};
```

---

[7] This is true across binary boundaries; inside a server, feel free to use all the features of your chosen language, including implementation inheritance.

```
void Grip(Handlebar &rhb);

Bicycle myBike; // instantiate a Bicycle
Grip(myBike); // treat it as a Handlebar
```

This code uses inheritance to reuse both Handlebar and Wheel, yet it makes little sense (for one thing it implements a unicycle, not a bicycle). Inheritance implies an *is-a* relationship, but a Bicycle is neither a Handlebar nor a Wheel. Chances are you wouldn't write code like this.

Here is another way to implement Bicycle, without using inheritance:

```
class Bicycle {
  Handlebar m_hb;
  Wheel  m_rgw[2]; // now it's a bicycle!
public:
  operator Handlebar & (void) { return m_hb; }
  ...
};
void Grip(Handlebar &rhb);

Bicycle myBike; // instantiate a Bicycle
Grip(myBike);  // treat it as a Handlebar
```

Now Bicycle contains an instance of the two classes it wants to leverage; it uses a *has-a* relationship. It still makes little sense, however, because of the user-defined cast operator. This method plays tricks on the C++ type system to make it appear that there's still an *is-a* relationship between Bicycle and Handlebar. You probably wouldn't write code like this either.

Here is a third way to implement Bicycle, again reusing both Handlebar and Wheel via containment:

```
class Bicycle {
  Handlebar m_hb;
  Wheel  m_rgw[2];
public:
  Handlebar & GetHandlebar(void) { return m_hb; }
  ...
};
void Grip(Handlebar &rhb);
Bicycle myBike; // Instantiate a Bicycle
Grip(myBike.GetHandlebar()); // Extract Handlebar
```

This code makes much more sense. Instead of using an implicit user-defined cast, `Bicycle` includes an explicit `GetHandlebar` method that provides access to its m_hb member. The `Handlebar` class is reused, and its conceptual relationship to `Bicycle` is made clear by the code. This code is cleaner, and in general, you are more likely to take this approach.

The `Bicycle` example is intended to demonstrate that objects can be reused without inheritance. You may take exception to this illustration because it seems contrived. After all, it's obvious that a `Bicycle` isn't a `Handlebar` and isn't a `Wheel`, and clearly classes associated with a *has-a* relationship shouldn't derive one from another. In fact, that's precisely why this example was chosen. If you choose any two associated classes in a C++ system on which you've worked, they are far more likely to have a *has-a* (or some other, less specific use) relationship than an *is-a* relationship. As a result, most reuse happens without inheritance of any kind. Think how many times you've reused a string class (e.g., `CString`, `std::string`, `ATL::CComBSTR`). How many times did that reuse involve derivation?

But what about classes that are in fact specializations of other classes? Consider a class `Vehicle`, which stores a current speed. Clearly a `Bicycle` *is-a* `Vehicle`, and traditionally reuse of the latter class would be achieved through derivation:

```
class Vehicle
{
  long m_nCurrentSpeed;
public:
  virtual long SetCurrentSpeed(long nSpeed)
  {
    return m_nCurrentSpeed = nSpeed;
  }
}

class Bicycle : public Vehicle
{
public:
  virtual long SetCurrentSpeed(long nSpeed)
  {
    if (nSpeed <= 40)
      return Vehicle::SetCurrentSpeed(nSpeed);
    else
      return -1;
  }
```

```
    ...
};
```

But reuse could also be accomplished without inheritance:

```
class Bicycle

{
  Vehicle m_v;
public:
  virtual long SetCurrentSpeed(long nSpeed)
  {
    if (nSpeed <= 40)
      return m_v.SetCurrentSpeed(nSpeed);
    else
      return -1;
  }
  ...
};
```

Using containment, this version of Bicycle is able to make use of Vehicle without deriving from it. Notice that this model is essentially equivalent to using private inheritance in C++ in that Vehicle's implementation (class) is reused but its interface (type) is not. Also, Bicycle can override individual methods of the Vehicle, which is what distinguishes private inheritance from a simple *has-a* relationship in C++. This is the model favored by COM.

Here is a COM version of Bicycle:

```
interface IHandlebar; // Defined elsewhere
interface IWheel;
interface IVehicle;
interface IBicycle;

class Bicycle : public IBicycle
{
  IHandlebar *m_phb;
  IWheel *m_rgpw[2];
  IVehicle *m_pveh;
public:
  virtual long SetCurrentSpeed(long nSpeed)
  {
    if (m_pveh && nSpeed <= 40)
      return m_pveh->SetCurrentSpeed(nSpeed);
    else
      return -1;
  }
```

```
    IHandlebar * GetHandlebar(void) { return m_phb; }
      ...
  };
```

There are two advantages to this approach. One is that, as you've come to expect in COM, interfaces and implementations are kept separate. `Bicycle` doesn't have to expose the `IVehicle` interface to reuse an implementation of it (although it could if it wanted to). The other advantage is that because `m_pveh` refers to an object indirectly, the actual implementation of `IVehicle` can be determined, and even changed, at runtime. This is an example of what's known as *prototype-instance specialization*, an alternative to implementation inheritance in which a "derived" object, `Bicycle`, refers to an entirely separate "base" object, in this case whatever implementation of `IVehicle` that `m_pveh` points to. Both these features, the ability to reuse interfaces and implementations independently and the ability to determine which object to reuse at runtime, provide significant extra flexibility in design.

Thus, the reuse of binary components in COM is easily achieved without implementation inheritance *and without either COM aggregation or COM containment*. COM aggregation and containment are fundamentally identity hacks, like the user-defined cast discussed earlier. COM aggregation is used primarily by the COM remoting infrastructure to allow the proxy manager to merge multiple COM objects into a single COM identity. Several NT 5 COM facilities are based on COM aggregation, but again, only to perform identity merges between multiple COM objects. The FTM also relies on COM aggregation, though only as a convenience not a necessity. COM containment is really just a subtle variation on COM aggregation that requires manual delegation of method calls, but semantically shares the fundamental purpose of exposing multiple COM objects as a single identity.

Go forth and design COM systems safe in the knowledge that while it's useful to understand how COM aggregation and COM containment work, the benefit is primarily in seeing why neither one is necessary for your system. In fact, most COM developers rarely use either of them. You may have heard that COM+ will actually bring back implementation inheritance. That may be true (we'll see when it ships), and it will be interesting to see how people use it. Like COM aggregation and COM containment, real implementation inheritance will have its place, perhaps in situations where you want to extend, but not otherwise modify, a base class's behavior. Once you go beyond that, the tight coupling issues may well begin to arise again. It's also likely that like COM aggregation, implementation inheritance will work only within an apartment, which may limit its appeal.[8]

---

[8] Imagine how hard it would be to debug a component in a single-threaded apartment that derives from a component in a multithreaded apartment (assuming it could be made to work at all)!

Apartments

Threads often add complexity to already complex software. Threads often introduce performance problems in software that is already too slow. Threads typically add defects to software that is already too buggy. Nonetheless, COM developers are forced to work in multithreaded processes all of the time. Fortunately, the COM apartment provides at least some semblance of order to what might otherwise be a completely chaotic environment. Unfortunately, the architecture of COM apartments has evolved over the years, leaving many developers confused—not because of any inherent complexity but rather because of the evolving story of the apartment. Although things have been fairly stable for a while, there is still a considerable body of literature that contains outdated information and terminology (the fact that the term *apartment model* still appears in print in 1998 is embarrassing, given that all of COM is based on apartments). This chapter investigates some of the common techniques that are used to ensure that a component has at least a fighting chance at surviving when deployed in the potentially toxic environment that is a Win32 process.

29. Don't access raw interface pointers across apartment boundaries.

Interface pointers live in apartments. They are bound to their apartments by court orders that don't allow them to leave without an escort. Break the law and you'll pay the penalty. Maybe not today, maybe not tomorrow, but you'll get hurt eventually. Case in point: imagine that an interface pointer to a proxy originates in apartment A. Being the threading wizard that you are, you choose to tuck this interface pointer into a global variable so that another thread in your process can have access to the interface:

```
STDMETHODIMP CFoo::Advise(IUnknown* pSink) {
  SetSink(pSink);
```

```
  }
  void SetSink(IUnknown* pSink) {
    (g_pSink = pSink)->AddRef();
    SetEvent(g_hEventSinkAvailable); //auto-reset event
  }
  void GetSink(IUnknown** ppSink) {
    WaitForSingleObject(g_hEventSinkAvailable, INFINITE);
    *ppSink = g_pSink;
    g_pSink = 0;
  }
```

Ignoring any potential race conditions (a critical section would solve this, but race conditions are irrelevant to this discussion), imagine how this code works. Some client of yours calls `Advise`, passing an interface pointer to an implementation of some outgoing interface that you plan to call out on eventually. You publish the sink by calling `SetSink`, allowing another thread to grab that sink pointer via `GetSink`. You even call `AddRef` for the new thread (good job—you obviously read Item 30). All seems well and good until you try to call out on the sink, at which time you immediately discover that the call fails with `RPC_E_WRONGTHREAD` (check those HRESULTs—see Item 2). What happened?

Apparently, you were fortunate enough to be dealing with a proxy from an external client. Proxies remember the apartment they were born in (each apartment is identified by a 64-bit object exporter ID, or OXID) and verify that they are being called on a thread executing in that apartment. Each thread that calls `CoInitialize` or `CoInitializeEx` has a thread-local storage slot that holds information such as the OXID of the apartment in which the thread is executing. Imagine what would happen if you didn't have a proxy (e.g., the interface pointer was obtained from an in-process server). The code would probably work most of the time but would fail randomly, during important demos at large conferences, because you have likely violated the object's concurrency requirements.

Apartments are designed to allow objects with different concurrency and reentrancy requirements to coexist peaceably with one another, but to make this happen, you must follow the rules: don't pass interface pointers between apartments. Marshal them across apartment boundaries instead.

So here's the code used to correct the problem:

```
  HRESULT SetSink(IUnknown* pSink) {
    HRESULT hr = CoMarshalInterThreadInterfaceInStream(
```

```
      IID_IUnknown, pSink, &g_pStream);
    SetEvent(g_hEventSinkAvailable); //auto-reset event
    return hr;
}
HRESULT GetSink(IUnknown** ppSink) {
    WaitForSingleObject(g_hEventSinkAvailable, INFINITE);
    HRESULT hr = CoGetInterfaceAndReleaseStream(
      g_pStream, IID_IUnknown, (void**)ppSink);
    g_pStream = 0;
    return hr;
}
```

Note that the long-winded function names used for marshaling are simply short-cuts for creating a memory-based IStream implementation and marshaling a MEOW packet[1] into it. (Note that this particular stream is implemented specifically to be usable across apartments.) The fundamental API used to marshal interface pointers is CoMarshalInterface, and for unmarshaling, CoUnmarshalInterface. You can easily imagine how the interthread marshaling APIs are implemented:

```
HRESULT CoMarshalInterThreadInterfaceInStream(
    REFIID iid, IUnknown* pUnk, IStream** pps) {
    HRESULT hr = CreateStreamOnHGlobal(0, TRUE, pps);
    if (SUCCEEDED(hr)) {
      hr = CoMarshalInterface(*pps, iid, pUnk,
        MSHCTX_INPROC, 0, MSHLFLAGS_NORMAL );
      if (FAILED(hr)) {
        (*pps)->Release();
        *pps = 0;
      }
    }
    return hr;
}
```

And similarly for unmarshaling:

```
HRESULT CoGetInterfaceAndReleaseStream(
    IStream* ps, REFIID iid, void** ppv) {
    HRESULT hr = CoUnmarshalInterface(ps, iid, ppv);
    if (FAILED(hr))
      *ppv = 0;
    ps->Release();
```

---

[1] *MEOW packet* is COM slang for a marshaled object reference. The term *MEOW* comes from the 4-byte signature (MEOW) used to identify marshaled object references.

```
      return hr;
  }
```

Bear in mind the basic rule that interface pointers, no matter where they come from (proxies or otherwise), should be marshaled across apartment boundaries and never used directly by a thread executing in a different apartment unless explicitly documented otherwise. The particular implementation of `IStream` returned by `CoMarshalInterThreadInterfaceInStream` is one of the canonical examples of an explicitly documented exception.

Should you be worried about ending up with multiple layers of proxies with all this marshaling? No. `CoMarshalInterface` is implemented such that if a standard proxy is marshaled, the resulting marshaled OBJREF will refer to the original object, not to the proxy.

You may discover a nasty limitation of `CoMarshalInterThread-InterfaceInStream` and friends if you attempt to modify the code in `GetSink` to allow multiple threads to unmarshal the interface pointer. It is easy to imagine a scenario in which multiple threads need to send notification messages. So you change `GetSink` to look like this:

```
HRESULT GetSink(IUnknown** ppSink, bool bLastReader) {
  WaitForSingleObject(g_hEventSinkAvailable, INFINITE);
  if (!bLastReader)
    g_pStream->AddRef(); // faulty attempt to keep
                         // OBJREF valid for next caller
  HRESULT hr = CoGetInterfaceAndReleaseStream(
    g_pStream, IID_IUnknown, (void**)ppSink);
  if (bLastReader)
    g_pStream = 0;
  return hr;
}
```

However, when you step through this new implementation of `GetSink` in the debugger, you'll notice that `CoGetInterfaceAndReleaseStream` fails when the second caller attempts to unmarshal the interface. It's not just for convenience that `CoGetInterfaceAndReleaseStream` releases the stream automatically; rather, it's because the stream was only good for a single unmarshal anyway. Notice how the implementation of `CoMarshalInter-ThreadInterfaceInStream` calls `CoMarshalInterface` with `MSHLFLAGS_NORMAL`. The semantics of a normal marshal (sometimes referred to as a *call marshal*) are that the marshaled OBJREF is good for *at most one* unmarshal. These semantics are enforced by `CoUnmarshalInterface`, which implicitly calls `CoReleaseMarshalData` on the OBJREF after a successful unmarshal. After `CoUnmarshalInterface` returns, the OBJREF is no longer valid.

It turns out that there is another type of marshal that is commonly used, the table marshal. Table marshals are designed to create MEOW packets that can be placed in tables for many consumers. These MEOW packets can be unmarshaled *zero or more times*, which is exactly what you want. Unfortunately, table marshaling a proxy is illegal for reasons outside the scope of this discussion, so it is not a general solution to the marshal-once-unmarshal-many problem at hand. Fortunately, modern[2] implementations of COM provide the Global Interface Table (GIT), which allows apartment-relative interface pointers to be converted into apartment-neutral "GIT cookies" that can freely be passed between apartments *within the same process*. The GIT will work properly with both real objects and with proxies, so it is possible to achieve the effects of table marshaling within a single process. Item 33 illustrates the most common application of the GIT in detail.

30. When passing an interface pointer between one MTA thread and another, use `AddRef`.

In Item 20, we discussed the importance of only using interface pointers that have been `AddRef`'ed. Threading adds an interesting twist to any talk about resource management, as threads tend to have distinct lifetimes. To see the potential problem, try to debug the following code:

```
struct CustomerID {
  CustomerID(long a, long b) : A(a), B(b) {}
  long A;
  long B;
};
DWORD WINAPI ThreadProc(void* pv) {
  CustomerID* pid = (CustomerID*)pv;
  // look up customer in remote database
  // perform analysis on customer info
  // spool report to printer...
  return 0;
}
void PrintCustomerInfoForJoe() {
  CustomerID id(100, 223); // joe's id
  DWORD tid;
```

---

[2] Windows NT 4.0 Service Pack 3 or later and DCOM95 Version 1.1.

```
    CloseHandle(CreateThread(0, 0,
                             ThreadProc, &id,
                             0, &tid));
  } // oops
```

Pretty obvious bug, agreed? The thread that calls `PrintCustomer-InfoForJoe` has a distinct stack on which it creates an instance of a `CustomerID` as an automatic variable. This thread then proceeds to create a second thread, passing a pointer to this local variable. As soon as the original thread returns from the function call, the customer ID goes out of scope and is overwritten by arbitrary stack "gunk." The secondary thread is out of luck. The problem is that the secondary thread had no control over the lifetime of a resource that it required to do its job. Here's the fix:

```
DWORD WINAPI ThreadProc(void* pv) {
  CustomerID* pid = (CustomerID*)pv;
  //...
  delete pid;
  return 0;
}
void PrintCustomerInfoForJoe() {
  CustomerID* pid = new CustomerID(100, 223);
  DWORD tid;
  CloseHandle(CreateThread(0, 0,
                           ThreadProc, pid,
                           0, &tid));
}
```

This example demonstrates how important it is for you to coordinate the lifetime of resources with the lifetimes of the threads that depend on them.

COM interface pointers are also resources that need to be managed. Each thread that you employ should maintain a reference on any interface pointers it plans to call through. By simply following this rule, you can avoid many nasty race conditions. Consider a similar example using interface pointers:

```
DWORD WINAPI ThreadProc(void* pv) {
  CoInitializeEx(0, COINIT_MULTITHREADED); // join MTA
  IUnknown* pUnk = (IUnknown*)pv;
  UseObject(pUnk);
  pUnk->Release();
  CoUninitialize();
  return 0;
}
```

```
void SpawnThreadWithInterface(IUnknown* pUnk) {
    // to avoid race conditions, be sure to AddRef
    // before the new thread is created
    // (assumes calling thread is also in MTA)
    pUnk->AddRef();
    DWORD tid;
    CloseHandle(CreateThread(0, 0,
                             ThreadProc, pUnk,
                             0, &tid));
}
```

Note that both threads in this example are running in a single apartment (namely the MTA for the process), so we don't have to worry about marshaling the interface pointer (see Item 29).

31. User-interface threads and objects must run in single-threaded apartments (STAs).

You may want a thread in your application to use COM and to service a Windows user interface (UI). If so, that thread needs to run in a single-threaded apartment (STA). The reason is simple: both user interfaces and STAs have thread affinity. MTAs do not have thread affinity and offer no guarantees about how their threads will be used. UI elements such as window handles are inexorably tied to the thread that created them. If that thread is in an MTA, the UI will break in a big way.

Imagine you're writing an application that wants to display a user interface and also make outbound calls to a collection of remote objects. For argument's sake, assume the client creates a number of additional worker threads to do some background processing and that these threads make calls to the same set of remote objects. It may seem reasonable to have all the client threads living in its MTA so they can share the remote objects' proxies without having to marshal them from thread to thread. You therefore decide to make all your threads enter the MTA, with the application's main thread taking on the further responsibility of creating the UI and then running a message pump.

In this scenario, the worker threads will be just fine. But during any outbound COM calls on the main thread, the UI will hang. This is because when the UI thread (which is in an MTA) makes a call to another apartment, it enters the appropriate proxy, marshals the current call stack, and heads into the channel. Inside the channel, it makes a blocking remote procedure call (RPC). While the thread is waiting inside the channel for the RPC response message, any window messages being posted to its queue simply stack up there. This has the effect of hanging the UI for any windows that that thread created, probably causing the end user to terminate the process prematurely.

This doesn't happen to a thread in an STA. When an STA thread enters the channel, it drops into a COM-managed message loop while COM creates another thread (or picks one up from a cache) and pushes this new thread into the black hole of RPC to wait for the response packet. This complex mechanism is necessary for STAs to service reentrant callbacks using the same thread, as described in Item 35. The loop also supports the dispatching of window messages and can keep a UI running.

The channel doesn't provide this behavior for MTA threads because it is unnecessary. An MTA supports reentrance implicitly; callbacks can be serviced directly by other RPC receive threads. This approach conserves resources; the channel doesn't consume an extra thread for each outbound call. Unfortunately, it also makes it impossible to implement an MTA-based user interface that works.

The solution is to leave the worker threads in the MTA but move the user-interface thread to an STA. Then, when the UI thread makes an outbound call, the channel will do the right thing: leave the calling thread in a message pump so that at a minimum, painting, task switching, and window activation messages are processed as necessary. In this case any proxy acquired in the MTA (via a worker thread) must be marshaled to the STA (the UI thread) before it can be used there.

Now imagine you are writing a server instead of a client. You're not planning on making outbound COM calls—you just want a set of objects that responds to requests by modifying the state of a user interface displayed wherever the server process is running. To maximize concurrency, you deploy all these objects in an MTA. The problem here is that user interface elements have thread affinity—the thread that created them must service them. Dropped in the MTA, however, these elements are subject to bombardment by random threads as incoming calls arrive.

If a thread in the MTA invokes a method on an object that creates a window, and then the thread returns to the RPC receive pool and is later destroyed, the window isn't going to work very well. In fact, when a thread is destroyed, any windows that were created by that thread are also destroyed automatically. To keep your windows alive and messages flowing properly, you need a thread that runs for the life of the user interface. The application's main thread is a reasonable choice for this since it has to hang around waiting to revoke the server's class objects. So, hell-bent on trying to make your UI run from the MTA, you modify your application's main thread to enter the MTA. You then register your class objects and spin in a message loop, instead of simply waiting for an event or whatever other signal you usually use for shutdown notification. Now you have to force that thread to create all the user interface elements so that it can dispatch their messages. You can't use COM to do this because all of the RPC threads are in the same apartment (the MTA), and no marshaling takes place between them. Instead you'd have to use some other interthread communication mechanism. Even if you got it to work, you still couldn't make outbound COM calls (from your UI thread) without freezing your windows. Clearly, this is not a good approach.

The solution is to move the objects that build the UI into an STA. If this is all the objects really do, then have the client deal with them directly. If the objects do other processing as well, and you want that work done concurrently, have the client send messages to objects in the MTA, which in turn send messages to objects in the STA whenever they need to manipulate the user interface.

In any case, live by this one simple rule: a thread that wants to expose a user interface and use COM needs to run in an STA.

32. Avoid creating threads from an in-process server.

COM is about hiding implementation details. Using interfaces to delimit component boundaries, COM protects clients from almost every aspect of an object's implementation, including where that component actually resides. Location transparency is one of COM's most useful and admired features. In theory, you can write the same client and object codes without worrying about the execution context of either. In practice this is largely true, with a few notable exceptions. Threading is one of them. Writing in-process servers that create their own threads is a dangerous business and should be avoided.

You may be thinking, What about the `ThreadingModel` named value I specify when I register my DLL? Isn't that supposed to make all the threading details work out right? The answer is yes, if you work under the assumption that your DLL is passive and it's the client executable that manages all the threads. Once your in-process server threads itself and becomes active in its own right, unpleasant issues start to arise.

Recall that in-process servers are loaded on demand and are unloaded (if not in use) when their client calls `CoFreeUnusedLibraries`. Internally, `CoFreeUnusedLibraries` walks the list of in-process servers currently loaded and calls each one's `DllCanUnloadNow` function. If the return value is `S_OK`, the server can be unloaded; if the return value is `S_FALSE`, the server must remain loaded. The typical implementation of `DllCanUnloadNow` simply checks the value of a server lock count that tracks outstanding references to objects.[3] If your in-process server starts up threads, you need to make sure that the DLL supplying their code doesn't get unloaded out from under them. If it does, your process will likely crash due to a hardware-generated exception the next time the thread is scheduled to execute. There are two ways to avoid this problem. One is to make sure your threads don't outlive the last outstanding reference to an object; therefore, when the server lock count goes to zero, the threads are no longer running and the DLL can be unloaded safely. The other is to treat a thread's existence as a reason to keep the server loaded and to increment the server lock count while the thread is running.

The second approach is more useful than the first because it decouples the lifetime of your threads from the lifetime of references to your objects, which the client controls. Allowing your thread to act totally independent from the client is desirable, but it isn't as simple as it seems. The trouble is that clients expect their in-process servers to be passive. When a client process decides to shut down, it releases all its references to objects and assumes its servers may be safely unloaded. This latter assumption is made inside the client's call to `CoUninitialize`, which doesn't bother to consult `DllCanUnloadNow` before it plucks each server from memory. You can't blame the client for this—it doesn't know any better and there is no way to tell it that a thread in the DLL is still actively pursuing some objective.

What happens if your client calls `CoUninitialize` while you still have threads running? `CoUninitialize` *will* unload your in-process server, so you have no chance to stop your threads. The obvious place for this code is inside `DllMain`:

```
HANDLE g_hStopEvent = 0;  // Shutdown event
HANDLE g_hThread = 0;     // Thread handle to wait for

// Assume g_hStopEvent and g_hThread are created
// when the worker thread is started
BOOL WINAPI DllMain(HINSTANCE h, DWORD dwReason, void*){
  switch(fdwReason) {
```

---

[3] For objects that implement reference counting, tracking outstanding references is the same as tracking the object's existence (which is often how the server lock count is implemented).

```
      case DLL_PROCESS_DETACH :
        SetEvent(g_hEvent);
        WaitForSingleObject(g_hThread, INFINITE);
        break;
  }
  return TRUE;
}
```

When the DLL is being unloaded, `DllMain` is called with the `DLL_PROCESS_DETACH` flag as its second argument. In this code, the DLL sets a Win32 event to signal its worker thread that it's time to shut down (the worker thread has to periodically check for this). Then the main thread blocks, waiting for the worker thread to stop.

This looks great, but it results in deadlock every time. The trouble is that access to `DllMain` is serialized. The main thread has entered the function and is waiting inside it. When the worker thread notices that `g_hStopEvent` has been signaled and exits, part of that shutdown is a notification to `DllMain` (with `DLL_THREAD_DETACH` as the second parameter), which must complete before the thread is destroyed. So the main thread holds `DllMain` waiting for the worker thread to signal, yet the worker thread needs `DllMain` to do this, and neither will let go until the other does: ergo, deadlock.

Calling `DisableThreadLibraryCalls` to stop the worker thread's call to your `DllMain` won't solve the problem. Even though your in-process server is willing to let the thread go without any sort of good-bye, other DLLs loaded in the process are not. Since the synchronization of calls to `DllMain` is done with a single lock that protects *all* the DLLs in a process, the worker thread's calls to these other libraries will cause the deadlock situation as well.

What if the code were modified so that the main thread didn't wait on the worker thread's existence, but rather on some per-thread event signaled by the worker thread function just before it exits? The trouble with this model is that the main thread's call to `WaitForSingleObject` returns as soon as the worker thread calls `SetEvent`, and the DLL can be unloaded before the thread function's final few instructions complete. Putting `DllMain` to sleep for a little while to avoid this issue would also be bad since you would probably freeze your client's user interface. Besides, you can never know how long it would have to sleep anyway, since the thread won't signal until it has acquired the global `DllMain` mutex and sent its `DLL_THREAD_DETACH` message.

So you can't wait for the thread to stop naturally without deadlocking. And you can't wait for another signal that the thread is about to stop because that inevitably introduces a race condition between the worker thread, which is trying to complete, and the main thread, which is trying to unload the DLL (and the worker thread's code). What if you took the gloves off, stopped playing nice, and called `TerminateThread`? In other words, have `DllMain` simply stop your worker threads when the library is being unloaded. This will work, sort of. The problem is that when you terminate a thread, it doesn't have a chance to exit cleanly. Specifically, it doesn't have a chance to notify all the DLLs in the process that it is going away. Any DLL expecting to clean up resources that were allocated on a per-thread basis will be disappointed. This sort of leak can lead to everything from degradation of performance to a horrible crash any time between the call to `TerminateThread` and the rest of your process's life.[4] Using this technique is incredibly dangerous.

Ultimately, there is no way to both disconnect the lifetime of your threads from the lifetime of references to your objects *and* to shut down your in-process server correctly. Accept it and move on. If you need to create threads, build an executable server instead. Inside an executable server, you have complete control of the lifetime of both threads and objects, and all of these shutdown problems vanish. Of course, access to an out-of-process server is slower, but it's not much worse than calling across apartments in the client process, if that's what you had in mind for your thread. And, of course, having a system that doesn't crash is something of a feature, too. All of this being said, someone reading this book will still try to create threads from in-process servers. But at least our consciences are now clear.

33. Beware the Free-Threaded Marshaler (FTM).

The Free-Threaded Marshaler may have remained shrouded in mystery but for two things. First, an author of this book who shall go unnamed[5] documented it in a well-read and well-respected technical journal.[6] Second, a certain COM component code-generating wizard[7] lists it as an option along with useful features such as whether the object supports `ISupportErrorInfo` and which apartment type the object would like. The only thing that could have made it worse is if the option were selected by default. You should not select this option yourself unless you are fully aware of the implications.

---

[4] Another problem is that you will leak the memory allocated for the thread's stack, and any critical sections held by the thread will never be released.

[5] OK, Don Box.

[6] OK, the September 1997 issue of *Microsoft Systems Journal.*

[7] ATL Object Wizard.

Recall that COM supports two types of apartments: single-threaded (STA) and multithreaded (MTA). STA components enjoy the convenience of handling only a single request at a time via the Windows message queue, whereas MTA components experience the scalability of being able to handle multiple requests simultaneously. This arrangement makes it advantageous for STA components to manage user-interface chores and then to create MTA components to handle background computational tasks. However, because these two kinds of components must communicate with one another, there is the overhead of a proxy and a stub, even when the components share the same address space. The FTM was invented to eliminate this overhead.

The logic goes something like this. By definition, MTA components are thread neutral and handle thread synchronization internally. If an MTA component shares the same address space with an STA component, why shouldn't the STA component be able to call *directly* into the MTA component, without going through a proxy?

When an object aggregates the FTM's implementation of `IMarshal`, two things happen. If an interface from the object is marshaled out-of-process, the FTM allows standard marshaling to happen just as you'd expect. On the other hand, if an interface from the object is marshaled within the process (i.e., `MSHCTX_INPROC` is used), the FTM custom marshals, filling the marshaling packet with the raw interface pointer value. When the interface is unmarshaled in a different apartment, the apartment receives an interface pointer directly on the component, instead of receiving an interface pointer to a proxy. In effect, objects using the FTM become apartment neutral:

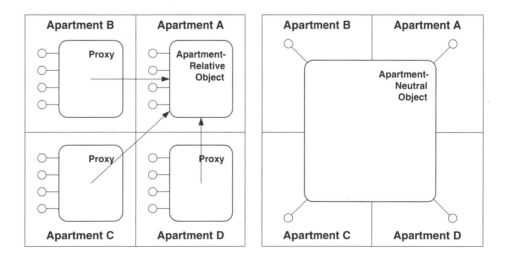

The good news is that being apartment neutral is often faster. The bad news is that it sometimes isn't, and unless you're careful, it doesn't even work. The problem lies not in the apartment-neutral object itself but in what it's holding. Objects often hold interface pointers to other objects. Those interface pointers either point to proxies or directly to other objects. In general, these interface pointers are apartment relative unless the underlying object is also apartment neutral. This means that a component using the FTM cannot safely hold interface pointers, as is shown below:

```
class CoPenguin : public IBird {
public:
  CoPenguin(IFoodSource* pfs)
  : m_cRef(0), m_pfs(pfs), m_pftm(0) {
    if( !m_pfs ) throw "Need food!";
    m_pfs->AddRef();
    // aggregate the FTM
    CoCreateFreeThreadedMarshaler(this, &m_pftm);
  }

  virtual ~CoPenguin() {
    m_pftm->Release();
    m_pfs->Release();
  }

  HRESULT QueryInterface(REFIID iid, void** ppv) {
    if (IID_IMarshal == iid )
      return m_pftm->QueryInterface(iid, ppv);
    // remainder of IUnknown left as an exercise
  }

  // IBird
  STDMETHODIMP Eat() {
    // Will return an error if m_pfs is a proxy
    // and the caller is in an apartment other than
    // the one used to construct the CoPenguin
    return m_pfs->GetFood();
  }

  // etc.

private:
  ULONG        m_cRef;
  IFoodSource* m_pfs;
```

```
    IUnknown* m_pftm; // FTM is apartment neutral
};
```

The reason that the proxy returns an error on a method call outside of its apartment is that interface pointers are apartment relative. To allow the component using the FTM to work from any apartment, interface pointers must be ditched in favor of an object reference that is apartment agnostic. To avoid the proxy's complaint, the interface pointer must be marshaled to the proper apartment *for each method call on the component using the FTM.* The intuitive way to solve this problem is to marshal an interface into an OBJREF using the `CoMarshalInterface` function and to store that rather than the interface pointer. An OBJREF is essentially an apartment-independent representation of an interface pointer, which is exactly what we're looking for.

When using `CoMarshalInterface`, there are two kinds of marshaling one could choose, *normal marshaling* (sometimes called call marshaling) and *table marshaling.* A normal marshal's properties are that it can only be unmarshaled once and that the data basically becomes invalid if the unmarshal has not yet occurred after a short timeout. A table marshal, on the other hand, can be unmarshaled any number of times and has no timeout. It seems perfectly suited for our use. Unfortunately, a table marshal is not allowed on a proxy, so cross-apartment interface pointers cannot be used with this technique (see Item 29 for more details).

Essentially, we need a component that has enough internal knowledge of COM to be able to marshal an interface pointer into an OBJREF and hold onto it for us; such a component must also allow us to unmarshal the OBJREF into several different apartments. The COM Global Interface Table (GIT) provides just this functionality. The GIT is a process-wide, apartment-neutral object that holds interface pointers and returns apartment-independent interface pointer identifiers (also called *GIT cookies*). The GIT can be accessed with `CoCreateInstance` using `CLSID_StdGlobalInterfaceTable`. The GIT provides its caching and retrieval function via the `IGlobalInterfaceTable` interface:

```
interface IGlobalInterfaceTable : IUnknown {
  HRESULT RegisterInterfaceInGlobal(
    [in] IUnknown *punk,
    [in] REFIID iid,
    [out] DWORD *pdwCookie);
  HRESULT RevokeInterfaceFromGlobal(
    [in] DWORD dwCookie);
  HRESULT GetInterfaceFromGlobal(
    [in] DWORD dwCookie,
```

```
      [in] REFIID riid,
      [out, iid_is(riid)] void** ppv);
};
```

Now an object using the FTM coupled with the GIT to hold its interface pointers can retrieve them on demand for every method call. This method will ensure
that each interface pointer is marshaled properly into whichever apartment the
calling thread belongs to. For example:

```
class CoPenguin : public IBird {
public:
  CoPenguin(IFoodSource* pFoodSource)
  : m_cRef(0), m_dwFoodSource(0), m_pgit(0), m_pftm(0)
  {
    // Cache the GIT
    // (error handling omitted for brevity)
    CoCreateInstance(
            CLSID_StdGlobalInterfaceTable,
            0, CLSCTX_INPROC_SERVER,
            IID_IGlobalInterfaceTable,
            (void**)&m_pgit);

    // Register the interface with the GIT
    m_pgit->RegisterInterfaceInGlobal(
                    pFoodSource,
                    IID_IFoodSource,
                    &m_dwFoodSource);

    // aggregate the FTM
    CoCreateFreeThreadedMarshaler(this, &m_pftm);
  }

  virtual ~CoPenguin() {
    m_pftm->Release();
    m_pgit->RevokeInterfaceFromGlobal(m_dwFoodSource);
    m_pgit->Release();
  }

  // IBird
  STDMETHODIMP Eat() {
    // Retrieve the IFoodSource interface
    IFoodSource* pfs;
    HRESULT hr = m_pgit->GetInterfaceFromGlobal(
```

```
                                m_dwFoodSource,
                                IID_IFoodSource,
                                (void**)&pfs;
      if (SUCCEEDED(hr)) {
        hr = pfs->GetFood();
        pfs->Release();
      }
      return hr;
   }

   // etc.

private:
   ULONG m_cRef;
   DWORD m_dwFoodSource;
   // note that FTM and GIT are both apartment neutral
   IGlobalInterfaceTable* m_pgit;
   IUnknown*              m_pftm;
};
```

Notice that the name of this item was not "Use the FTM with wild abandon." Even with the GIT, the use of the FTM should be avoided unless you have a really compelling reason to become apartment neutral (e.g., an Active Server Page expects objects at application or session scope to be apartment neutral). One of the problems is the sheer complexity associated with the FTM. Having an object that holds references to other objects—an extremely common thing to do—is now much more complicated. However, the complexity can be dealt with. The main problem is efficiency.

One of the main reasons to group components into the same apartment is so that they can share the same concurrency model (i.e., they can work together without the overhead of the proxy/stub). However, unless all closely cooperating components use the FTM, there will be a proxy/stub pair when using the GIT on held interfaces. In the case in which one method call on a component using the FTM translates into several method calls on numerous cached interfaces, you're paying the interapartment hop cost *many* times rather than just once. The promise of the FTM is efficiency, but the reality is that it is often less efficient unless you're willing to enforce apartment neutrality on all closely cooperating components.

34. Beware physical locks in the MTA.

If your objects live inside an MTA they can, by definition, be concurrently accessed by more than one thread. It is up to you to make them thread safe by protecting both their data members and any global data they share. You can do this
using any of the standard Win32 synchronization mechanisms for locking (e.g.,
critical sections, mutexes). Methods that need to access either type of data in a
thread-safe way—avoiding a simultaneous read and write or simultaneous
writes—must acquire a lock before doing so and release it after they're done. The
code fragment below shows a simple implementation class that needs to protect
its state with a mutex.

```
class Long : public ILong
{
   long m_l;
   HANDLE m_lock;   // Maintained in ctor/dtor
public:
   …
   STDMETHODIMP ReadValue(long *pl) {
     WaitForSingleObject(m_lock, INFINITE);
     *pl = m_l;
     ReleaseMutex(m_lock);
     return S_OK;
   }

   STDMETHODIMP WriteValue(long l) {
     WaitForSingleObject(m_lock, INFINITE);
     m_l = l;
     ReleaseMutex(m_lock);
     return S_OK;
   }

   STDMETHODIMP DoubleValue(void) {
     WaitForSingleObject(m_lock, INFINITE);
     m_l *= 2;
     ReleaseMutex(m_lock);
     return S_OK;
   }
};
```

Every access to the m_l member variable is bracketed by calls to acquire and release the m_lock mutex so that only one operation touches m_l at a time.

Notice that this code is very careful to release m_lock before returning from each method. What would happen if you wrote code that returned from a method *without* releasing a lock?

```
STDMETHODIMP Long::Start(void) {
  WaitForSingleObject(m_lock, INFINITE);
  return S_OK;
}

STDMETHODIMP Long::DoubleValue(void) {
  m_l *= 2;
  return S_OK;
}

STDMETHODIMP Long::End(void) {
  ReleaseMutex(m_lock);
  return S_OK;
}
```

The goal is to allow your client to lock the object by calling Start, hold any number of other clients at bay while calling DoubleValue to update m_l any number of times, then unlock the object by calling End. Attractive as this might be, and assuming all clients followed the protocol, this code won't work!

In this case, threads spell trouble with a capital T. Many of the Win32 synchronization objects (including the mutex) have thread affinity. That is, they must be acquired and released by a specific physical thread. It is impossible for one thread to get a mutex and for another thread to consequently release it, so for the code above to work, the same physical thread must call Start and End. Since calls to objects in the MTA are dispatched immediately using arbitrary RPC receive threads, there is absolutely no way you can guarantee this for objects running inside the MTA. The essence of this quandary is that the Start method returns, allowing its thread to leave the MTA while holding a physical lock. Once the thread has left, there is no way to know if, when, or where that particular thread will be used again. The best you can hope for is that the locking thread exits and the lock is abandoned (this isn't much of a hope . . .).

A similar issue arises if your code makes outbound calls to other objects while holding a physical lock.

```
// Implementation of Doubler object
STDMETHODIMP Doubler::DoubleLong(ILong *pl) {
  long l;
  pl->ReadValue(&l);
  l *= 2;
  pl->WriteValue(l);
```

```
    return S_OK;
  }

  // Implementation of Long object
  STDMETHODIMP Long::ReadValue(long *pl) {
    WaitForSingleObject(m_lock, INFINITE);
    *pl = m_l;
    ReleaseMutex(m_lock);
    return S_OK;
  }

  STDMETHODIMP Long::WriteValue(long l) {
    WaitForSingleObject(m_lock, INFINITE);
    m_l = l;
    ReleaseMutex(m_lock);
    return S_OK;
  }

  // New implementation of DoubleValue,
  // delegates to Doubler
  STDMETHODIMP Long::DoubleValue(void) {
    WaitForSingleObject(m_lock, INFINITE);
    // delegate to Doubler object
    m_pDoubler->DoubleLong(static_cast<ILong*>(this));
    ReleaseMutex(m_lock);
    return S_OK;
  }
```

This modified implementation of Long::DoubleValue delegates to an instance of a Doubler object. The Long sends a pointer to its own interface as input to m_pDoubler->DoubleLong so that the Doubler object can call back to Long::ReadValue and Long::WriteValue to get and set the data it manipulates. All this works great, unless the Doubler object is in another apartment.

Since Long is implemented in an MTA, the delegating call to m_pDoubler->DoubleLong is genuinely blocking—that thread is blocked in the channel waiting for the outbound RPC call to complete. Note that before blocking, the thread acquired m_lock. When the Doubler object calls back through the ILong* it was passed, the call is directly dispatched by an arbitrary RPC receive thread. That thread enters ReadValue and immediately waits to acquire m_lock. The result is deadlock, which is definitely not the desired result. Again, the problem is that many Win32 synchronization objects, in this case the m_lock mutex, have thread affinity, whereas the MTA does not.

How can you solve these problems? The second problem is easier, so let's tackle it first. There are a number of options here. One is to avoid making outbound calls while holding a physical lock. In other words, DoubleValue shouldn't make the outbound call to m_pDoubler->DoubleLong because m_lock has been acquired. This may seem somewhat harsh, but it means you never have to worry about this sort of deadlock.

A slightly looser constraint can also be used: avoid making any outbound call that can possibly result in a callback that may cause deadlock. In this case, DoubleValue shouldn't make the outbound call to m_pDoubler->DoubleLong because m_lock has been acquired *and* because DoubleLong will call back to Long::ReadValue, which will result in deadlock. If you choose to use this more flexible policy, realize that you are shouldering a heavy burden—you must carefully analyze your code for all potential deadlock situations.

A third approach is to never use INFINITE as the second parameter to WaitForSingleObject (or any of its siblings), so that deadlock can be broken (albeit rather harshly).

```
STDMETHODIMP Long::ReadValue(long *pl) {
  // Wait for up to 1 minute
  DWORD dw = WaitForSingleObject(m_lock, 60000);
  if (WAIT_TIMEOUT == dw)
    return E_UNEXPECTED;
  *pl = m_l;
  ReleaseMutex(m_lock);
  return S_OK;
}
```

If ReadValue were written this way, the callback wouldn't cause deadlock, but it would result in a runtime error. This is better than hanging the system, but only just barely (also, it may be impossible to choose a timeout interval that will not erroneously reject valid lock requests).

Finally, you could protect your state using a handmade lock based on a *logical* thread of execution. The calls from DoubleValue to m_pDoubler->DoubleLong and back to ReadValue are causally related; that is, they are all part of the same logical thread. If you could identify a logical thread of execution, you could use that information to control access to m_l. To make this work, you have to propagate some token that identifies your logical thread. You can do this either explicitly, by passing the token as a parameter that is forwarded through each call, or implicitly, by using a channel hook[8] that forwards the value

---

[8] Channel hooks are a powerful but currently undocumented feature of COM.

through each call. In the first case, your interfaces have to be designed with this in mind because each method has to carry an extra parameter. In the second case, you have to have a channel hook registered in every process through which the logical thread passes.

You can apply this final solution, using a logical lock, to the first problem as well—wanting to hold a lock across multiple method invocations—but it's harder. By having a client acquire a logical lock, again represented as a token, and passing it back into each method, you can deal with the fact that the call to Start and the call to End are dispatched on different physical threads. However, if you want your logical lock to have the same semantics as a physical lock (e.g., a mutex), you have to implement Start such that any threads attempting to acquire the logical lock wait until the first client is done. When the client finally calls End, you must allow only one of the threads waiting in Start to proceed. In addition, your logical lock has to be prepared to deal with abandonment in case the client that holds it never returns to release it.[9]

The moral of the story is: be very careful about how you synchronize your threads inside the MTA. Don't return from a call to the MTA while holding a physical lock. Don't call out of the MTA while holding a physical lock unless you can guarantee that the call won't result in a callback that deadlocks or that you'll detect such a deadlock if it occurs and break it. Finally, if you just can't do one of these things, implement some protocol for logical locking instead.

35. STAs may need locks too.

Many developers realize that writing thread-safe components for the MTA is hard. They like to spend their evenings and weekends at home, so they choose to deploy their components in STAs instead. If you are one of them, be aware that although the STA environment is certainly more forgiving, locking may still be an issue.

Consider a process that uses multiple STAs. If components in separate apartments access shared data (global or static variables, for example), that data must be protected using critical sections or the like. In this scenario, multiple STAs present problems very similar to those arising in the MTA.

You shouldn't write code that acquires a lock in one method and releases it in another. Your client may never call back, and the lock won't be abandoned until the STA that owns it is destroyed. This style also leaves the data open to access from

---

[9] The latter problem is dealt with for you when you are using physical locks: they are abandoned when the owning thread terminates.

any method of any object in the apartment that owns the lock. You also shouldn't write code that acquires a lock and then makes an outbound call if there is any possibility that it can result in a call to an object in another STA in the same process that then tries to acquire the lock. This restricts direct calls into other apartments in the same process as well.

Multiple STAs make you nervous, so you decide to stick with just one. That means one thread to worry about and no locking issues, right? Wrong. But how can that be, since by definition a single STA provides no concurrency? The answer is simple: STAs have to support reentrance.

Consider the case in which a client passes a reference to object A (which lives in its own apartment) to an object B (which lives in another apartment). Assume that object B makes a call back to object A within the scope of the client's initial outbound call. For this to work, the client's apartment must be reentered.

```
interface IBackward;

interface IForward : IUnknown {
  HRESULT Call([in] IBackward *pBack);
}

interface IBackward : IUnknown {
  HRESULT Callback(void);
}

// IForward implementation
HRESULT ObjectB::Call(IBackward *pBack) {
  HRESULT hr = pBack->Callback();
  assert(SUCCEEDED(hr)); // callback must succeed
  return hr;
}

// IBackward implementation
HRESULT ObjectA::Callback(void) {
  return S_OK;
}

// Client code
IForward *pf = 0;
if (SUCCEEDED(GetObjectB(&pf))) {
  IBackward *pb = new ObjectA;
  pf->Call(pb);
```

```
    pf->Release();
    delete pb;
}
```

If this code didn't work for all apartment types, COM wouldn't be very useful. So the COM remoting layer goes to great pains to make sure it does work, even if both apartments in this scenario are STAs.

Frankly, this is highly unintuitive. The call out of the client apartment to object B is synchronous (as all COM calls are as of this writing[10]). The callback from object B to object A must be serviced by a thread that has entered object A's apartment. In the case of an STA, that means the apartment's one and only thread, which is waiting for the initial outbound call to return. You'd expect this to result in deadlock, but it doesn't. It turns out that calls out of an STA aren't really blocking, they're actually quasi-blocking. To make an outbound call, your STA thread calls into a proxy, marshals the call stack for transfer to the target apartment, and then calls into the channel, which is COM's wrapper around RPC. But the STA thread doesn't actually make the RPC call; RPC *is* blocking and stops the calling thread cold. So the channel starts a separate thread (or grabs an existing one from a cache) to make the blocking RPC call, and the STA thread waits, spinning in a message pump. Remember that inbound requests are dispatched to STA-based objects by queuing a message for the appropriate thread. This is why STA-based servers need to pump messages. It also explains how STA reentrance works. As shown below, when a callback is made to an STA whose thread is in an outbound call, the invocation is posted to the thread's message queue and will be dispatched by the pump inside the channel.

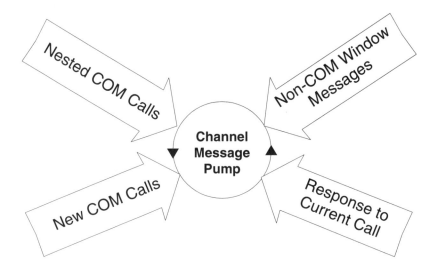

---

[10] Asynchrony will be offered in a future release of COM.

Note that this technique allows the callback to be serviced on the correct thread, keeping COM's apartment laws intact.

Without the message pump hidden in the channel, it would be impossible to call back into an STA. So the presence of the message pump is good. What happens if your client is in an outbound call to object B and some other client calls into your client's apartment trying to access object A? The other client's inbound call gets queued, as you'd expect, and is dispatched by the pump inside the channel. The presence of the message pump in this case may or may not be good. What if the other client's invocation on object A will modify some state that your client thread expected to remain unchanged during its outbound call to object B? In this case, unconstrained reentrance is a problem.

When state needs to be protected, mutexes (and other synchronization objects) spring to mind. Unfortunately, they won't help you here because a mutex is designed to mutually exclude access between distinct threads, and each STA consists of only a single thread. If your client thread acquires a mutex before calling out to another apartment, don't expect the lock to stop some other client's call into your apartment from accessing the state the lock is supposed to protect. The channel will service the inbound call on your own thread (which has been "borrowed" for exactly this purpose). Besides, a typical use of an STA is to house a user interface, and blocking a UI thread by waiting on a mutex is a cardinal sin (see Item 31).

To solve this problem, you need some kind of logical lock, and COM provides one via the `IMessageFilter` interface. `IMessageFilter` provides the hooks necessary to extend the channel's message pump logic to control reentrance by selectively blocking incoming requests:

```
interface IMessageFilter : IUnknown {
  DWORD HandleInComingCall(
    [in] DWORD dwCallType,
    [in] HTASK htaskCaller,
    [in] DWORD dwTickCount,
    [in] INTERFACEINFO* pInterfaceInfo
  );
  DWORD RetryRejectedCall(
    [in] HTASK htaskCallee,
    [in] DWORD dwTickCount,
    [in] DWORD dwRejectType
  );
  DWORD MessagePending(
    [in] HTASK htaskCallee,
```

```
    [in] DWORD dwTickCount,
    [in] DWORD dwPendingType
  );
}
```

Each STA can register its own custom implementation of `IMessageFilter` by calling `CoRegisterMessageFilter`. The filter's implementation of `HandleInComingCall` allows it to control whether an inbound call is processed or rejected. The default filter provided by COM lets everything through. A custom filter can postpone other clients' inbound calls when your thread is in an outbound call:

```
DWORD CustomFilter::HandleInComingCall(
  DWORD dwCallType, HTASK, DWORD, INTERFACEINFO*) {
  if (dwCallType == CALLTYPE_TOPLEVEL_CALLPENDING)
    // a new top-level call is inbound, but the STA
    // thread is currently making an outbound call
    return SERVERCALL_RETRYLATER;
  else
    return SERVERCALL_ISHANDLED;
}
```

The `dwCallType` flag indicates what sort of call is coming in. `CALLTYPE_TOPLEVEL_CALLPENDING` indicates a new request from some other apartment while your thread is making an outbound call. The sample above chooses to postpone such calls by returning `SERVERCALL_RETRY-LATER`. A `dwCallType` value of `CALLTYPE_NESTED` would have indicated a nested callback (as was discussed earlier), which should typically be allowed through.[11] The sample above allows all such calls to be processed by returning `SERVERCALL_ISHANDLED`. A third value, `SERVERCALL_RE-JECTED`, is also available to force a client to cancel the call.

Interestingly, `HandleInComingCall` is called whenever an inbound request arrives, whether or not your STA thread is currently in an outbound call. This is useful if you want to protect state for other reasons. For example, if your STA thread is providing a user interface in addition to servicing COM calls, it might want to display a modal dialog box to allow the user to edit some data. If the same data can be modified via calls to objects in the STA, the dialog processing code has to be prepared to deal with state changes that take place between the time it was displayed and dismissed. If you don't expect much (or any) contention, and resolving the dialog's inaccurate view of the world isn't difficult, you can be optimistic and write the code to reconcile the differences when necessary.

---

[11] Nested calls are detected via the causality ID (CID) propagated through a series of calls as part of the ORPCTHIS structure, the implicit first argument to all cross-apartment method calls.

If you expect a lot of contention, or resolving the dialog's inaccurate view of the world is difficult, you can be pessimistic and stop the inbound COM calls that corrupt the dialog's view by changing the state underneath it.

```
DWORD CustomFilter::HandleInComingCall(
  DWORD dwCallType, HTASK, DWORD, INTERFACEINFO*) {
  // a new top-level call is inbound, but the STA
  // thread is currently in an outbound call
  if (dwCallType == CALLTYPE_TOPLEVEL_CALLPENDING)
    return SERVERCALL_RETRYLATER;
  // a new top-level call is inbound, but the STA
  // thread is currently servicing the user
  // interface and doesn't want the world to change
  // while it does so
  else if (dwCallType == CALLTYPE_TOPLEVEL &&
           g_bLockStateBecauseUserInterfaceIsBusy)
    return SERVERCALL_RETRYLATER;
  else
    return SERVERCALL_ISHANDLED;
}
```

This version of the custom filter blocks any incoming calls whenever the global `g_bLockStateBecauseUserInterfaceIsBusy` flag is set. Note that the `INTERFACEINFO*` argument indicates the particular object, interface, and method being used. This information can be used to make finer-grained decisions about calls to accept or reject. For example, you could accept calls that you were certain wouldn't modify protected state.

Even with these reentrance issues, it is usually easier to write components for an STA than for the MTA. If you choose this path, however, remember two things: using multiple STAs introduces many of the problems of the MTA, and even with a single STA, locking issues arise out of the necessity to support reentrance and callbacks.

36. Avoid extant marshals on in-process objects.

Examine the following code:

```
STDMETHODIMP CoPaint::CreateBrush(REFIID iid,
  void** ppv) {
  return CoCreateInstance(CLSID_CoBrush, 0,
    CLSCTX_LOCAL_SERVER, iid, ppv);
}
```

```
STDMETHODIMP CoPaint::CreatePen(REFIID iid,
  void** ppv) {
  return CoCreateInstance(CLSID_CoPen, 0,
    CLSCTX_INPROC_SERVER, iid, ppv);
}
```

See any potential problems? Imagine that the CoPaint server is implemented
as a simple, single-threaded (STA-based) out-of-process server. Note that
CoPaint relies on Helper objects to implement various Child objects.
Conceptually, this is a great way to partition an application, since a separate development team can own each server. However, beware of arbitrarily handing out
pointers to objects implemented in DLL (in-process) servers. Recall that a DLL
simply makes a guest appearance in the client's apartment; it has no control over
the lifetime of that apartment. Therefore, when an external client calls
CoPaint::CreatePen in the code above, an in-process instance of CoPen
is created inside the apartment (in a separate DLL) and a reference to that object
is marshaled back to the caller.

Traditional COM servers allow external clients to control their lifetimes, so
imagine that the CoPaint server is implemented similarly, such that when the
last client disconnects, the server will shut down. But it is impossible to really
know if all objects living in the server's apartment have no external clients, since
CoPen is implemented in a separate DLL, with a separate lock count, invisible
to CoPaint. The effect is that any external references to CoPen will be left
dangling when all external references to objects implemented in CoPaint are
released and the server shuts down.

Note that instances of CoBrush do not experience this phenomenon, since the
CreateBrush method exports a pointer to a proxy, and standard proxies marshal in such a way that the caller gets a duplicate proxy that references the original object in the out-of-process CoBrush server. The CoBrush server has a
lifetime that is completely independent of the CoPaint server.

Note that if you could hook CoPen's implementation of AddRef and
Release, then the problem would be solved, since you would know when
there were no outstanding references to the object. This is the case with aggregation (the inner object delegates to the outer's implementation of IUnknown), so
this rule doesn't apply to aggregated objects, whose lifetimes are intrinsically controlled by the outer object. In fact, given this, it would be perfectly acceptable to
simply create a generic implementation of IUnknown that aggregated an object
from an in-process server and blindly delegated QueryInterface calls for

everything except `IID_IUnknown` to the inner object. This would allow you to hand out pointers to the in-process object while retaining knowledge of the object's lifetime. Unfortunately, this "blind aggregation" mechanism only works with objects specifically written to support aggregation.

For objects that do not support aggregation, you could provide a wrapper class that simply delegates all calls to the in-process object, but this is a lot of work if written manually for each object. One of the authors of this book created a generic delegator that automates this approach and is even more efficient in delegating method calls than a simple hand written implementation.[12]

There are other techniques for dealing with this lifetime issue. The first is simply to avoid the problem in the first place. Don't ever export pointers to in-process objects implemented in separate DLLs. If you're not willing to settle for this conservative approach, you might try explicitly documenting lifetime restrictions within the semantics of the interfaces you design. For instance, you could document a hierarchy of objects such that Child objects must be released before Parent objects (although this is somewhat restricting for clients).

A more invasive technique is possible if you can convince the DLL implementers to notify you when it is OK to shut down. OLE documents use such a protocol (see `IOleContainer::LockContainer` for an example). However, when using general-purpose components not written against such a protocol, there is not much you can do to discover when it is reasonable to exit your process.

Since it is generally unsafe to export pointers to in-process objects, you may wonder how surrogates work. Isn't their entire job in life to create instances of objects in DLL-based servers and expose them out-of-process so they can be used off-host? Well, yes. However, the surrogate plumbing has incestuous knowledge of how many extant marshals exist within the process. When the surrogate plumbing detects that the number of marshals has dropped to zero, it notifies the surrogate process (usually `dllhost.exe`) that it is safe to shut down. Unfortunately, there is no documented way to detect when there are no extant marshals within a process, so this technique is not an option for our lowly out-of-process object broker.

It would be possible to run the DLL within the system-supplied surrogate process and then explicitly ask for a local server implementation of `CoPen`. Although safe, this would now require a change to the component's configuration to assign it an AppID (which is required for surrogate activation).

---

[12] Look for Keith Brown's Universal Delegator sample at http://www.develop.com/kbrown.

37. Use `CoDisconnectObject` to inform the stub when you go away prematurely.

It is sometimes necessary to destroy an object with a nonzero reference count. In general, this is a bad idea, since it is likely that other parties are expecting you to stay around (they are holding extant references, after all). This caveat being stated, it still may be necessary to leave this earth prematurely either due to fail-fast policies or when a server is shut down via some out-of-band technique (e.g., COM servers that run as NT services responding to a net stop request from the administrator).

When an object shuts down with a nonzero reference count, it must ensure that no other calls are dispatched by parties that may hold extant references. If the only other parties that hold references are simply in-process objects from the same source base, this can be achieved using some sort of global switch that indicates that a process-wide shutdown is taking place:

```
MyClass::~MyClass(void) {
  if (m_pSomeOtherObject && !g_bShuttingDown)
    m_pSomeOtherObject->Release();
}
```

While this code assumes that all users of the object are aware of this idiom, that is often not the case inside a particular object hierarchy.

The previous example does not take into account clients that live outside the process of the object. In this case, it is possible that the client may issue a call to a proxy after the object has decided to destroy itself. If this happens, then the call will arrive at the stub, which now holds a dangling reference to the once-healthy object. When the stub dispatches the call through its dangling reference, the results will be less than pretty, since it is likely that the memory once occupied by your object now contains a completely random vptr/vtable combination. To avoid this problem, the object should call `CoDisconnectObject` to inform the stub that the object is going away.

`CoDisconnectObject` does two things. First, it informs the stub to release any held references to the actual object. Second, it informs the stub to no longer dispatch calls from extant proxies. If a call arrives after the call to `CoDisconnectObject`, the issuing proxy will be notified immediately that the object is dead. This fact is communicated to the caller via a well-known HRESULT (RPC_E_DISCONNECTED). This is considerably more pleasant than having random code execute in the server.

Security

What can one say about security? If you don't get it right, at best your system will not function and at worst will introduce gaping security holes in your network. Of course, computer and network security is not a required course in most computer science curriculums, so few developers even have a clue what the issues are, let alone the basic vocabulary or concepts. To make matters worse, most development organizations do not make security an integral part of every project. Rather, one lonely person is typically assigned the job of security oracle and the rest of the development team tries to ignore his or her existence until a scapegoat is needed to sacrifice to the missed deadline gods. It is no wonder that the majority of deployment problems are security related. While security is actually an extremely interesting and well-documented field, most COM developers can survive with a basic understanding of the three core concepts of security: authentication, access control, and security principals. This chapter provides several guidelines that, when combined with a basic understanding of these three concepts, will reduce the time it takes to deploy and develop a distributed application.

38. `CoInitializeSecurity` is your friend. Learn it, love it, call it.

Very few distributed applications can ignore security and escape being mauled by the NT security gods. If you plan to use COM to develop distributed applications, consider spending some time reviewing the NT security model and familiarizing yourself with access tokens, impersonation, and access control lists (ACLs).

Unlike remote procedure call (RPC), where you must explicitly turn on security and verify authentication levels of incoming calls, COM provides a certain level of security automatically. Incoming calls are screened based on process-wide settings that you can control by calling `CoInitializeSecurity`. In fact, these settings are required, so if you neglect to call `CoInitialize-Security`, it will be called on your behalf when you make your first interesting COM call (e.g., registering a class object, importing or exporting an interface pointer). This API can only be called once per process, and it sets up critical defaults that affect your code both as a server and as a client of COM interfaces. We will cover all the parameters of this subtle API in a logical progression from authentication to access control to client trust.

```
HRESULT CoInitializeSecurity(
    void* pSecDesc,              // access control
    LONG cAuthnSvc,              // authentication
    SOLE_AUTHENTICATION_SERVICE*
        prgAuthnSvc,             // authentication
    void* pReserved1,            // m.b.z.
    DWORD dwAuthnLevel,          // authentication
    DWORD dwImpLevel,            // client trust
    void* pReserved2,            // m.b.z.
    DWORD dwCapabilities,        // misc
    void* pReserved3             // m.b.z.
);
```

In any secure distributed system, authentication is the first task at hand. Authentication is the process of one security principal proving its identity to another security principal. Several protocols have been defined for authentication, and most involve some form of handshake that avoids sending passwords across the wire. These protocols are abstracted by a COM-like interface known as SSPI (security support provider interface). This allows Microsoft and third-party vendors to plug in loadable security support provider (SSP) dynamic-link libraries (DLLs) to support authentication protocols such as NTLM and Kerberos (see Item 40).

The `cAuthSvc` and `prgAuthnSvc` parameters to `CoInitialize-Security` allow you to choose which SSPs you wish to use in the current process. Unless you have a compelling reason not to, simply pass -1 for `cAuthSvc` and NULL for `prgAuthnSvc` to get the default authentication packages for your machine. Under Windows NT 4.0, NTLM is the only SSP available; however, Windows NT 5.0 will add Kerberos and possibly others. By simply choosing the defaults, your code will transparently use the best authentication protocol available. Once you've selected which SSPs to use, it is important to understand the different levels of service they can provide, as summarized in the following table.

RPC_C_AUTHN_LEVEL_NONE	Do not authenticate.
RPC_C_AUTHN_LEVEL_CONNECT	Authenticate caller's credentials at connection request.
RPC_C_AUTHN_LEVEL_CALL	CONNECT, plus sign first packet header of each call to ensure RPC header is not tampered with.
RPC_C_AUTHN_LEVEL_PKT	CALL, plus sign each packet header of each call to ensure RPC header is not tampered with.
RPC_C_AUTHN_LEVEL_PKT_INTEGRITY	PKT, plus sign each packet payload to ensure RPC parameters are not tampered with.
RPC_C_AUTHN_LEVEL_PKT_PRIVACY	INTEGRITY, plus encrypt each packet payload to ensure RPC parameters are protected from packet sniffers.

Ultimately, the proxy controls the level of authentication for each call. In fact, the `CoSetProxyBlanket` API allows you to adjust the level of authentication on each individual interface proxy (see Item 41). During a call, the server can obtain information about the level of authentication in use and decide whether to reject a call.[1] This check can be performed on a call-by-call basis via CoQueryClientBlanket:

```
const DWORD MY_MIN_AUTHN = RPC_C_AUTHN_LEVEL_CONNECT;
HRESULT CoBankAccount::Withdraw(long cBucks) {
    DWORD dwAuthnLevel = 0;
    HRESULT hr = CoQueryClientBlanket(
                        0,0,0,
                        &dwAuthnLevel,
                        0,0,0);
    if (FAILED(hr) || dwAuthnLevel < MY_MIN_AUTHN)
        return E_ACCESSDENIED;
    // normal code goes here...
}
```

[1] Note that depending on the actual underlying transport and security provider, certain authentication levels (CONNECT or higher) may be promoted automatically, so a good practice is to look for a range of values (e.g., `dwAuthnLevel >= MY_MIN_AUTHN` as opposed to `dwAuthnLevel == MY_REQUIRED_AUTHN`). A good example of this is same-machine activities—in this case, COM promotes the authentication level to PRIVACY because local communications are implicitly private. Note that this particular promotion does not cause encryption to occur. The privacy is implicit in that no bits actually go across the wire.

This forms the basic model of authentication in COM. The caller chooses the level of authentication for a call (via a setting on the proxy), and the callee decides whether it's good enough. However, for most servers that care about security, having to write this gatekeeper code to watch for unauthenticated clients is tedious and error-prone. For this reason, COM allows applications that export interface pointers to set an automatic low-water mark for authentication via the dwAuthnLevel parameter to CoInitializeSecurity. If a call comes in below this level, it is automatically rejected with E_ACCESSDENIED.

From a server's perspective, this feature makes it pretty easy to secure access to all the objects within the process from illegitimate callers. However, it leaves the client guessing what level of authentication to choose for a given proxy in order to avoid getting E_ACCESSDENIED. One approach to solving this would be to have the proxy default to RPC_C_AUTHN_LEVEL_PRIVACY, but this has two drawbacks. The first should be obvious: performance will suffer dramatically if all packets are encrypted. The second is much more subtle: a proxy with this authentication setting will always attempt authentication, even if the server does not require it. If authentication fails (e.g., the client is running Windows CE at home and doesn't even have a user account to authenticate against), the client will be denied access. In this case, the client would need to explicitly set the authentication level to RPC_C_AUTHN_LEVEL_NONE on each interface proxy. Once again, we leave the client guessing.

COM solves this problem elegantly by providing security hints. When a proxy is first created at unmarshal time, it knows exactly what the exporting process chose for a low-water mark (specifically, the client obtains this information during object export identifier [OXID] resolution). The proxy can then use this information to set a reasonable authentication level.

There is a devious twist to this story, however. The dwAuthnLevel parameter is actually overloaded so that it works for importers as well as exporters. When a proxy is created in the client's apartment, it looks not only at the hint obtained from the server but also at the authentication level specified by dwAuthnLevel in the client's call to CoInitializeSecurity. The proxy then chooses the highest of the two levels. While this tends to make systems more secure (because it tends to push authentication levels higher), it can also trip you up. If you want to export *and* import interface pointers (this symmetry is one of the greatest features of COM), you have only a single setting with which to play. Understanding this dichotomy is essential to developing distributed COM applications that function in predictable ways.

With that said, here are some general rules of thumb[2] for using the dwAuthnLevel parameter of CoInitializeSecurity:

1. Servers: if you want *any* anonymous callers to be allowed into your process, you must choose RPC_C_AUTHN_LEVEL_NONE.

2. Servers: if you don't want anonymous callers, but prefer rather to know who your clients are (so you can control access, audit, etc.), choose CONNECT or PKT.

3. Clients: always choose RPC_C_AUTHN_LEVEL_NONE. This will allow you to leverage the security hints provided by COM and use only the level of authentication that each server requires. If you need something different, you can always adjust the proxy settings explicitly. This setting will also allow you to receive unauthenticated callbacks (authenticated callbacks are often difficult in systems based on NT 4 because of missing trust relationships between domains).

After determining your authentication settings, the next step is to choose an access control policy to determine who is and who isn't allowed to perform privileged operations. Once again, it is completely possible for an object to trap each incoming call and explicitly grant or deny access to a user (see Item 42); however, this is tedious and error-prone. COM provides four built-in mechanisms for choosing an overall access control policy for a process, and they are all overloaded in the first parameter (pSecDesc) of CoInitializeSecurity:

1. Pass NULL. COM will not perform any automatic access checking. (Note that this is the only setting you can use if you choose RPC_C_AUTHN_LEVEL_NONE.)

2. Pass a pointer to a security descriptor. The DACL[3] controls who can enter the process via a COM call.

3. Pass a pointer to an implementation of IAccessControl. This is just a platform-independent way to perform option 2.

4. Pass a pointer to an AppID (a globally unique identifier [GUID]). COM looks in the registry for all of the settings for CoInitialize-Security. This setting is designed for surrogate processes such as DLL-HOST.EXE, and you should generally avoid it.

---

[2] Rules of thumb don't excuse you from understanding the underlying model and thinking long and hard about how to deal with authentication levels in your designs.

[3] Discretionary access control list.

Passing a security descriptor is trivial except for a few gotchas.[4] IAccess-Control is an interface that abstracts the implementation of a DACL and allows platforms that don't have a full implementation of NT security to play (e.g., Windows 9X). The EOAC_XXXX flags that you pass for dwCapabilities help COM figure out exactly what sort of pointer you are passing (IAccess-Control or AppID), if you are not simply passing a security descriptor.

No matter how you choose to implement your access control policy, be extremely careful to always grant access to the System account. The COM Service Control Manager (SCM) runs as this principal, and denying access to the SCM leads to various indecipherable error messages, the most notorious of which is E_OUT-OFMEMORY. The OXID resolver also runs under the System account and needs access to COM processes to provide rundown services (i.e., unwinding references from clients that have stopped sending liveness notifications). The following code shows how to form the SID for the System account that does not depend on names (remember that well-known account names are localized, so avoid using LookupAccountName):

```
void* AllocLocalSystemSID() {
    SID_IDENTIFIER_AUTHORITY a = SECURITY_NT_AUTHORITY;
    void* psid = 0;
    AllocateAndInitializeSid( &a, 1,
                          SECURITY_LOCAL_SYSTEM_RID,
                          0, 0, 0, 0, 0, 0, 0, &psid );
    return psid;
}
```

So far, we've discussed using CoInitializeSecurity to specify the default SSP, default authentication level, and access control policy. There is one final setting that applies purely to proxies that you import. This is the default impersonation level, dwImpLevel. Impersonation level specifies a degree of trust in the objects that you use and ranges from zero trust (anonymous) to infinite trust (delegation):

---

[4] At the time of this writing (NT 4, Service Pack 3), this security descriptor has several odd requirements. First of all, it must be in absolute format (not self-relative). Second, the owner and primary group security identifiers (SIDs) must be set (this is mainly an annoyance since they are never used anyway). Most frameworks deal with this by obtaining these SIDs from the process token (via OpenProcessToken and GetTokenInformation). Failure to properly form this rather fragile parameter to CoInitializeSecurity causes the function to return E_INVALIDARG, much to the developer's chagrin.

`RPC_C_IMP_LEVEL_ANONYMOUS`	Do not allow server to see or use client's log-on token.
`RPC_C_IMP_LEVEL_IDENTIFY`	Allow server to see (but not use) client's log-on token.
`RPC_C_IMP_LEVEL_IMPERSON-ATE`	Allow server to see client's log-on token and use it to make system calls up to one machine hop away from client's actual log-on.
`RPC_C_IMP_LEVEL_DELEGATE`	Allow server to see client's log-on token and use it to make system calls any number of machine hops away from client's actual log-on.

The Anonymous setting is not currently implemented, and there are no plans (as of this writing) to include it in NT 5. If you specify this level, COM will automatically promote it to IDENTIFY. Delegation is not supported as of this writing, but Kerberos in NT 5 will provide support for it, although you should temper your anticipation of this feature (see Item 40).

That leaves you with IDENTIFY and IMPERSONATE. It is extremely useful to understand the implications of these settings. If you make an authenticated call to an object, the object can obtain your token regardless of the impersonation level you specify. The impersonation level simply says *what the object can do with your token*. The mechanism provided by Windows NT for obtaining a client's token is impersonation (followed by a call to `OpenThreadToken`), so this implies that as long as a call is authenticated, the object can always call `CoImpersonateClient` to obtain your token, regardless of the impersonation level. This is somewhat counterintuitive to the naming of the impersonation-level settings. Once the object has obtained your token, that token will be annotated with the level of impersonation you chose. This is how the system limits the object's use of the token.

`RPC_C_IMP_LEVEL_IDENTIFY` allows the object to peek inside the token to determine your identity, the groups you belong to, and so on, but does not allow the object to open any secured executive objects (e.g., NTFS files and registry keys) under the auspices of that token. `RPC_C_IMP_LEVEL_IMPER-SONATE`, on the other hand, allows the object to open executive objects using your credentials, but this privilege only extends to the machine on which the object is running. Delegation (when supported) extends this privilege infinitely.

Since you should generally avoid running code under an impersonation token (see Item 40), it is a good practice to use `RPC_C_IMP_LEVEL_IDENTIFY` unless absolutely necessary. Remember, this is only the default setting for proxies; you can always adjust this setting via `CoSetProxyBlanket`.

So what happens if you forget to call `CoInitializeSecurity`? Well, in order to support legacy applications that were written before COM security was introduced, there are settings in the registry that can be manipulated using a tool called DCOMCNFG.[5] COM uses these settings to implicitly call `CoInitializeSecurity` on your behalf. Be afraid. Be very afraid. In fact, how does COM determine which AppID to use for your application if, for instance, you simply launch it by double-clicking it? Taking a peek at the registry under `HKEY_CLASSES_ROOT\AppID` will give you a clue (go look for yourself!). There are lists of EXE files (just filenames, no paths) that point to AppIDs.

Even if COM happens to find the correct AppID for your server, how do you know what settings it will find there? DCOMCNFG is a developer's tool and is not at all end user friendly. For example, as of this writing, the administrator must know to include the System account in your access permission list in order for your application to function correctly.

If you are deploying your components in Microsoft Transaction Server (MTS), the story is considerably better. The MTS Explorer provides a much cleaner and more reliable interface for security configuration. If you configure your components to run in a server package (that is, out-of-process), the MTS surrogate (MTX.EXE) will call `CoInitializeSecurity` with the appropriate parameters. MTS surrogates allow the administrator to configure the process-wide authentication level and nothing else. MTX.EXE will use the default SSPs. MTX.EXE turns off COM access control by registering a NULL DACL. It can safely do this because it layers its own role-based access control scheme on top of COM authentication.

The message is: if you don't use MTS, seize the reins and call `CoInitializeSecurity`. Do not force your users to rely on DCOMC-NFG to make your application work. For the few settings that must be in the registry,[6] put them there yourself and provide your own simplified user interface for letting the end user configure them (if they need configuring at all).

Take time to understand the security issues you face. Take control over your application's environment. It is virtually impossible to have a stable COM server that does not deal with security, because administrators are not perfect. They will occasionally screw up machine-wide default registry settings that you might be counting on implicitly. Design security into your application from the start.

---

[5] DCOMCNFG is notorious for being rather buggy.

[6] `LaunchPermission` is an obvious one, as well as `RunAs` (see Item 39).

39. Avoid As-Activator activation.

The COM infrastructure is lazy. Proxies don't aggregate in interface marshalers until receiving a client's `QueryInterface` for an interface. COM servers don't start listening on a network transport until a client using that protocol requests service. In fact, a COM application isn't even brought to life as a process unless a client needs to use objects hosted in that application. This last aspect of COM laziness is what this item deals with.

When it comes time for the SCM to launch a process to service an incoming activation request (via a client's call to `CoCreateInstanceEx`, `CoGetClassObject`, etc.), it must first obtain a security token with which to create the new process. Normally when you log in interactively to Windows NT, you present your credentials (authority, principal, password), and the log-on daemon starts the shell (typically EXPLORER.EXE) using a token that holds your identity and the groups to which you belong, as well as any privileges you hold on that machine. Whenever you launch an application from the shell, `CreateProcess` simply reaches up and copies your token for use by the new process. Every user mode process running on Windows NT must have a token.

So which token should the SCM choose for your server process? The token of the interactively logged-on user? What if no user is logged on? How about the Administrator account? The Guest account? Clearly, this is an important decision over which you would like to have some control as a COM developer.

If you don't deal with this explicitly, the SCM uses the principle of least surprise (pardon the pun) and chooses a policy of Run As Activator. This implies that when your server is launched, it will run with the client's security token. This certainly seems reasonable as the default, since the system must choose *some* policy for picking a token for your application. Typically, there is no interactive user logged in on a server machine anyway, and using well-known accounts like Administrator or Guest would seldom be appropriate or appreciated by end users.

Imagine the implications of this default setting on a distributed application. First of all, in order to make this work, your server must be able to obtain a meaningful token for the client, which means you must be able to authenticate the client. So right off the bat, the SCM simply cannot launch a COM application on behalf of an anonymous client if that application uses the Run As Activator policy.

Let's say all your clients can be authenticated. What happens when your server attempts to access remote secure resources, such as a file on a network share, or a remote COM server? This effectively requires delegation of the client's security token, which as of this writing is not supported by the default SSP (Kerberos will provide this in the future).

Fine; as an experienced COM developer, you know there's always a workaround. Why not just call `LogonUser` and get access to local and remote resources under the guise of some distinguished security principal? So off you go to create a special account in the domain for your server and to write the code to call `LogonUser`/ `ImpersonateLoggedOnUser`. You soon discover that in order to call `LogonUser`, you must have a special privilege known as TCB, or Trusted Computing Base. Great. You are so close to a solution you can feel it. Now all you need is to somehow get this TCB privilege into your token so you can call `LogonUser`. But to whose account should you grant the TCB privilege? It's simple: since you run as activator, you must grant the privilege to all clients that could possibly call into your application. For a moment you actually consider granting everyone the right to call `LogonUser`. If you are lucky, by this time one of your colleagues has realized what you are about to do and has jarred you out of your security-induced nightmare. Granting everyone the right to call `LogonUser` would leave a gaping security hole where anyone who could log on locally could execute code that looped until it guessed the administrator's password (or anybody else's password for that matter). This is an extremely bad idea!

Obviously, this is not a solution. Before we discover the real solution, there is yet one more issue that the Run As Activator policy raises: the notion of resource sharing and `REGCLS_MULTIPLEUSE` semantics.

Most distributed applications aim to scale to support reasonably large numbers of users. To make this happen, servers are written with the goal of sharing resources carefully between clients. When a COM-based server publishes class objects, it always specifies `REGCLS_MULTIPLEUSE` to designate a preference for a single instance of the server to service all client activation requests. This allows the server to manage concurrency and cache resources that can be shared among clients. So if your application is supposed to run as activator, how can there possibly be a single instance of it? If Susan activates an object in your server, the SCM starts an instance of your server running with an impersonation token from Susan. If Rick comes along ten minutes later and activates an object in your server, the SCM happily creates another instance running with Rick's token. By the way, if the client is on a remote machine, the server process will not be able to access secure network resources such as remote file servers, unless delegation is enabled (see item 38). Obviously, this is not what you want in a scalable application.

Hopefully, the answer is becoming clear. Why not tell the SCM up front about a distinguished principal whose token should be used to launch your server no matter who the activator is? This is in fact the recommended way to configure distributed servers. It solves many problems. Unauthenticated clients can call the server (if the authentication policy allows for this—see Item 38). The server can access local resources. The server can access remote resources. The server is now a first-class citizen!

The way to specify this preferred setting is to create a RunAs named value under your AppID key (this is one of the few settings that must be configured via the registry, since your process is not yet running when it is evaluated). By default, if no such named value exists, your application gets the Run As Activator policy, which is clearly bad for a distributed system. Specify the key as follows:

```
HKEY_CLASSES_ROOT/AppID/{...}
    RunAs="Domain\User"
```

This looks great so far. So the SCM simply looks up this value and calls LogonUser—but doesn't LogonUser require a cleartext password? Where does that come from? It turns out that the Local Security Authority (LSA) sub-system keeps a special encrypted dictionary of local secrets that is used for storing passwords such as this. The DCOMCNFG tool uses the LSA API to set the RunAs secret. Check out the DCOMPERM example that ships with the Platform SDK as an example of programming the LSA. Be aware that Administrator privileges are required to read or write this password, which is why DCOMCNFG complains if you try to run it under a security principal that is not a member of the local Administrators group.

You should also consider extending your setup program to automatically add this account when your product is installed. Be sure to grant the new account the "Log on as a Batch Job" privilege (again this can be done via the LSA API); otherwise, activation requests will fail (the SCM calls LogonUser using a batch log-on). DCOMCNFG automatically adds this privilege when you use the Identity tab to specify the RunAs principal.[7]

There is a special account that you might want your server to run as: System. The LocalSystem account (a.k.a. System) is the most privileged account on any machine. It is a member of the local Administrators group and has many privileges that even administrators do not have. This represents the "operating system" and is implicitly trusted. LocalSystem is so trusted it is included as part of the trusted computing base and can call LogonUser at will. The only way to

---

[7] However, as of this writing (NT 4, Service Pack 3), DCOMCNFG fails to do this correctly on backup domain controllers. But it's the thought that counts.

run as LocalSystem is to write your setup program so that it installs your COM server as an NT Service (via the `CreateService` API), which itself is a privileged operation that requires a member of the local Administrators group to run your setup application. It is worthwhile to discuss the benefits and drawbacks of running under the LocalSystem account.

By default, LocalSystem has access to almost all resources on the local machine, including the interactive window station (e.g., LocalSystem can programmatically scrape the screen of any locally logged-on user who doesn't explicitly say otherwise). LocalSystem has virtually unlimited access to the registry, all kernel resources created by any application that passes NULL for the `SECURITY_AT-TRIBUTES` parameter, and most files in a secure NTFS partition.

As of this writing, LocalSystem has no network credentials.[8] This means you cannot access remote secure resources such as shared file systems or COM servers. However, since LocalSystem is part of the trusted computing base, you could easily call `LogonUser` (or for COM, fill out a `COAUTHIDENTITY` structure and call `CoSetProxyBlanket`) to obtain a token with network credentials and remedy this. So it is safe to say that when running as LocalSystem, you can have your cake and eat it too, although you may have to do a little more typing.

No matter what identity you choose in your AppID, COM will hold you to it. When you call `CoRegisterClassObject`, COM checks the class identifier (CLSID) you are registering and verifies that you are in fact running as the principal specified in the `RunAs` named value of the associated AppID. This prevents rogue users from spoofing COM servers by launching a process that calls `CoRegisterClassObject` before the legitimate server is launched by the SCM.

This feature makes it difficult to debug your application's startup code. In this scenario, you'd typically launch your application from an interactive log-on in a debugger. If you do this, you will probably be logged on as "Joe Programmer," rather than as the distinguished principal normally used by your server. If this is the case, COM will complain that "Joe Programmer" is not the user who is designated as the `RunAs` principal by returning `CO_E_WRONG_SERVER_IDENTITY` when you call `CoRegisterClassObject`. Another nasty problem that creeps up when debugging COM applications launched by the SCM is that of window stations. Normally COM servers do not provide their own user interface (see Item 3), but what happens when you run a debug build of your application and an `ASSERT` macro fires? COM applications started by the SCM that are designated to run as a distinguished principal normally run in a noninteractive window station, where

---

[8] NT 5 is slated to correct this for those using the Kerberos SSP.

it is totally legal to put up modal dialog boxes (as the `ASSERT` call will do). However, no live human is there to see this dialog or press the OK button to dismiss it, so your thread is effectively hung. If you were in the middle of processing a client's call, the client will appear unresponsive. At this point, you will probably start checking network cables to make sure none have been chewed on recently by the mice that seem to have infested your lab since you started using COM to develop distributed systems.

These are the reasons for the third possible setting for `RunAs`. Run As Interactive User is a simple policy that you can use when debugging your application. While extremely useful for debugging, you should generally avoid Run As Interactive User for production code, as it is very difficult to predict who the interactive user will be at any given time. If an administrator is logged in, the code will run with administrative privileges. This could be good or bad, depending on how trusted the code is. If Joe User is logged in with guest privileges, your code will run with guest privileges. This could be good or bad, depending on whether your code needed to do anything useful. If no one is logged on interactively, all activation requests to your server will fail. This is almost always bad. So, prefer `RunAs="SomeUser"` for release code, make use of `RunAs="Interactive User"` for debugging, and avoid Run As Activator altogether.

40. Avoid impersonation.

Impersonation is the mechanism in NT that allows a thread in your server to temporarily take on the identity of a client in order to attempt some operation that the client may or may not have permission to perform. This is an incredibly simple model and, as such, works well for simple programs. Unfortunately, the naïve use of impersonation doesn't scale well to more sophisticated systems.

Let's step back and recall the basic access control technique used by Windows NT. Take the registry as an example. When you open a registry key, say for `KEY_READ` access, the Security Reference Monitor (SRM) is consulted to determine whether the security principal opening the key has been granted the permission to use the access mask being requested (`KEY_READ`). If you do in fact have these permissions, you will be given a valid handle to the key, and the handle will be annotated with the access mask you requested (`KEY_READ`). You can now use this handle at will, and all further access checks will be performed against the mask cached in the handle. This is a great performance win when compared with making another call to the SRM at each system call. This technique provides reasonable security with reasonable performance.

Now imagine an interactive application that wishes to run forever.[9] Some principal, say a clerk in the company, launches the application, and throughout the lifetime of the process, a manager may occasionally wander by the terminal and need to perform some privileged operation. Rather than log out and log back in (that takes time, you know), the application simply displays a dialog to collect new credentials (authority, principal, password). The application then logs on the new user and starts impersonating the token on the main application thread (via `LogonUser`/`ImpersonateLoggedOnUser`).

Consider the problems inherent in this technique. Any handles already opened by the application have cached access masks that do not reflect the manager's access permissions and must be closed and reopened (`DuplicateHandle` is also an option) to gain the manager's level of access. Handles opened with the `MAXIMUM_ALLOWED` access mask are the most obvious case.

What about when attempts are made to call out of the process using COM? COM ignores the thread token (the impersonation token) and prefers the process token for the default identity of a proxy (unless you explicitly cloak[10]). This means that *each interface proxy* must be annotated with the credentials of the user being impersonated. Does this sound like a fun application to develop or debug?

There is another obvious flaw in the above scheme. The clerk must be granted the TCB privilege to allow the `LogonUser` call to succeed. The danger of granting the TCB privilege to wide groups of users is discussed in Item 39. Not to mention that interactively collecting credentials from a user opens the possibility of a trojan horse that simulates your application's log-on dialog to learn a user's password.[11]

Given this background, consider a COM server that impersonates a client (via `CoImpersonateClient`). If you choose to require client authentication (see Item 38), you will not need to call `LogonUser` to get the client's token, since the token will be obtained automatically during the authentication handshake. However, the other issues (and some we have not yet discussed) still apply.

---

[9] Or until the next service pack is released, whichever comes first.

[10] Cloaking is a feature that will be available in NT 5. By calling `CoSetProxyBlanket`, COM will capture the identity of the currently executing thread on your next outgoing call through the proxy.

[11] This is why you press Ctrl+Alt+Delete to get a log-in dialog in Windows NT. This *secure attention sequence* is trappable only by privileged driver code.

The naïve use of impersonation as an access control tool can easily lead to a proliferation of DACLs that becomes difficult to manage. Imagine the following code (with irrelevant error checking omitted for brevity):

```
HRESULT CoBank::GetAccount( long nID,
                            REFIID iid, void** ppv ) {
  CoImpersonateClient();
  HANDLE hf = CreateFile( GetAccountFile( nID ),
                   MAXIMUM_ALLOWED,
                   0, 0, OPEN_EXISTING, 0, 0 );
  CoRevertToSelf();
  // check for potential access denied errors
  if ( INVALID_HANDLE_VALUE == hf )
    return HRESULT_FROM_WIN32( GetLastError() );

  CoAccount* pAccount = new CoAccount( hf );
  pAccount->AddRef();
  hr = pAccount->QueryInterface( iid, ppv );
  pAccount->Release();
  return hr;
}
```

This code demonstrates the classic pattern for impersonation: impersonate the client, attempt to access some resource (which may fail with E_ACCESSDENIED), then revert to your original identity. The code seems rather straightforward, but note that a DACL must be kept on each bank account file. What if a bank account were stored in several files? What if you need to access registry keys? What if you need to write to a shared memory section? Each of these elements would require a DACL, and managing these DACLs is terribly difficult in a distributed system because they are associated with disparate resources that may be distributed across many hosts. What if you decide to change your implementation to use a database rather than a file?

Another subtle problem with the code is this: what if the bank account file is not on the local machine, but rather resides on a network share? The call to CreateFile will fail unless the client has enabled delegation by specifying RPC_C_IMP_LEVEL_DELEGATE in a call to CoInitializeSecurity or CoSetProxyBlanket. The NTLM SSP does not support delegation, so NT 4 clients using NTLM will be excluded. Even with NT 5 and the Kerberos SSP, clients should be wary of granting delegation authority. Even the above code assumes the client is using RPC_C_IMP_LEVEL_IMPERSONATE; otherwise, the call to CreateFile would have failed.

When developing a sophisticated COM application, consider taking a different approach for access control. Use impersonation to determine whether a client has rights to perform the logical operation at hand. Do this at a designated entry point into your application (e.g., for the bank application, this might be when creating an instance of the Bank object or opening a particular bank account). Try to *impersonate only for the purposes of obtaining the client's token.* Then use the client's token to verify access (see Item 42), but do so while running under your own token, not the client's. The following code takes this approach:

```
HRESULT CoBank::GetAccount( long nID,
                            REFIID iid, void** ppv ) {
  // impersonate temporarily to get the client's token
  CoImpersonateClient();
  HANDLE htok = 0;
  OpenThreadToken( GetCurrentThread(), TOKEN_QUERY,
                   TRUE, &htok );
  CoRevertToSelf();

  // use token to determine the maximum access rights
  // client has to account. Note SD is not necessarily
  // associated with the physical account file...
  DWORD grfAccess = 0;
  BOOL bAccessGranted = FALSE;
  AccessCheck( GetSDForAccount( nID ), htok,
               MAXIMUM_ALLOWED, ...,
               &grfAccess, &bAccessGranted );
  CloseHandle(htok);
  if ( !bAccessGranted )
    return (*ppv = 0), E_ACCESSDENIED;

  // CreateFile won't fail due to security constraints
  HANDLE hf = CreateFile( GetAccountFile( nID ),
                          GENERIC_READ | GENERIC_WRITE,
                          0, 0, OPEN_EXISTING, 0, 0 );

  // cache the access mask with the account
  CoAccount* pAccount = new CoAccount( hf, grfAccess );
  pAccount->AddRef();
  hr = pAccount->QueryInterface( iid, ppv );
  pAccount->Release();
  return hr;
}
```

The new version works for clients that specify impersonation levels of IDENTIFY or greater. Also, the call to `CreateFile` will not have difficulty accessing remote files because the call is made with the token of the bank application rather than attempting to use the client's token. Security descriptors can be kept in a single location for easy management (e.g., as a blob in a database or as a memory-mapped file). For more strategies for fine-grained access control, see Item 42.

There is one final issue that deserves mentioning. If your application needs to scale to support hundreds, thousands, or hundreds of thousands of users, it needs to share resources carefully among clients. The naïve use of impersonation (e.g., our first version of `GetAccount`) impedes the ability to share security-sensitive resources. As an example, imagine that you decided to store the actual data for all bank accounts in a relational database, and you planned to access this data via ODBC or OLE DB. If you needed to perform operations on the database using the client's credentials (in order to let the database system determine the client's permissions), each client must have a separate connection to the database. This would be incredibly expensive.

If, on the other hand, you choose to simply impersonate the client to obtain the client's token and do access checking yourself, clients can share database connections because the database assumes that your application has already performed an access check. Generally speaking, it's much easier to do access checks closer to the client (e.g., in the middle tier) than further away from the client.

The moral of the story is to use impersonation with care. As a rule of thumb, your main application logic and resource acquisition code should execute under the process token rather than under an impersonation token. Take time early in your design iterations to consider how you plan to control access to objects, and avoid being seduced by the deceptive simplicity of impersonation.

41. Use fine-grained authentication.

Authentication is a fascinating topic.[12] It is defined as the mechanism by which one security principal proves its identity to another security principal. You participate in authentication every day when you see people you know on the street—visually and audibly you are assured that they are who they claim to be. However, if you weren't sure of the identity of the other person (maybe they just looked like someone you used to know), you might ask them questions before making any assumptions about their identity. One type of question you could ask would disclose a secret that only you and the other person remembered (like the name of the movie that the two of you saw on your first date). This would make you feel

---

[12] Read Bruce Schneier's excellent book, *Applied Cryptography*, if you want to be captivated.

reasonably comfortable that you knew to whom you were talking. In fact, there is an authentication protocol based on this idea: basic authentication.

Basic authentication is a protocol often used on HTTP and FTP servers to prove the identity of clients. It is a simple protocol. The connecting client (Alice) prepends the request message with her name and a secret that only she and the server (Bob) know (this takes the form of a password). This is a very efficient mechanism; however, if this information is sent in the clear (i.e., not encrypted), it will only work at most one time. Any eavesdropper can see this information (via NetMon and friends) and can later impersonate Alice's identity and talk to Bob, so Bob can never really be sure the caller is Alice.

To avoid sending secrets over the wire, you could take a slightly more sophisticated approach and use a simple challenge-response scheme. This is the mechanism used by Windows NT up through version 4.0, via the NTLM security support provider. This protocol is also very simple. Alice sends a message to Bob indicating that she wishes to be authenticated via NTLM. Bob crufts up an 8-byte random number that represents the challenge[13] and sends this back to Alice. Alice takes the challenge plus her password as input to a one-way function that produces a 24-byte response. She sends this response back to Bob along with her authority and principal name (e.g., "CorporateDomain\Alice"). Bob then forwards the challenge/response pair (along with Alice's authority and principal name) on to the Local Security Authority (LSASS.EXE) running on his own machine.

Ultimately, what Bob needs is a security token representing Alice, and the LSA is the subsystem responsible for producing these tokens. The LSA simply peeks at Alice's password[14] and calculates the response from the challenge to verify that the caller is really Alice. However, unless Bob is running on a domain controller for "CorporateDomain," Bob's LSA does not know Alice's password. In this case, Bob's LSA simply forwards the request to his domain controller. If Bob is also a member of "CorporateDomain," then the LSA on Bob's domain controller can satisfy the request. Otherwise, the request is forwarded (yet again) to a domain controller in "CorporateDomain" if a trust relationship exists.[15] The main drawbacks to this mechanism are as follows:

---

[13] The challenge is not completely random because Bob is not allowed to send the same challenge twice (this avoids potential replay attacks).

[14] Actually, the LSA sees a hash of Alice's password, but this is the same hash that Alice used to calculate the response.

[15] This mechanism is commonly known as *pass-through authentication*.

1. Domain controllers can be saturated by authentication requests.

2. Bob knows who Alice is, but Alice doesn't know who Bob is (NTLM only offers one-way authentication).

A more secure and scalable solution is the Kerberos authentication protocol, which scales better because it amortizes the cost of authentication over three subprotocols. When Alice logs on, the first subprotocol of Kerberos authentication takes place (obtaining a ticket-granting ticket from her domain controller). When Alice connects to Bob for the first time, the second subprotocol takes place (obtaining a server ticket from the domain controller for Bob). From here on out, each new connection from Alice to Bob is not nearly as expensive and does not require round-trips to a domain controller.[16] Also, Kerberos allows for an extra leg in the third subprotocol to provide mutual authentication, so Alice can also ascertain Bob's identity, all without hitting a domain controller.

No matter what authentication protocol you choose, it is interesting to consider what happens when Alice executes the following code:

```
void TalkToBob( IBob* pBob ) {
   pBob->SendMessage( OLESTR("Hello Bob,") );
   pBob->SendMessage( OLESTR("this is Alice!") );
   }
```

Assuming Bob has required authentication for all incoming clients, then clearly the first call Alice makes to Bob will require some sort of authentication handshake, which may require extra round-trips. However, what happens when Alice makes a second call to Bob using the same proxy? Is this second call authenticated? The answer is that it depends on the level of service you request from your security support provider. RPC_C_AUTHN_LEVEL_NONE turns off authentication completely. RPC_C_AUTHN_LEVEL_CONNECT will perform the authentication handshake on the first outgoing call. After this, as long as you hold the object proxy, no further authentication will be provided. So Bob is not guaranteed that the second call in the above code really came from Alice. How could an intruder (Mallory[17]) take advantage of this? If Bob held valuable resources that made it worth his while, Mallory could compromise a router and hijack Alice's connection and have his way with Bob. To protect against this, Bob might prefer to require RPC_C_AUTHN_LEVEL_PKT authentication. This level ensures that every request and response packet header is digitally signed by the sender

---

[16] Tickets expire after eight hours (by default), so eventually Alice will go back to the domain controller, but the number of round-trips is negligible compared with NTLM.

[17] The names Alice, Bob, Mallory, and Eve are classic names used in cryptography circles to denote **A** sending a message to **B** with a **Mal**icious active attacker or a passive **Eaves**dropping attacker trying to subvert the process.

using a shared secret known only to Alice and Bob. This makes it easy for Bob to verify that each packet is really coming from Alice.

This raises an interesting question: how do Alice and Bob get this shared secret in the first place? It turns out that this is the second great feature of all interesting authentication protocols (including NTLM and Kerberos). During the handshake, both Alice and Bob discover a random set of bits (they both end up with the same bits) that they can use to do cool tricks like per-packet authentication to foil attackers like Mallory. This is called a *shared secret*.

Mallory is unhappy. He cannot impersonate Alice and make authenticated calls to Bob to complete his evil plans (whatever they might be). But Mallory still owns a router that Bob and Alice are using to communicate. After some experimentation, he realizes that he can alter the payload of Alice's message in such a way that the simple IP checksum will not be disturbed. Hah! He can now make small changes in just the right places, such as the bank account numbers in an electronic transfer of funds, and skip town before anybody notices!

Bob counters this by leveraging the secret he shares with Alice. He requires Alice to use `RPC_C_AUTHN_LEVEL_PKT_INTEGRITY`. At this level, the RPC runtime instructs the SSP to calculate a cryptographic hash of the headers *and payload* in the packet and to encrypt this hash (forming a digital signature). A cryptographic hash typically consists of 128 bits (or more) that appear to change completely randomly when a single bit of the hashed message changes. Mallory is foiled again! He cannot deterministically alter the messages without being detected. However, when Alice sends a large message to Bob, she notices some extra CPU cycles being dedicated to this hashing operation.

Mallory throws his keyboard down in disgust and gives up. Meanwhile, on the other side of town, Eve has picked up where Mallory left off. Eve (a jealous coworker at Bob's company) has decided to start listening in on Alice and Bob's conversation. So she fires up NetMon and starts listening on Bob's subnet, watching all the traffic between Alice and Bob. However, Bob looks over the cubicle wall and sees what she is up to and decides the next day to start requiring Alice to use `RPC_C_AUTHN_LEVEL_PKT_PRIVACY`. Now the RPC runtime encrypts the entire payload of each packet passed between Alice and Bob, using their shared key. This adds significant CPU cycles for large messages, but hey, Bob thinks Alice is worth it. Now the only information Eve can garner is related to traffic. She can see the host to which Bob is talking (by looking at the IP header or equivalent), as well as how often they communicate, but she cannot see the actual conversation. This is known as *end-to-end encryption*, in which routing information is exposed but the payload is encrypted. This is also the strongest security COM provides.

For completeness, RPC_C_AUTHN_LEVEL_CALL is also provided, but as of this writing it is always promoted to RPC_AUTHN_LEVEL_PKT anyway. If supported, this setting would only protect the first fragment of a call over connectionless transports such as UDP.

It should be clear that you take an ever-greater performance hit as you move into the higher levels of authentication quality-of-service. While Bob could certainly call CoInitializeSecurity and require PKT_PRIVACY for all clients all the time, this setting is unnecessarily high for most applications. Well-written secure COM applications use a higher granularity of authentication than just all-or-none. COM provides a gatekeeper for you (see Item 38), and you need to select the lowest allowable authentication level for your process when you call CoInitializeSecurity. Any client that tries to get in under the wire with a lower authentication level will be rejected at the front door. You will never even see those calls. To enforce higher levels of authentication, you'll need to do a little typing. Assuming Bob has chosen RPC_C_AUTHN_LEVEL_CONNECT as his low-water mark, he could do the following:

```
HRESULT CoBob::SendProtectedMessage(const OLECHAR*) {
    HRESULT hr = CoQueryClientBlanket(0, 0, 0,
                                      &dwAuthnLevel,
                                      0, 0, 0 );
    if (FAILED(hr) ||
        dwAuthnLevel < RPC_C_AUTHN_LEVEL_INTEGRITY)
        return E_ACCESSDENIED;
    // implementation goes here...
}
HRESULT CoBob::SendSecretMessage(const OLECHAR*) {
    HRESULT hr = CoQueryClientBlanket(0, 0, 0,
                                      &dwAuthnLevel,
                                      0, 0, 0 );
    if (FAILED(hr) ||
        dwAuthnLevel < RPC_C_AUTHN_LEVEL_PRIVACY)
        return E_ACCESSDENIED;
    // implementation goes here...
}
```

Bob should document the elevated authentication requirements of his methods so that Alice (or anyone else for that matter) will know the semantics of the method and will not be denied access. Assuming Alice has chosen

RPC_C_AUTHN_LEVEL_NONE as her default setting for proxies, she could write the following code (error checking omitted for brevity):

```
void TalkToBob(IBob* pSharedBob) {
    // default proxy will be set to CONNECT18
    IBob* pBob = 0;
    CoCopyProxy(pSharedBob,
                reinterpret_cast<IUnknown**>(&pBob));
    pBob->SendMessage(OLESTR("Hi Bob, this is Alice!"));

    DWORD dwAuthnSvc, dwAuthzSvc, dwImpLevel, grfCaps;
    CoQueryProxyBlanket(pBob, &dwAuthnSvc, &dwAuthzSvc,
                        0, 0, &dwImpLevel, &grfCaps);

    CoSetProxyBlanket(pBob, dwAuthnSvc, dwAuthzSvc, 0,
                      RPC_C_AUTHN_LEVEL_INTEGRITY,
                      dwImpLevel, grfCaps);
    pBob->SendProtectedMessage(
    OLESTR("Transfer $9000 from checking to savings,"));

    CoSetProxyBlanket(pBob, dwAuthnSvc, dwAuthzSvc, 0,
                      RPC_C_AUTHN_LEVEL_PRIVACY,
                      dwImpLevel, grfCaps);
    pBob->SendPrivateMessage(
       OLESTR("and meet me at the Ritz at eight."));

    pBob->Release();
}
```

Alice is a tough-as-nails developer. She writes client code that runs in the multi-threaded apartment (MTA), and she is very careful not to introduce race conditions into her code. In her application, she has designed pSharedBob as a shared resource in the MTA that many threads use, so Alice carefully uses CoCopyProxy to get her own private copy of the IBob interface proxy. This will allow her to change the security settings on her private copy of the proxy without affecting any other threads that happen to be using pSharedBob as well. If you aren't worried about race conditions and concurrency, you'll probably never need to use CoCopyProxy. Also note that Alice first called CoQueryProxyBlanket so she wouldn't accidentally muck up any other default settings on the proxy, such as the impersonation level. This makes her code easier to maintain since she doesn't hardcode things like

---

[18] Connectionless protocols normally promote CONNECT to CALL, and since CALL is always promoted to PKT, technically, the proxy will default to PKT if the underlying transport is connectionless (e.g., UDP), which is the default in Windows NT 4.

`RPC_C_AUTHN_WINNT` for the NTLM authentication service. Obviously, she wants to use Kerberos as soon as NT 5 ships!

Before we leave the discussion of fine-grained authentication, it is useful to understand the mechanism used by COM when dealing with activation requests such as `CoGetClassObject` and `CoCreateInstanceEx`. Recall that the `dwAuthnLevel` and `dwImpLevel` settings you specify when calling `CoInitializeSecurity` from a client application help determine the default settings for *proxies*. This has absolutely no effect on the security settings used for activation calls. If you want to control security settings for activation calls, you must explicitly provide them via a `COAUTHINFO` structure (recall that the `COSERVERINFO` structure points to one of these):

```
typedef struct _COAUTHINFO {
    DWORD                   dwAuthnSvc;
    DWORD                   dwAuthzSvc;
    LPWSTR                  pwszServerPrincName;
    DWORD                   dwAuthnLevel;
    DWORD                   dwImpersonationLevel;
    COAUTHIDENTITY *        pAuthIdentityData;
    DWORD                   dwCapabilities;
} COAUTHINFO;
```

This structure contains the same parameters used to control proxy security settings via `CoSetProxyBlanket`. Unless you explicitly provide your own settings, COM uses the following algorithm:

1. Attempt to execute the request using connect-level authentication and impersonate-level trust.

2. If step 1 fails, attempt to execute the request without authentication (i.e., `RPC_C_AUTHN_LEVEL_NONE`).

While these are reasonable defaults, you should consider using a finer-grained approach. Clients who know ahead of time that they cannot be authenticated (e.g., Internet-based clients) should either explicitly turn off authentication for activation requests or should provide alternate credentials that *can* be authenticated (via `COAUTHIDENTITY`). Turning off authentication results in a significant improvement in responsiveness during activation calls, since you don't have to wait for step 1 to fail (typically several network round-trips, which can sometimes take minutes due to timeouts) to fail. On the other hand, you might want to raise the authentication level for a highly secure application. In any case, be aware that you must always specify at least impersonate-level trust in the COAUTHINFO structure; otherwise, the remote SCM will not be able to perform the activation on your behalf. It is also important to understand that the proxy you obtain via remote activation still uses the default-negotiated authentication level (as discussed in Item 37), rather than the setting you specified via COAUTHINFO, so you may also need to explicitly adjust the authentication level on the proxy.

Be aware of the powerful service your SSP bestows upon you. You do not need to use the CryptoAPI to send private messages. You do not need to have every single message encrypted to have a secure application. Don't settle for a single level of authentication quality-of-service in your secure COM application. Use fine-grained authentication.

42. Use fine-grained access control.

Access control in any secure system is predicated upon the knowledge of a client's identity. Distributed systems, including COM, rely on authentication protocols to determine this identity. So before you embark on defining an access control policy for an application, realize that without authentication, access control is meaningless. Take CoInitializeSecurity, for example. The first parameter to CoInitializeSecurity is the access control policy for the application, but unless you choose RPC_C_AUTHN_LEVEL_CONNECT or higher, it is illegal to pass anything other than NULL. With that said, let's talk about some realistic strategies you can use to develop a meaningful access control policy.

COM provides two automatic access control checks, typically referred to as *access permissions* and *launch permissions*. COM uses the access permission policy to simply block callers at the door if the policy does not grant them access. On the other hand, COM only evaluates launch permissions when an incoming activation request would require the SCM to launch a COM application. Since the process is not yet running, you cannot specify launch permissions via CoInitializeSecurity, so you must place your launch permission policy in a named value (LaunchPermission) under your application's AppID key.

Both of these mechanisms are extremely coarse-grained. The decisions you make for these policies affect your entire application, not just a particular class, interface, or method call, so if you want a higher level of granularity, you'll have to do some typing. Ultimately, you will leverage the authentication service provided by COM to determine the client's identity, and then explicitly grant or deny access depending on what the client is trying to do. There are several approaches you might take. The first is to leverage impersonation.

Most developers who are forced to deal with access control first try to solve the problem by leveraging as much of the access control infrastructure built into the operating system as possible. This is a logical strategy. The most obvious way to provide fine-grained access control without having to do much typing is this: `CoImpersonateClient`. It seems so incredibly easy—just impersonate the client during every method call and let the underlying operating system deal with access checks. This way you don't have to bother developing a user interface for manipulating access control lists, and the administrator can simply set DACLs directly on the files, registry keys, and so forth on which your application relies. This works well for simple applications, but breaks down for most nontrivial systems, especially where the appropriate access control scheme is based on operations, not objects (see Item 40).

If you agree that impersonation will not be a good long-term solution for a fine-grained access control policy, the next logical step is to simply add security descriptors to your objects and call `AccessCheck` yourself. With this approach, you can provide your own security descriptor for each logical object in your application to which you want to control access:

```
HRESULT CoWidgetMaker::Shutdown() {
    // impersonate temporarily to get the client's token
    CoImpersonateClient();
    HANDLE htok = 0;
    OpenThreadToken(GetCurrentThread(), TOKEN_QUERY,
                    TRUE, &htok);
    CoRevertToSelf();

    // explicitly perform an access check to see whether
    // this client is allowed to shut down the reactormachine.
    BOOL bAccessGranted = FALSE;
    AccessCheck(m_pSecurityDescriptor, htok,
                SHUTDOWN_MACHINE, ...,
                &bAccessGranted );
    CloseHandle(htok);
    if (!bAccessGranted)
        return E_ACCESSDENIED;
    // do shutdown
    return S_OK;
}
```

Win32 provides plenty of support for this style of programming (see `CreatePrivateObjectSecurity` et al.), since this is the basic model of access control used in the operating system. It is a totally reasonable model with few drawbacks. The main drawbacks are that you must now develop an access control list editor (not a trivial task) and you must manage your own security descriptors. While these tasks are feasible, there is another access control model that is a bit simpler and may work for your application: role-based access control.

Each user who makes requests to your COM application can be assigned roles that are specific to your problem domain, and you can verify membership in the role at runtime. Windows NT provides support for roles via aliases. Unfortunately, all of the literature on NT security, as well as the user interface that NT provides for configuring them, refers to aliases as *Local Groups*, so most people overlook the potential for role-based security purely because of nomenclature. An alias (or Local Group) can be defined on any machine and can include a collection of zero or more users and groups (however, it cannot include other aliases, so you cannot nest alias definitions). The beauty of aliases is that when your server authenticates an incoming client, the token you get from the authentication handshake is produced by the LSA on the machine on which your server is running. The token therefore includes not only the security identifier (SID) for the client and the domain-wide groups (also known as *Global Groups*) to which the user belongs but also any aliases that have been assigned to the user on the local machine.

Using roles, you can now write code that looks like this:

```
HRESULT CoWidgetMaker::Shutdown() {
    // impersonate temporarily to get the client's token
    CoImpersonateClient();
    HANDLE htok = 0;
    OpenThreadToken(GetCurrentThread(), TOKEN_QUERY,
                    TRUE, &htok);
    CoRevertToSelf();

    // supervisors are allowed to shut down the machine
    BOOL bInRole;
    CheckTokenMembership(htok, g_SupervisorSID,
                         &bInRole);[19]
    if (!bInRole)
        return E_ACCESSDENIED;
    // do shutdown
```

---

[19] `CheckTokenMembership` is new for NT 5, but it is trivial to implement yourself via `GetTokenInformation(TokenGroups)` and `EqualSid`.

```
        return S_OK;
    }
```

There is a significant difference in the programming model here. With a role-based access control policy, you focus on discovering roles that users play that distinguish them from one another, rather than on placing explicit permissions on each object in the system. Not all systems lend themselves to this model, but many do. The obvious benefits of this model are that you don't have to manage security descriptors on each object or bother implementing an ACL editor. Your setup application should create the required aliases during installation (via the Net APIs on NT 4 or ADSI on NT 5), and the administrator can assign these aliases to arbitrary users and groups via the built-in account manager (e.g., User Manager in NT 4).

Another benefit of role-based access control is that it maps well onto the natural flow lifecycle of a software development project. During analysis, you not only discover interfaces and classes but also strive to discover roles. In the design and implementation phases, developers rely on these roles to implement a fine-grained access control policy. During deployment, you'll rely on the administrator to determine which users should be in which roles, which is often a considerably easier task than explicitly specifying access control on each and every object in your system. If you choose clear role names, this step will considerably simplify the administrator's job.

One interesting application of this idea would be to provide declarative support for per-interface or per-class role-based access control. Imagine that you could write the following IDL:

```
#define ALLOW(roles) custom(ALLOW_GUID, roles)
#define DENY(roles) custom(DENY_GUID, roles)
[uuid(...), ALLOW("Operators;Supervisors")]
coclass WidgetMaker {
    interface IWidgetMaker;
    [DENY("Operators")] interface IWidgetControl;
}
```

Using a type library, it would be possible easy to develop a generic shim object (see Item 25, flyweights) that acted as a gatekeeper and delegated calls to your real object only if they satisfied the access control policy supplied by the interface definition. Instead of handing back a pointer to the widget maker, you would hand back a pointer to the shim object, which in turn would forward calls to your widget maker, if appropriate, or return E_ACCESSDENIED to unauthorized callers. In fact, this is the exact technique used by Microsoft Transaction Server.

If you plan to deploy your COM application in MTS, support for role-based security is built into the infrastructure. MTS's context wrapper provides the access-checking shim described earlier. MTS allows you to declaratively set per-class and per-interface[20] access control policies based on roles. For finer-grained access control, MTS's IsCallerInRole method hides (and optimizes) all the grungy code required to scrape out the caller's token and check it for membership in a role. MTS itself doesn't rely on NT aliases, but rather provides its own mapping (and user interface) that allows administrators to map users and groups to your own logical roles. Your setup application doesn't need to worry about installing NT aliases; you simply need to declare the roles for the application.

With that said, here are some general guidelines for implementing an access control policy:

1. Access permissions (specified via CoInitializeSecurity) must include *all users* who are allowed to call into your process.

2. Launch permissions (specified via your AppID in the registry) should be at least as restrictive as access permissions (to avoid a user launching a server and then being denied access to call into it).

3. Avoid the shortsighted solution of running code under an impersonation token as an easy way out of dealing with fine-grained access control.

4. Consider using operating system primitives (e.g., security descriptors) to implement object-based access control.

5. Even better, consider using roles to implement fine-grained access control (this is free in MTS).

The coarse-grained access control policies provided by COM were designed to make your life easier, not to solve all your security problems. For systems that care about security, prefer fine-grained access control.

---

[20] Per-method access control is not supported as of this writing. There are also no custom IDL attributes to map roles to interfaces; instead, the MTS Explorer provides this service graphically.

Transactions

In Microsoft Transaction Server (MTS), the transaction is all. Many DevelopMentor-ites (including at least two of the authors) initially tried to ignore this and view MTS as simply a "better COM." To do this is to overlook the most powerful abstraction in the MTS programming model: the transaction. As pivotal as the interface is to COM, the transaction unifies an MTS developer's view of concurrency management and recovery from failures. MTS is but one technology that marries transactional programming with interface-based programming, but due to its grounding in COM, it is likely to be one of the most widely used and therefore the most influential. Transactional programming, especially *outside* the scope of databases, has as pervasive an effect on one's view of software as interface-based programming does. This chapter provides transactional programmers with some hints as to how to use the programming model correctly and effectively.

43. Keep transactions as short as possible.

Transactional programming is fundamentally about lock management. The "I" in the ACID properties mandates that concurrent transactions must be isolated from one another. To achieve this, most systems use some sort of locking to keep one transaction from interfering with another transaction. The literature has formalized three degrees of isolation to represent the levels of protection one can expect from a system. MTS transactions run at degree 3 isolation, which is the highest level. This level is often referred to as *serializable*.

To achieve degree 3 isolation, any read or write locks acquired during a transaction are held until the transaction (not just the read or write operation) completes. While one transaction is holding a lock, it is likely that other transactions are blocked from doing their work. This reduces overall system throughput, particularly on multiprocessor machines. To maximize throughput and scalability, it is critical that transactions complete as soon as possible to release the locks that are held by the transaction.

To enforce short transaction times as well as to resolve deadlocked transactions, MTS creates transactions that auto-abort if not committed within a short period of time. This transaction timeout defaults to 60 seconds but is configurable using MTS Explorer or the MTS catalog. It is a bad idea to arbitrarily raise this timeout threshold, because throughput will likely suffer due to reduced concurrency.

One way to ensure that a transaction ends as soon as possible is to leave each method in the `SetComplete` state. This tells the context wrapper that your object is happy with the current state of the system and has no more work to do inside this transaction. Of course, this also means that your object will be destroyed once your method returns control to the context wrapper, but this is the cost of keeping transactions as short as possible. This does not mean that leaving a method while in the `EnableCommit` or `DisableCommit` state is never useful. `DisableCommit` in particular can be very effective at ensuring that the current transaction cannot commit until after your object receives another method call. However, both `EnableCommit` and `DisableCommit` tell the context wrapper that your object would like to keep the transaction running. This is especially problematic if your object is the root object in a transaction, because the transaction will not complete until your object is deactivated, which of course will not happen until either the client releases its references or your object enters the `SetComplete` state.

The discussion so far has ignored the fact that client applications often want to program in terms of long-running transactions. Performance considerations aside, MTS's transaction timeout makes this impractical. Client applications achieve long-running *logical* transactions by using multiple *physical* transactions that execute sequentially. This style of programming requires the application to become much more aware of the ACID properties than might normally be required. When composing long-running logical transactions out of a sequence of physical transactions, it is the responsibility of the application to ensure that the ACID properties hold for the logical transaction. If an intermediate physical transaction fails, it is the application's job to apply compensating transactions to undo the results of the physical transactions that have executed successfully so far. To do this, the application will likely need a recovery strategy to handle the case of complete application failure, such as looking at a recovery queue or table at startup to see if any compensating transactions need to be applied. It is also the job of the application to use some form of application-level concurrency control, since no physical locks will be held for any significant duration of time. This is typically done using either optimistic policies based on aborting transactions when overwriting a given piece of state that has changed since it was last read or pessimistic policies in which application-level locks are associated with shared pieces of state. Optimistic locking approaches tend to result in lower effective throughput for heavily loaded systems due to increased abort rates. Optimistic locking is also the harder of the two to implement.

44. Always use `SafeRef` when handing out pointers to your own object.

MTS is based on the concept of interception. At creation time, MTS places a context wrapper between the outside world and your object. The context wrapper implements the same set of interfaces as your object and is all the outside world ever sees. When clients issue method calls against your object, it is the context wrapper that actually receives the method requests. The context wrapper preprocesses the call prior to passing control to your object. Once your object returns control to the context wrapper, the context wrapper postprocesses the call prior to returning control to the client.

The context wrapper's preprocessing work includes (1) inhibiting concurrent access to a single object,[1] (2) ensuring that transactional objects have a Distributed Transaction Coordinator (DTC) transaction, (3) ensuring that an instance exists and has been activated to service the call (see Item 50), and (4) performing declarative security checks. The context wrapper's postprocessing work includes (1) controlling transaction outcome based on the last call to `SetComplete` or `SetAbort`, (2) potentially deactivating the instance, and (3) releasing certain resources acquired during the method call (e.g., SPM locks).

Given the nontrivial amount of work performed by the context wrapper, it should be obvious that bypassing it would be a bad idea. In general, the runtime ensures that clients only call into your object via your context wrapper. MTS catches the result of your class factory's `CreateInstance` method and only returns the context wrapper to the client. Additionally, when the client calls `QueryInterface` on the context wrapper, the context wrapper is careful to hand out references only to itself and not to the raw underlying object. However, if references to your raw object are passed via any other means, it is your job to ensure that the receiver gets a pointer to your context wrapper and not the raw object. This is why there is a `SafeRef` function in the MTS API.

---

[1] Technically, the current implementation of MTS relies on COM's intrinsic single-threaded apartment (STA)-based serialization; however, future versions of MTS may not work this way.

The `SafeRef` function takes two parameters: your `this` pointer and the interface identifier (IID) of the interface you wish to pass around:

```
[iid_is(riid)] void *
SafeRef([in] REFIID riid, [in] IUnknown *pThis);
```

The `SafeRef` function simply finds your context wrapper, calls `QueryInterface` on it, and returns the resultant interface pointer. This, of course, means that you now have an additional reference on the context wrapper that you must properly manage by calling `Release` when appropriate.

There are two common situations in which `SafeRef` is necessary. You must use `SafeRef` when returning your `this` pointer as an `[out]` parameter of your own methods. You must also use `SafeRef` when passing your `this` pointer as an `[in]` parameter to another object. Consider the following interface and co-class definitions:

```
interface  IYou;
interface IMe : IUnknown {
  HRESULT HereIAm([out] IMe **ppMe);
  HRESULT UseYou([in] IYou *pYou);
  HRESULT DoSomeWork(void);
}
interface IYou : IUnknown {
  HRESULT UseMe([in] IMe *pMe);
}
[ TRANSACTION_REQUIRES_NEW ]
coclass Me {
  interface IMe;
}
[ TRANSACTION_REQUIRES_NEW ]
coclass You {
  interface IYou;
}
```

Given these interface definitions, the following implementation of `Me::UseYou` would be wrong:

```
STDMETHODIMP Me::UseYou(IYou *pYou) {
  return pYou->UseMe(this); // ouch, no context wrapper!
}
```

Note that a raw `this` pointer is being passed to the You object. This means that when the You object calls back to the Me object,

```
STDMETHODIMP You::UseMe(IMe *pMe) {
  return pMe->DoSomeWork();
}
```

the callback will not go through the context wrapper, bypassing interception.

If both objects are in the same activity and process, then the worst problem is that the DoSomeWork callback will execute in the transaction of the You object, which is not correct. If the two objects are in different processes, then (1) the callback will not have a transaction at all, and (2) no declarative security checks will be performed. In fact, the object will have no context, and none of the MTS services you've grown to expect will work properly. To avoid this problem, the raw this pointer should never be passed outside of a method call. Instead, the UseYou method should use the SafeRef function:

```
STDMETHODIMP Me::UseYou(IYou *pYou) {
  // grab the context wrapper
  IMe *pMe = (IMe*)SafeRef(IID_IMe, this);
  // pass the context wrapper instead of raw this
  HRESULT hr = pYou->UseMe(pMe);
  // release the context wrapper
  pMe->Release();
  return hr;
}
```

With this code in place, all is well. Interception has been restored.

It is also important to use SafeRef when passing your this pointer as an [out] parameter. The following implementation of Me::HereIAm would be wrong:

```
STDMETHODIMP Me::HereIAm(IMe **ppMe) {
  (*ppMe = this)->AddRef(); // ouch, no context wrapper!
  return S_OK;
}
```

Note that the raw pointer is being passed back to the caller. Thus, any calls that are issued through the resultant pointer will completely bypass MTS's interception. The correct version of this code is as follows:

```
STDMETHODIMP Me::HereIAm(IMe **ppMe) {
  // give out reference to context wrapper
  *ppMe = (IMe*)SafeRef(IID_IMe, this);
  // don't bother to AddRef, since SafeRef already did!
  return S_OK;
}
```

Note that now the caller will receive a reference to the object's context wrapper and all will be well.

It is important to note that you only need to use `SafeRef` when dealing with pointers to your own object. References returned from `CoCreateInstance`, `IObjectContext::CreateInstance`, or any other COM or MTS method or API are always safe to pass around (except for the caveats on cross-activity object sharing discussed in Item 45). It is actually quite simple to understand exactly when to call `SafeRef` or not. Here are two simple rules: (1) only pass references to your own object to `SafeRef`, and (2) don't pass references to your own object to anyone else without using `SafeRef`.

45. Don't share object references across activity boundaries.

Much of the popular MTS literature does not put enough emphasis on one of the most fundamental aspects of the programming model: the activity. Because of this, people are often confused when their traditional COM-style designs don't work properly or efficiently when applied to MTS.

An MTS activity is a set of objects that act in concert on behalf of a *single* client. An activity can contain objects from multiple packages potentially running on multiple host machines. Each MTS object exists in exactly one activity, although an activity can contain multiple objects. Each MTS transaction exists in exactly one activity, although an activity can contain multiple transactions due to the use of the `[TRANSACTION_REQUIRES_NEW]` attribute. Each object created using `CoCreateInstance` belongs to a new activity. Objects created using `IObjectContext::CreateInstance` belong to the activity of their creator. While not formally specified, the client thread that begins the activity by calling `CoCreateInstance` should be considered part of the activity as well, although a single thread can begin multiple activities simply by calling `CoCreateInstance` multiple times.

The MTS programming model implies (but does not enforce) that MTS objects should not be shared across activity boundaries. This means that given the following simple interface definition,

```
interface IFriendly : IUnknown {
  HRESULT UseMe([out, retval] long *pn);
  HRESULT HereIAm([in] IFriendly *pMe);
}
```

the following client code would cause an object in one activity to use an object in another activity:

```
// error handling code deleted for clarity
IFriendly *pf1 = 0, *pf2 = 0;
// create one object in a new activity
CoCreateInstance(CLSID_Friend, ..., &pf1);
// create another object in a new activity
CoCreateInstance(CLSID_Friend, ..., &pf2);
// pass reference from one activity to another
pf1->HereIAm(pf2);
```

Note that the first object can now call into the second object to perform its work.

At the very least, crossing the activity boundary presents an opportunity for violating the isolation of both transactions, assuming that the coclass `Friend` is marked `[TRANSACTION_REQUIRED]` or `[TRANSACTION_RE-QUIRES_NEW]`. If the first object were to receive intermediate results from the second object's transaction as `[out]` parameters from a cross-activity method call, dirty or unrepeatable reads become possible, since the first object's transaction may never commit (or may not be finished modifying the state returned from the method).

To see the potential for problems, consider the following implementation of the `HereIAm` method:

```
STDMETHODIMP Friend::HereIAm(IFriendly *pf) {
  // read results from a second transaction and
  // cache for use in this transaction
  return pf->UseMe(&m_nData);
}
```

This method caches a long integer returned by the second object passed as a parameter. If the implementation of `UseMe` used the intermediate results of its transaction (e.g., the results of a query against modified data) to produce its output, this method call has violated the serializability of both transactions. This happens because the object that called `UseMe` may use this result even if the second transaction is not done modifying the underlying data. Of course, the second transaction could also abort, which means that the results of `UseMe` never really happened. In either case, the object in the first transaction will never know that its cached result from `UseMe` is now invalid.

A more interesting problem arises when passing references to MTS objects across threads. Although MTS does guarantee that a single MTS object will never be accessed concurrently, MTS only loosely guarantees serialized access throughout an entire activity. The programming model implies that at most one logical thread (causality) will be active within a given activity; however, this is only guaranteed within a particular process. If an activity spans two or more processes or hosts, MTS does not attempt to perform any cross-process or cross-host serialization of calls. Therefore, if you pass references to MTS objects to secondary threads, there is a potential for concurrent execution inside a single activity. This can occur even if you follow the laws of COM apartments religiously.

By having two threads issuing method calls to an activity concurrently, it is possible that concurrent execution within the activity can happen if the two threads issue calls to objects in different processes. Since MTS does not attempt to serialize across process boundaries, there is no protection against this concurrency. Concurrency within an activity is extremely dangerous, as it is possible that an object working on behalf of one thread might attempt to commit the transaction while an object working on behalf of the second thread is in the middle of performing work inside the same transaction. If the transaction were to actually commit, this would likely result in data inconsistency due to committing a partially formed transaction.

It turns out that the problem of concurrency within an activity is not limited to threads calling into objects in multiple processes. Consider the case in which two threads call into the same object concurrently. By definition, one of the thread's requests will be serviced first, since MTS does serialize method execution on a single instance. However, if the first method were to call out to an object in another apartment, the MTS runtime thread that is servicing the call will enter a message filter while waiting for the response. Because the MTS-provided message filter does not block calls from different causalities (e.g., CALLTYPE_TOPLEVEL_CALLPENDING), the thread is susceptible to reentrance from other incoming calls (such as the one issued by the second thread). Again, this can cause unexpected results, as it is now possible for one thread to issue a request that would attempt to commit the current transaction while another thread is in the middle of doing work in the same transaction.

Despite the fact that MTS is built on top of COM, it is a different programming model. COM objects can be accessed freely from any thread in the system, provided marshaling has been properly addressed. MTS objects, on the other hand, are likely to malfunction if accessed by any thread other than the one that started the activity (or an MTS runtime thread servicing a method call in the same activity).

To get around this limitation, it is important to remember that the MTS programming model is based on shared state, not shared objects. If you need a second thread to access shared state, that thread needs to create its own private object hierarchy in its own activity. This is the only way to take advantage of MTS's concurrency management facilities and correctly share state between multiple clients.

46. Beware of exposing object references from the middle of a transaction hierarchy.

The MTS programming model implies that clients create a single object that may itself create other objects to help perform its work. This is certainly the model implied by MTS activities, and MTS transaction management also assumes this. While there is nothing that explicitly prohibits an object from exposing its subobjects to clients, it must be done carefully when transactions are involved.

To see the problems with passing out references to subobjects inside a transaction, consider the following interface and coclass definitions:

```
interface ISubObject : IUnknown {
  HRESULT DoSomeWork(void);
}
interface IMainObject : IUnknown {
  HRESULT CreateSubObject([out, retval] ISubObject **);
  HRESULT FinishTransaction(void);
}
[ TRANSACTION_REQUIRED ]
coclass MainObject {
  interface IMainObject;
}
[ TRANSACTION_REQUIRED ]
coclass SubObject {
  interface ISubObject;
}
```

Given this simple object hierarchy, assume that MainObject's implementation of CreateSubObject is

```
STDMETHODIMP
MainObject::CreateSubObject(ISubObject **pp) {
  IObjectContext *poc = 0;
  HRESULT hr = GetObjectContext(&poc);
  if (SUCCEEDED(hr)) {
    hr = poc->CreateInstance(CLSID_SubObject,
```

```
                    IID_ISubObject, (void**)pp);
    poc->Release();
  }
  return hr;
}
```

and that `MainObject`'s implementation of `FinishTransaction` simply leaves the object in the `SetComplete` state:

```
STDMETHODIMP MainObject::FinishTransaction() {
  IObjectContext *poc = 0;
  HRESULT hr = GetObjectContext(&poc);
  if (SUCCEEDED(hr)) {
    hr = poc->SetComplete();
    poc->Release();
  }
  return hr;
}
```

As an aside, these two methods are identical to the stock implementations of `ITransactionContextEx::CreateInstance` and `ITransactionContextEx::Commit`, respectively.

Given the object hierarchy just described, consider the following client code that executes 100 transactions using this object hierarchy:

```
IMainObject *pmain = 0;
HRESULT hr = CoCreateInstance(CLSID_MainObject, 0,
        CLSCTX_ALL, IID_IMainObject, (void**)&pmain);
if (SUCCEEDED(hr)) {
  for (int n = 0; n < 100; n++) {
    ISubObject *psub = 0;
    hr = pmain->CreateSubObject(&psub);    // begin tx
    if (SUCCEEDED(hr)) {
      hr = psub->DoSomeWork();
      if (SUCCEEDED(hr))
        hr = pmain->FinishTransaction();  // end tx
      psub->Release();
    }
  }
  pmain->Release();
}
```

This code is perfectly reasonable and will work as expected. A new transaction will start at each call to the `CreateSubObject` method. Each transaction will end when the client calls `FinishTransaction`. Granted, the objects themselves will be created and destroyed at each transactional boundary, but this is to be expected given the isolation requirements of each transaction.

While the previous example will work fine, it is important to note that once a transaction has completed, a new transaction will be started when a method call comes in for *any* object in the hierarchy. This means that the following example would work equally well:

```
IMainObject *pmain = 0;
HRESULT hr = CoCreateInstance(CLSID_MainObject, 0,
          CLSCTX_ALL, IID_IMainObject, (void**)&pmain);
if (SUCCEEDED(hr)) {
  ISubObject *psub = 0;
  hr = pmain->CreateSubObject(&psub);    // begin tx 0
  if (SUCCEEDED(hr)) {
    for (int n = 0; n < 100; n++) {
      hr = psub->DoSomeWork();            // begin tx 1-99
      if (SUCCEEDED(hr))
        hr = pmain->FinishTransaction();// end tx
      psub->Release();
    }
  }
  pmain->Release();
}
```

Note that in this example, the `CreateSubObject` method is called exactly once and the context wrapper for the subobject is reused across all transactions. Given the object hierarchy with which we started, this would be a more efficient way to achieve the same effect as the previous example.

The potential problem with using subobjects in a transactional object hierarchy is that if the root object of the transaction is never reactivated, the transaction can never commit. To see the problem in action, consider the following client code:

```
IMainObject *pmain = 0;
ISubObject *psub = 0;
CoCreateInstance(CLSID_MainObject, 0,
          CLSCTX_ALL, IID_IMainObject, (void**)&pmain);
pmain->CreateSubObject(&psub);     // starts tx
hr = psub->DoSomeWork();
pmain->FinishTransaction();        // commits tx
psub->DoSomeWork();                // starts new tx
Sleep(61000);
```

Note that there is no way for the second transaction to ever commit, since the root object in the transaction has never been reactivated. For the transaction to actually commit, the client would have needed to issue at least one call against the root object in order to reactivate it. The reason that reactivation is necessary is that a transactional commit happens only when the root object in the transaction is deactivated (either by the client releasing all of its references or by the object itself entering the `SetComplete` state).

Note that this item recommends that you beware of handing out references to subobjects in a transaction. That doesn't mean that it is never useful. It does mean that you must carefully document your object hierarchy to ensure that clients understand that the root object is significant and must be used to end a transaction. This is exactly the approach taken by the `ITransactionContextEx` interface and implementation. If you decide to use this approach, use this interface as your inspiration.

47. Beware of committing a transaction implicitly.

Because the lifetime of a transactional object is scoped to its transaction, MTS tries to commit the transaction when the root object is deactivated. Normally, this means that the root object has returned from a method in `SetComplete` state. However, if the client releases all of its references to the object's context wrapper prior to the object's entering the `SetComplete` state, MTS will attempt to commit the transaction anyway. Since the object will be deactivated when the context wrapper goes away, this is consistent with the relationship between transactions and objects. When the context wrapper attempts to commit the transaction in this way, it is said that the transaction has committed *implicitly* (i.e., the transactional object does not initiate the commit explicitly).

Implicit commits are actually a reasonable idea. They allow the client to create an object, submit some method requests, and release the object, all within the scope of a single transaction. The primary problem with implicit commits is that, unlike an explicit commit (or abort), the client cannot easily discover the outcome of the transaction. Recall that when a root transactional object returns from a method in `SetComplete` state, it is telling the context wrapper to attempt to commit the transaction prior to returning control to the caller. If the transaction commits successfully, the client will receive the successful HRESULT from the object. If, however, the commit attempt fails, the context wrapper will modify the HRESULT to indicate that the transaction has been aborted. This allows the client to deal with the failed transaction in whatever manner it deems appropriate.

In the case of an implicit commit, however, the commit attempt is not made until the client's final call to `IUnknown::Release`. Unfortunately, there is no way for the context wrapper to communicate the outcome of the transaction through this method call.[2] If the client doesn't care about the outcome of the transaction, this is not a limitation. However, most clients care. If implicit commits are important to your design, your object needs to communicate the success or failure of the transaction by modifying system state as part of the transaction. This might mean inserting or deleting a record in a well-known database table. Or it might mean enqueuing or dequeuing a message on a well-known queue. In either case, the client would need to query the system state after using the object to see if the transaction actually ran to completion successfully.

One additional problem related to using implicit commits relates to transaction times. When an object explicitly tries to commit a transaction by leaving a method in `SetComplete` state, it is trying to bring the current transaction to a close as soon as possible (see Item 43 for why this is a good idea). If the object relies on implicit commits at client release time, it is possible that the client may not release its references in a timely manner. At best, this will simply reduce overall system throughput due to prolonged transaction times. At worst, the transaction will abort if the client doesn't release its references before MTS's auto-abort timeout.

Implicit commits are a good idea because they are consistent with the relationship between transactions and objects. However, in practice, having an explicit operation that commits the transaction is almost always easier to use properly.

48. Use nontransactional objects where appropriate.

People often mistakenly characterize MTS as having two kinds of objects: stateful and stateless. This myth has been propagated by much of the early writing on MTS. In fact, MTS does have two fundamental types of objects; however, statefulness is not the primary distinguishing factor. Rather, the fundamental characteristic that distinguishes MTS objects is whether or not the object is running inside a transaction.

A nontransactional object exists outside the scope of a transaction. A transactional object exists inside the scope of a transaction. All instances of classes marked [TRANSACTION_NOT_SUPPORTED] are nontransactional. All instances of classes marked [TRANSACTION_REQUIRED] or [TRANSACTION_REQUIRES_NEW] are transactional. Instances of classes marked [TRANSACTION_SUPPORTED] are nontransactional if they are created via

---

[2] For one thing, the method returns a ULONG, not an HRESULT.

`CoCreateInstance` or if they are created by other nontransactional objects. Instances of classes marked [`TRANSACTION_SUPPORTED`] are transactional only if they are created by other transactional objects using `IObject-Context::CreateInstance`.

A nontransactional object is just like any other COM (or C++) object. It is created when the client makes an activation call, and it remains in memory until the client releases its last reference. In contrast, a transactional object lives within the boundaries of a single DTC transaction. The object is initialized while a transaction is active, and its lifetime will be terminated soon after the transaction commits or aborts. When a new transaction is started, MTS will create a new instance of the class to service requests inside the new transaction. Despite some popular misconceptions, this is done to enforce transactional isolation and consistency, not to save resources.

Although much of the MTS programming model focuses on transactional programming, there are occasions where using nontransactional objects is necessary. One common application of nontransactional objects is to hold state across transaction boundaries. If an object hierarchy needs to keep *transaction-invariant* state across two or more transactions, the only way to do this is to put the state into a nontransactional object that can reinitialize the transactional objects at each transaction. A simplistic way to achieve this is to have the client create a [`TRANSACTION_NOT_SUPPORTED`] object that then creates the subordinate transactional objects.

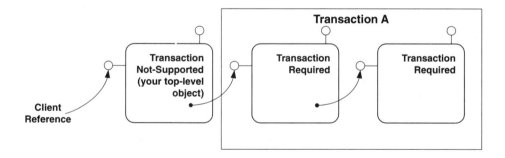

Note that if the nontransactional object is deployed in a library package, the state will be held on the client machine, which provides a better opportunity for load balancing across transactions. Since transactional objects are destroyed at the end of each transaction, future versions of MTS can potentially activate the transactional objects on different machines at each transaction.

The problem with using the approach just described is that it limits composability of the object hierarchy, since the nontransactional object will stop transactional propagation when the object hierarchy is composed into another transactional hierarchy. To solve this problem, one should use [TRANSACTION_SUPPORTED] instead of [TRANSACTION_NOT_SUPPORTED] to allow the transaction to flow from the context of the activator. This will yield the same results when a base client or nontransactional object creates the hierarchy. However, when a transactional object creates the hierarchy, the transaction will flow through to the subordinate objects, as shown in the figure below.

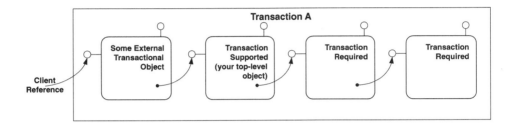

While this will cause the [TRANSACTION_SUPPORTED] object to become transactional and therefore have a limited lifetime, this is not a problem because the object's client is a transactional object that shares the same limitation and will need to recreate the hierarchy at the next transaction anyway.

Another common reason to use nontransactional objects is to support database calls at lower isolation levels. Some resource managers (e.g., SQL Server 6.5) extract the transaction isolation level from the DTC transaction on which they are enlisted. When using MTS declarative transactions, this isolation level is degree 3, or serializable. While always correct, this isolation level reduces the overall transaction throughput of the system due to the use of two-phase read locks.[3] For transactions that do not update state and can accept minor inconsistencies, it is sometimes desirable to hold read locks for a shorter duration to increase throughput. Unfortunately, there is no way to do this from a transactional object.[4] To solve this problem, read operations that need to run at degree 2 (committed read) must be issued by a subordinate *nontransactional* object. Since no enlistment happens for nontransactional objects, the object is free to change the isolation level using standard data access techniques.

---

[3] That is, the read lock is held to the end of the current transaction, not just the current read operation.

[4] SQL Server will recognize the NOLOCK attribute for select statements, lowering the isolation level to degree 1 (uncommitted read).

49. Move nontrivial initialization to `IObjectControl::Activate`.

The MTS programming model imposes a two-phase initialization sequence on all objects. When the client first creates an MTS object, the MTS runtime creates an instance of the requested class; however, in MTS terms, the object is not yet activated. MTS postpones activating the object until the first method call. MTS informs the object that it is being activated by calling the object's `IObjectControl::Activate` method.

The primary implication of the MTS activation model is that until your object is activated, the context for your object is unavailable. This means that in your object's constructor,[5] you cannot do anything that requires context. Constructors therefore cannot take advantage of declarative transactions, auto-enlistment, or MTS security features. Additionally, constructors cannot create other objects in the same activity. Finally, you cannot pass references to your object's context wrapper to other objects in a constructor. All things considered, constructors are fairly limited in the MTS programming model.

MTS objects must postpone these nontrivial types of operations until the `IObjectControl::Activate` method is called. At this point, the object has been associated with a context wrapper and the object's context is fully formed. Calls to `GetObjectContext` and `SafeRef` will now work properly. Although this two-phase initialization model may seem inconvenient, it actually enhances the scalability of the system, since nontrivial resources are not acquired until the client issues the first method call. Additionally, the implicit transaction will not begin until the first object in the hierarchy is activated, keeping transaction times as short as possible. Finally, if the object is poolable (i.e., it returns `TRUE` from `IObjectControl::CanBePooled`), it is critical that *all* initialization happen inside the `Activate` call, since it will be called multiple times as the object is moved from context wrapper to context wrapper.[6]

On a related note, it is a good idea *not* to wait until `IObject-Control::Deactivate` time to release nontrivial resources. Due to the way MTS works, your object may not be deactivated until the *next* transaction begins (this is definitely true of objects that leave a method in the `DisableCommit` or `EnableCommit` state). This means your object might hold expensive resources longer than is necessary. Also, be aware that while your object does have context during the `Deactivate` call, the current transaction

---

[5] Or any other code that executes inside of `IClassFactory::CreateInstance`, such as ATL's `FinalConstruct` method.

[6] Note that at the time of this writing the current implementation of MTS (2.0) does not support object pooling.

may have already completed by the time your object has been deactivated. In fact, MTS may be on the verge of starting the next transaction and is simply notifying your object that it needs to go away. This argues that objects that need to do transactional work at deactivation time should always leave methods in the `SetComplete` state, since only then is your object's `Deactivate` call guaranteed to happen under the current transaction.

50. Don't rely on JIT activation and ASAP deactivation to achieve scalability.

Many developers, writers, and lecturers look at just-in-time (JIT) activation and as soon as possible (ASAP) deactivation as the keys to scalability under MTS. The argument goes like this: if your objects are "stateless" and only live for the duration of a method call, then that alone will allow your application to scale to millions of clients. This view is at best naïve and at worst blatant hucksterism. Here's why.

JIT activation and ASAP deactivation (from here on simply referred to as JIT activation) are pitched as a mechanism that allows a small number of objects to satisfy requests for a large number of clients. While this is technically true, this will not enhance scalability as much as some would like you to believe. For one thing, the actual memory consumed by your instance is probably insignificant when compared with the memory consumed by the COM and MTS runtimes to keep the context wrapper alive. Since JIT activation assumes that the client will hold a long-lived reference, the COM stub manager and interface stubs need to remain in memory until the client has released the proxy. This consumes about 400 bytes per object under the current implementation of COM. The context wrapper remains in memory during this time as well, which adds another 600 to 700 bytes of overhead. Now, if your object was indeed several thousand bytes, JIT activation might represent a big win. But given the short life span of transactional objects, it is unlikely that a transactional object will get a chance to consume much more than a few hundred bytes over its lifetime, often less. The fixed overhead of the stub and context wrapper infrastructure certainly makes JIT activation less effective than some would have you think.

A more substantial impact of JIT activation is that expensive resources (e.g., database connections) that are shared via resource dispensers will get released faster. Unfortunately, given the composable nature of MTS components, JIT activation isn't going to help as much as one would like. Consider the following pseudocode that uses a database connection and a subordinate component:

```
STDMETHODIMP MyClass::Method(void) {
  m_pADOConn->Open("DATASERVER");
```

```
    m_pADOConn->Execute("Some SQL statement");
    m_pSomeOtherObject->DoSomeWork();
    GetObjectContext(&poc);
    poc->SetComplete(); // enable JIT activation
    poc->Release();
    return S_OK;
}
```

If the subordinate object that is used in this method were to do the following,

```
STDMETHODIMP YourClass::DoSomeWork(void) {
    _Connection *pConn = CoCreateInstance(CLSID_ADOConn);
    pConn->Open("DATASERVER"); // note: same DSN string
    pConn->Execute("Some other SQL statement");
    pConn->Release();
    return S_OK;
}
```

the benefits of resource pooling are lost. Since the first object held the database
connection until the object deactivated, the second object would need its own
private connection. If resource pooling were important, the first object should
have closed the connection immediately after using it and not waited for ASAP
deactivation:

```
STDMETHODIMP MyClass::Method(void) {
    m_pADOConn->Open("DATASERVER");
    m_pADOConn->Execute("Some SQL statement");
    m_pADOConn->Close(); // put connection back into pool
    m_pSomeOtherObject->DoSomeWork();
    return S_OK;
}
```

Note that this object doesn't bother to call SetComplete. If it is not transactional, it doesn't need to. It does, however, hold shared resources for as short a period of time as possible. This deliberate act of letting go of shared resources is far
more effective at achieving scalability than simply writing "stateless" objects.
SetComplete exists to allow transactional objects to speed up transaction
completion. Period.

Epilogue

So, you either made it through the entire book or you skipped to the back to see how it ends. Either way, here are some meta-guidelines we recommend that you follow.

Read the COM specification.

To date, nothing has come close in terms of importance or conciseness.

Read *Principles of Transaction Processing* by Philip Bernstein and Eric Newcomer.

Although not an MTS book, this is the only worthwhile book currently on the market that has anything significant to say to MTS developers.

Be a skeptic.

Form your own personal COM belief system through empirical study and research. Don't blindly believe Microsoft. Don't blindly believe popular opinion. Don't blindly believe this (or any) book.

Distrust your tools.

The COM group produces COM, and various tool groups at Microsoft proceed to butcher it. Even ATL (perhaps the finest COM development tool around) has its flaws (albeit fairly minor ones as of version 3). Just because a tool happens to work a certain way does not mean that it is the best way. This is especially true if the tool doesn't allow statements to end with semicolons.

Learn MTS.

MTS is the future of COM. If you want to be prepared for COM+ (or whatever it is called when it is released), master MTS as soon as possible.

Learn Java.

Java may be the future of COM. Future COM+ features are likely to be highly inspired by various Java-isms. In particular, look at Java reflection and curse the Visual Basic team for the abomination that is `IDispatch`.

Be a part of the COM community.

Go to COM-friendly conferences (WinDev, Microsoft Professional Developer's Conferences, USENIX COOTS). Form COM user groups in your organization. Share your experiences and innovations with the world on the DCOM mailing list.

About the Authors

The four authors have worked together as COM educators at DevelopMentor, a leading COM education firm. All four authors have been active participants in the COM programming community and have a combined 20 years' experience working in the field of distributed object computing.

Don Box

Don Box is a contributing editor to *Microsoft Interactive Developer* and *Microsoft Systems Journal*, where he writes the bimonthly COM column. Don is a former columnist and associate editor for the *C++ Report* and wrote the book *Essential COM* for Addison-Wesley in 1997. Don is a co-founder of DevelopMentor and has consulted on a variety of COM-based projects, including Microsoft Transaction Server and Software AG's port of COM to Sun's Solaris operating system. Don holds a master's degree in computer science from the University of California, Irvine.

Keith Brown

Keith Brown has been working with COM since its first public appearance in late 1993. After spending several years in the COM space, he was captivated by Bruce Schneier's book, *Applied Cryptography*, and decided to spend a year digging around in the bowels of Win32 security. The result of this ongoing research is a short course taught at DevelopMentor, and the "Security Q&A" column in *Microsoft Systems Journal*. Keith has agreed to share his fascination for distributed security in an upcoming book. Keith holds a bachelor's degree in electrical engineering from the University of California, Irvine.

Tim Ewald

Tim is a principal scientist at DevelopMentor, where he focuses his efforts on COM-related research and development projects and on the evolution of DevelopMentor's COM curriculum. Tim is the former COM columnist for *DOC Magazine*. Before joining DevelopMentor, Tim spent many years as a consultant helping corporate clients leverage COM and other object technologies across a variety of problem domains. Tim holds a bachelor's degree in computer science from Hampshire College.

Chris Sells

Chris Sells is an independent consultant specializing in designing and building distributed systems using COM. He is also a long-time instructor for DevelopMentor, where he has developed and taught several C++ and COM courses. Chris is currently completing the book *ATL Internals* for Addison-Wesley with Brent Rector. Chris also wrote *Windows Telephony Programming: A Developer's Guide to TAPI* and coauthored *The Downloader's Companion for Windows 95* with, ironically enough, Scott Meyers and Catherine Pinch. Chris holds a master's degree in computer science from the Oregon Graduate Institute of Science and Technology.

Index